T0342575

Are Markets Moral?

ARE MARKETS MORAL?

Edited by

Arthur M. Melzer

and

Steven J. Kautz

UNIVERSITY OF PENNSYLVANIA PRESS

PHILADELPHIA

Published by
University of Pennsylvania Press
Philadelphia, Pennsylvania 19104-4112
www.upenn.edu/pennpress

Printed in the United States of America on acid-free paper
10 9 8 7 6 5 4 3 2 1

Library of Congress Cataloging-in-Publication Data
Names: Melzer, Arthur M., editor. | Kautz, Steven J., editor.
Title: Are markets moral? / edited by Arthur M. Melzer and
    Steven J. Kautz.
Description: 1st edition. | Philadelphia : University of
    Pennsylvania Press, [2018] | Includes bibliographical
    references and index.
Identifiers: LCCN 2018004258 | ISBN 9780812250527
    (hardcover : alk. paper)
Subjects: LCSH: Capitalism—Moral and ethical aspects. |
    Economics—Moral and ethical aspects.
Classification: LCC HB501 .A659 2018 | DDC 174/.4—dc23
LC record available at https://lccn.loc.gov/2018004258

CONTENTS

Introduction

Arthur M. Melzer and Steven J. Kautz

The eleven essays gathered here explore the vexed relationship between moral values, on the one hand, and free market economics, on the other. Is it somehow the case that the essential principles of the capitalist system are at odds with morality or, less drastically, do the practical workings of the system eventually but inevitably weaken or overturn moral practices and outcomes? Or, on the contrary, is the capitalist system of economic freedom actually a direct demand of morality or at least something compatible with, supportive of, or even necessary to moral practices and outcomes?

The necessity for these questions springs from the collision of two undeniable facts. First, free market economics has been slowly but constantly spreading around the globe. Second, it has been the subject of varied but constant moral attack, even in the countries that adopt it. Clearly, there is something very attractive about capitalism and something morally suspicious about it. Our aim is to investigate both.

Of course, we could be accused of arriving rather late at a question that has been around for several centuries. But clearly the issue is not yet settled. It is not even stale. It is kept alive and vibrant by the inescapable importance that it has for our lives. It is kept alive also by something else: the new evidence and new developments that keep arising. These flow from the ever-evolving character of capitalism in the West, but also from the continuing spread of capitalism to non-western parts of the world, most impressively, in our time, to Asia. Indeed, this process constitutes a remarkable historical experiment conducted on a vast scale.

During the infancy of capitalism in the West, many of its philosophical proponents tried to identify the precise moral and religious conditions that were necessary for it to grow and flourish. Great emphasis was put on certain western ideas of individualism and liberty and especially on Protestant ideas of work and frugality. People wondered out loud whether capitalism could ever really thrive in Catholic countries. But as time has gone on, events have rushed ahead of theory, demonstrating that capitalism is a plant that can thrive in many more soils than was ever supposed. The experience of capitalism in Asia is thus a crucial event for the world, helping us to open our eyes more fully to a phenomenon we thought we knew well. It is with that idea in mind that we made nonwestern capitalism one focus of this work and chose to present many of these essays first in New Delhi. In this way and others, we have tried to broaden and freshen the old discussion of markets and morals.

Two other ways are worth mentioning. We have sought to include chapters from a broad array of academic disciplines—economics, political science, philosophy, history, and law—and also from people with a background in activism (Forman), business (Das), and culture criticism (Lawler).

This diversity, however, also carries with it a potential difficulty that could be jarring to the unalerted reader. The chapters gathered here deploy a greater variety of vocabularies and styles than is typical in academic collections. Just to mention the most obvious of these differences, some chapters employ a traditional scholarly format (Epstein, Tomasi, Bibby, McNamara, McCloskey) while others adopt a looser, essayist style as more appropriate to the kind of arguments they seek to make (Melzer, Lukes, Lawler, George, Das, Forman). Within the broad audience that this book seeks to address, the second group of chapters will be more immediately appealing for the general reader and better adapted for classroom use. Scholars, we hope, will appreciate the full range of narrative approaches.

*   *   *

The volume opens with a brief chapter by Arthur Melzer providing an initial overview of this long debate. It seeks to illuminate the intellectual terrain by supplying a map (or one possible map) of the most prominent points and counterpoints in the debate. It focuses primarily on alternative attitudes toward the "profit motive" as well as toward "private property" (distribution by production as distinguished from need).

The next five chapters—collected under the heading "The Glories and Miseries of Marketization"—take widely differing positions on this issue and also recommend fundamentally different methods for addressing it. It makes sense to begin with John Tomasi, who, as a distant disciple of John Rawls and F. A. Hayek, still hopes to do political theory in the grand style. Building on his book *Free Market Fairness*, his chapter makes the most ambitious effort in the volume to provide a universal foundational argument for the moral necessity of capitalism, beginning from a fundamental human right. The fundamental right to which he appeals, however, is not the right of property but the right to free economic activity. Our economic activity—our lives, not as needy consumers, but as self-actualizing producers—constitutes the true locus of positive freedom. It is through such activity, he argues, through our economic careers broadly construed, that we have agency and become the responsible authors of our own lives.

Richard Epstein, also not shy of foundationalism and grand theory, shares Tomasi's ambition to ground the capitalist system as a direct demand of morality. But having long since left behind, as he explains here, his wayward youth as a juvenile deontologist, he takes his pro-market stand as a radical consequentialist, suspicious of all recourse to universal rights or anything with the lingering odor of Kantian moral absolutism. His thesis is that "the *only* way in which to understand capitalism is in terms of its overall social utility measured, not in the aggregate, but by the Pareto and Kaldor-Hicks standards that construct collective social indices out of individual preferences, without seeking to sum the utilities of one person, in some cardinalist fashion, with those of all others."

The ensuing three chapters, by Steven Lukes, Robert George, and Peter Lawler, have a common methodological spirit, even though it brings them to different conclusions. More suspicious of foundationalism and grand theory, they attempt to break down large questions and proceed on a more case-by-case basis. They seek to steer a course between market fundamentalists and anti-market fundamentalists, between excessive faith in markets and excessive fear of them. Markets are fine things in their proper place; the moral danger comes from spillover, from markets in spheres where they don't belong—excessive, unfettered marketization. In this approach, the task becomes to identify and understand where markets are more helpful than harmful, or the other way around. In other words, without directly confronting the deontology versus consequences issue raised by Epstein, they essentially hold that, even if one agrees that one must look to consequences (among other things), the question remains: what kinds of consequences? These must include not just economic results like production and distribution, but moral and cultural ones as well.

Steven Lukes approaches this general task by putting primary emphasis on the moral dangers of creeping "commodification," while underlining the need to unpack this much-employed concept and the difficulties of applying it.

Robert George, by contrast, focuses on the "social capital" issue. Capitalism tends—although it is a tendency that we can resist, he insists, if we are fully conscious of it—to undermine the very mores and habits on which it depends, especially the values bred by strong families and a culture of individual dignity.

Peter Lawler emphasizes a still different site of primary vulnerability: the universities. He offers a complex meditation on the negative effects of late capitalism and globalization on higher education (indeed, on higher anything), especially through their tendency to sap our patience for noble and useless things.

The three chapters comprising the next section, "Non-Western Capitalism," examine various experiences and experiments to be found outside our borders and beyond the usual suspects. In "Dharma, Markets, and Indian Capitalism," Gurcharan Das supplies a quick summary of the last two millennia of Indian political economy, which suggests that India's sharp turn in the 1990s away from British socialism to a more spontaneous commercial order was less an abandonment of its ancient ways than a return to them. And, with echoes of Robert George's essay, Das argues that the unique moral/religious concept of *dharma*—duty, justice, law, harmony, well-being—has played an indispensable role in the rise and maintenance of Indian capitalism.

Continuing in this vein, Deirdre McCloskey suggests that giving due attention to the experiences of capitalism in contemporary India, China, Singapore, and other Asian nations can transform the capitalism debate. These new histories, when combined with a closer examination of the older ones in the West, demonstrate, first, how misguided the old speculation was about the preconditions of capitalism: it is not the preserve of any race or religion, of any aspect of "deep culture," or even of economic conditions such as the slow, centuries-long accumulation of capital. The primary requirement is what she calls "the Bourgeois Revaluation . . . the coming of a business-respecting civilization." A society must simply come to appreciate the acquisitive posture toward life of its entrepreneurial class, and above all it must learn to trust, liberate, and protect the disruptive innovations that class introduces—with special emphasis on "protect," since, by definition, innovation will always face organized hostility from established interests. This simple prescription has proven not only remarkably universalizable but amazingly rapid and transformative in its consequences: "A country honoring and liberating its bourgeoisie can achieve a modern standard of living for even its very poor in a couple of generations. Three at most. . . . Look at, say, Singapore . . . once Asian-poor, [its] income per capita is now higher than that of the United States."

Simply taking in the spectacle of these revolutionary events, McCloskey suggests, tends to place the whole contemporary capitalism debate in a very different perspective—an older but more solid one. There are, as we have been seeing, numerous and ever-renascent critiques of capitalism, but they continue to remain somewhat speculative and uncertain. Standing in sharp contrast are capitalism's extraordinary and unmistakable accomplishments: the rescue of literally billions of our fellow human beings from the direst poverty, and this before our very eyes in just "a couple of generations." How is it that we do not give thanks for these wonders every day? "Long may it triumph," McCloskey intones, "for the good of the wretched of the earth." Measured against these accomplishments, don't all our precious moral objections seem a bit beside the point?

Still, those embracing a case-by-case approach might reply to McCloskey, in a kind of reversal of Marx, that robust capitalism is indeed the best thing for the poor, but not necessarily for the rich or for wealthy societies, where our moral objections become more relevant.

In the next chapter, Fonna Forman—who continues the case method as well as the use of non-western cases—goes further. Looking especially to the experience of Latin America, she argues that, in practice, capitalism and the contemporary neoliberal movement, with their attacks on government action and calls for privatization, have succeeded only in corrupting both the public sphere and the private one: undermining civic dedication or public-spiritedness, while producing, not genuinely free markets, but crony capitalism, which has done little to benefit the poor. In her pursuit of solutions, as well as her analysis of the problem, Forman continues to focus on Latin America, although not its states but smaller units, cities like Bogotá, Medellín, São Paulo, and the Tijuana-San Diego border region. She highlights the actions of various reformist mayors who have attempted to create public-private partnerships, not in the old way by collaborating with powerful business interests, but by first mobilizing and then partnering with the people. The formula is investing top-down resources to catalyze bottom-up capacities—a new synthesis of state and market action.

Forman's chapter also provides a transition to the last section of the volume, "Revisiting Locke, Montesquieu, and Smith," where we continue the political debate on the literary front. To ground her new synthesis, Forman makes a point of returning to Adam Smith, arguing that the neoliberalism that has distorted our public policy has likewise distorted our reading of this founding father of capitalism. When Smith is seen whole, she contends, it becomes clear that he never regarded economics as an independent, stand-alone field, but rather saw it as inextricably bound up with both morality and politics. It is and should be subject to moral ends as well as to top-down, political means.

In "Capitalism and the Moral Sentiments," Peter McNamara agrees that Smith—like Locke—is not an economist in the contemporary sense, but a moralist and political thinker. Through a close comparison of the moral psychologies of these two thinkers, he shows how and why Locke was far less certain than Smith regarding the Enlightenment *doux commerce* faith that (capitalist) economic progress would also bring moral progress.

In the final chapter, this issue is further explored by Andrew Bibby in a study of Montesquieu, the ultimate case man. *The Spirit of the Laws* explores the effect of capitalism on morality and religion and also the reverse. But Montesquieu distinguishes multiple types of capitalism, markets, and morality. And on the crucial *doux commerce* thesis, he maintains, according to Bibby, that commerce both undermines and strengthens morality: it undermines the lofty and severe moralities of the ancient republics and biblical religions, but it softens and improves the barbarous ones, promoting the bourgeois virtues of frugality, economy, moderation, work, wisdom, tranquility, order, and rule.

CHAPTER 1

The Moral Resistance to Capitalism: A Brief Overview

Arthur M. Melzer

The danger in a volume of independent essays by multiple authors is that the big picture gets lost in the sequence of rival snapshots. It may be useful to begin, then, with a bird's-eye view of the terrain—or at least with one bird's view—outlining some of the major points and counterpoints of the long-standing debate about markets and morals.

I would argue that, from a moral point of view (as distinguished from an economic one), the capitalist or free market system is defined most clearly by two things. The system is driven by the "profit motive" as its psychological or motivational source. And, relatedly, it is based on the moral principle of "private property," a view of justice that bases the rightful ownership of goods on production as distinguished from need. To be sure, there are also other morally important features of capitalism (commodification and creative destruction, to name two), but these are essentially derivative—eventual consequences of these more fundamental features.

To investigate the morality of capitalism in a systematic way, we should begin by exploring and evaluating these two defining features. What is meant by the "profit motive" is somewhat obscured by its misleading name, as if it denoted any concern for one's own profit or good: that is, selfishness of every kind, as distinguished from pure altruism. Actually, it denotes a very specific and peculiar kind of selfishness, which grounds what might called the "acquisitive posture toward life." Human lives can be built on many different inclinations: the desire for security, for pleasure, for wealth, for love, for honor, for justice, for God. The profit motive is distinct from all of these in-clinations (many of them selfish, some altruistic). It is the open-ended desire for material gain, the embrace of acquisitiveness more or less for its own sake, neither grounded in nor limited by some clear final end or purpose be-yond it. Thus, in particular, it is not the love of wealth—of the use and enjoy-ment of money—but of endlessly increasing one's wealth. It is the hope and desire for continuous improvement, for always moving up, for constantly getting ahead. It is rooted in no clear vision of life's consummation—of ful-fillment, rest, and happiness. It is rather a dynamic view of life: a delight in endless forward movement for its own sake.

Through most of human history, the profit motive, this curious acquisi-tive posture toward life, was a well-recognized human temptation, but viewed with suspicion and dislike. To be sure, within limits it is unobjectionable: it is natural and indeed necessary to tend to one's own material good. But great emphasis was always placed on the need to control it, to prevent it from breaking out of those narrow, natural limits—to hedge it in politically through laws regulating economic activity and morally through customs and ethical principles that condemned the endless and unfettered pursuit of gain as both senseless and socially harmful.

The great revolution that gave rise to modern capitalism, I would argue, was the self-conscious effort—made by early modern philosophers like Hobbes, Locke, Hume, Montesquieu, and Smith—to largely (although never completely) unfetter acquisitiveness or profit-seeking from its ancient politi-cal and moral constraints and to place this newly liberated and rehabilitated motive at the center of social life.

If this picture or something like it is true, then it already helps us to un-derstand the puzzle referred to in the Introduction, that capitalism, even while spreading, constantly provokes moral disapproval. For we see that cap-italism was from its start a self-consciously iconoclastic movement, a rebel-lion against and reversal of deeply rooted values, a "disruptive innovation" on the moral level well before its creative destruction on the economic level. (This is not to say, of course, that all of its early philosophic proponents openly presented themselves as moral rebels and disruptors. Certainly Hobbes and Mandeville did, as did Machiavelli before them. But their more cautious and ultimately more influential successors like Locke and Smith largely confined themselves, on the surface of their writings, to quietly and incre-mentally reinterpreting prevailing moral and religious traditions in the di-rection of commercial society and the acquisitive life.)

To understand the morally disruptive character of capitalism more concretely, we need to ask exactly what is wrong with the profit motive. What is the basic moral objection to it? Here things get a bit complicated, since there have been not just one but a confusing variety of such moral objections. To put some order into this multiplicity, it is useful to make a basic distinction between what I will (loosely) call the left-wing and right-wing critiques of capitalism (although each camp will typically borrow some elements from the other side as well). Let us begin with this reflection: any human passion or motive may be morally evaluated from two different standpoints. Is one's motive good or harmful for other people, for society, and is it good or bad for oneself?

Thus, a basic category of moral objections to the profit motive is that it is harmful to others: by unfettering human selfishness it leads to injustice and exploitation. A second category is that it is harmful and degrading to oneself because it induces one to lose oneself in the endless chase for material goods, which is fruitless and irrational in itself while also distracting one from higher, nobler, and thus more intrinsically rewarding activities. The first category of critique—characteristic of the Left—looks upon capitalism with fear and indignation, denouncing it as oppressive and unjust. The second—characteristic of the Right—looks down upon it with lofty contempt, dismissing it as stunting and ignoble.

These two different forms of critique, moreover, tend to map onto differences of social class. Historically, the acquisitive life is most characteristic of the middle class—the commercial class squeezed between the laboring class below and the leisure class above. The proletarian class tries to make the bourgeoisie feel guilty for its purported injustice at the same time that the aristocratic class tries to make it feel ashamed of its baseness and vulgarity. Thus one reason the commercial life has been so consistently embattled and insecure is that it tends to be attacked from both sides (especially in societies with lingering aristocratic traditions, as in Europe and much of the developing world).

The right-wing or aristocratic critique is less well known and less powerful today than it once was, owing to the decline of genuine aristocracy (although it remains prevalent among social conservatives, as well as intellectual and artistic elites). Its central claim is simply that there are ends in life that are higher and more intrinsically satisfying than the continuous pursuit of wealth—such as the intellectual life, the artistic life, the life of moral and political activity, and the religious life. A society that has liberated and legitimated the human impulse for continuous gain tends to produce a materialistic culture that hinders people from hearing the call of their higher longings. To be sure, in a liberal capitalist society people remain nominally free to follow any way of life they choose, but in practice it is not so easy to escape the pervasive influence of one's society and culture.

In response to this critique, the defender of capitalism has at least three primary avenues of reply. The first would be to argue that, on the contrary, the individual has greater freedom to resist his or her culture than is commonly assumed today, so that a materialistic culture does not necessarily squeeze out other, higher ways of life. Indeed, the increase in general prosperity and security it produces might rather expand people's range of possible life choices. Second, one might concede that a commercial society does perhaps lower the ceiling with respect to moral character, but at the same time it raises the floor. Perhaps the highest, most strenuous human virtues have become less common, but certain real if lesser virtues have become far more so—the so-called bourgeois virtues such as basic honesty, self-discipline, prudence, and self-reliance. Furthermore, the commercial life at its peaks—among the great innovators and entrepreneurs—is actually far more intellectually challenging, morally impressive, and humanly fulfilling than has typically been seen, especially by the hostile intellectuals and artists to whom we principally owe our understanding of this life. Third, one might embrace a value relativist view and simply deny the original premise that any way of life can be said to be intrinsically higher or lower than any other.

Turning to the left-wing critique of capitalism, the claim here is that the profit motive is morally objectionable because it is harmful to others—it makes one unjust and exploitative. The most famous and extreme version of this critique is found, of course, in Marx, who claims that in the capitalist world of selfish and competitive individuals, the rich are forced by the system itself continually to squeeze more and more out of their workers, lest they lose out to their competitors. Thus, as the rich grow richer, the poor will and must grow poorer, until they are horribly oppressed. The philosophical founders of capitalism, like John Locke and Adam Smith, had of course argued just the opposite. They thought that it was precisely in a capitalist economy, which releases so many productive forces, that continuous economic growth would redound to everyone's benefit, rich and poor alike, if unequally.

As almost everyone will agree, in this fundamental debate, if Marx had been right, then every decent human being would be a communist. But as most will also agree, Marx has been proven wrong. Although conditions have naturally varied from country to country and decade to decade, the overwhelming evidence from the last two centuries of capitalist development around the world is that the poor have gotten not poorer, but a great deal richer.

In light of this widely recognized failure of the primary left-wing critique of capitalism—the inevitable immiseration of the poor—the Left has largely pursued two alternative lines of argument. The first is the theory of imperialism, the second the critique of inequality. Capitalist countries have managed to avoid exploiting their own workers, so the first argument goes, by exploiting the workers of other countries. They have outsourced their oppression. In this way, the phenomenon of imperialism has temporarily kept capitalism alive. It has certainly kept the left-wing accusation of capitalist oppression alive. And here the historical record would seem to be far more friendly to the Left, since no one can deny that many capitalist countries of the West have engaged in a great deal of colonialism and imperialism.

Still, the question is whether those imperialist policies were a direct consequence of capitalism and indeed necessary to its survival. Defenders of free enterprise would answer, No, pointing to the fact that the colonial empires eventually proved to be, not helpful and sustaining to capitalist economies, but actually harmful, and that western countries in fact grew far more rapidly (and with continuing uplift of the poor) in the period of retreat from imperialism than in its heyday.

As the issue of imperialism has gradually waned—at least as the fundamental basis for the left-wing critique of capitalism—the Left has slowly turned to another line of argument. It consists in a frank retreat from the claim of oppression and immiseration to the claim of inequality. Let us grant—this argument goes—that, over time, a capitalist economy does not impoverish the poor, but enriches all classes. Still, it does not do so equally. It allows economic inequality to persist and often to widen, sometimes dramatically.

Now, most people would agree with this statement, but the defender of capitalism would ask why income inequality is a grave moral problem. Human beings may be equal in some respects, but surely not in all. They are certainly not equally productive, so why should they be equally remunerated?

And, of course, the incentive of receiving more, of surpassing others, through greater productivity is precisely what energizes economic development, creating the growth—in jobs, wages, and products—that eventually redounds to the benefit of everyone.

To this, the common replies on the left are these. First, the issue is not to have complete equality, but to avoid extremes of inequality. Extreme inequality is a very harmful thing because it too can stifle economic growth and because economic inequality inevitably spills over into political inequality, thus threatening democracy. Second, while it is true that people are not equally productive, it is far from clear that the inequalities of wealth produced by capitalism are proportioned in any tolerably accurate way to these differences in ability or production. Indeed, in an individualist and capitalist society, full of so-called "self-made men," there is a widespread tendency among the successful to deceive themselves about how much their success is or can be due to circumstances of their own creation. Can anyone truly claim to be self-made?

There is much more to be said, many further rounds of point and counterpoint, in the debate over income inequality (which we plan to explore in a separate volume). But let me jump to the larger issue that stands behind the inequality debate—the second defining element of capitalism, the principle of private property. This principle is the fundamental source of income inequality, since it distributes goods according to people's unequal productivity. Isn't this principle of distribution fundamentally unjust and—since the decline of the immiseration argument—the deepest ground of the left-wing critique of capitalism?

In matters of distribution and ownership, human beings are and have always been moved by two rival ideas of justice. Every economic good necessarily has two aspects: it must be produced, but it is only produced for the purpose of being used or consumed. And we all have within us a set of moral intuitions connected to the need for production and a rival set connected to the ultimate aim of use. Thus, everyone feels that when people put their labor into the creation of something, along with their time, their skill, and their investment, they acquire some claim to that thing—otherwise they are slaves. This notion of ownership and property is found in every society and in every two-year-old. If you have made something, you are entitled to it; if you work harder, you deserve more. Everyone knows and gets this idea. And while we are under its spell, it seems absolute and unassailable.

But everyone also knows and gets a rival idea that does assail it. For when a very rich man passes a very poor one on the street, the rich man knows that if he gave the other a hundred dollars, he himself would never miss it, he would not even know that it was gone, but it would mean a great deal to the poor man. And this simple thought gives rise in all of us to a new moral idea, very much at odds with the previous one. We feel that it would be a better distribution of things—more rational and more just—if the poor man had that money. Not because he has produced it—he has not—but because he can use it more. The potential good inherent in that money is realized more in the poor man's hands than in the rich one's. The good is more or less wasted on the rich man, and is it not wrong for goods to be wasted when people are in need? Again, if a rich woman buys a very fine piano on a whim, although she cannot play it, while a true musician is hindered from developing her gift for want of such a piano, there is something irrational and unjust in this distribution. This is the morality attaching to the use or consumption of goods: things ought to be given to those who need them more in preference to those who need them less. Commodities should be distributed so as to maximize the good they do. (We think of this as a socialist or communist principle of distribution, egalitarian and beneficial to the poor, but it can equally be used—and was used—by aristocrats, who justified their unequal riches, not by the claim to have worked for them, heaven forbid, but through the claim that they alone put wealth to its highest and truest use: to lift men above necessity, to free them for the life of genuine excellence and nobility.)

These two antithetical moral ideas are present in all human beings. Throughout history, the conflict between the two has riven our societies and torn our hearts. Since ancient times, philosophers have highlighted this problem. Most of them have seen the morality of use, of "to each according to his need," as the higher and more ideal principle (since consumption is the end and purpose of production), but the morality of "to each according to his production" as the more necessary one (since, if there is no effective incentive for production, there will be no goods for anyone to consume). Thus, Plato, in his utopian writing, the *Republic*, calls for the abolition of private property in favor of distribution according to need or the ability to use well. But in his more realistic dialogue, the *Laws* (739d–e), he acknowledges that such a policy is fit for gods but not men.

Contemporary capitalism, which is to say welfare capitalism, has sought to combine the two principles by applying the principle of use or need to those below a certain level of income and that of production to those above it. This compromise has taken much of the edge off of the moral critique of capitalism arising from the former principle. In some cases, indeed, it has given the proponents of the principle of need something of a stake in the opposite principle through the growing awareness that the welfare state, being very costly, is not really sustainable without the higher economic growth generated by capitalism. This has produced a relative truce—whether temporary or permanent it is hard to say—in this fundamental moral conflict that has been perhaps the greatest and most enduring source of the debate over markets and morals.

PART I

The Glories and Miseries
of Marketization

CHAPTER 2

Economic Liberties and Human Rights

John Tomasi

Introduction

Should the private economic liberties of market society be recognized as universal human rights? I believe so: all people, everywhere, have powerful rights to engage in private economic activity. The most familiar arguments in favor of economic liberty emphasize social benefits that are often associated with the protection of economic liberty. But in making my case for recognizing private economic liberties as human rights, I shall explore another aspect of economic liberty. I call this the *personal argument* for economic liberty.

The Institutional Argument for Economic Liberty

Many publications lay out the economic case for private economic liberty. Typical of these is the *Index of Economic Freedom*, jointly published each year by the *Wall Street Journal* and the Heritage Foundation. The *Index of Economic Freedom* ranks each country in the world by the degree of protection afforded to ten economic liberties collected under four headings: the rule of law (property rights, freedom from corruption); limited government (fiscal freedom, government spending); regulatory efficiency (business freedom, labor freedom, monetary freedom); and open markets (trade freedom, investment freedom, monetary freedom).[1]

Readers of the *Index of Economic Freedom* will be familiar with the political and material case for economic liberty. There is a robust positive correlation between the protection of economic freedom and the achievement of important goals such as material prosperity and political liberty. As the authors of the *Index* recently summarized their findings, "Countries with higher levels of economic freedom substantially outperform others in economic growth, per capita incomes, health care, education, protection of the environment, and reduction of poverty."[2] We may call this the *institutional argument* for economic freedom.

Now, if we believe that it is important that people everywhere enjoy goods such as decent health care, a clean environment, and rising per capita wages, then, in drawing attention to the link between economic freedom and the production of these political and material values—that is, in making the institutional case for economic liberty—we are ipso facto making a moral case for economic freedom too. Let me say straightaway that I affirm the importance of defending the moral dimension of economic freedom in these institutional terms. This is a vital point and I shall return to it by the end. However, I also wish to call attention to another aspect of the moral case for economic freedom. For in addition to the institutional case for economic freedom, there is also what I call the *personal case* for economic liberty. And this personal case for economic liberty, I believe, may support my thesis that the private economic liberties of capitalism should be recognized as basic human rights.

The *personal case* for economic liberty rests on a simple idea. We should defend economic liberty not merely because such liberties have a proven record of securing political and material benefits—vitally important as those goods may be—but also because by protecting economic liberty, we respect other people as our *moral equals*. In particular, when we insist that governments protect private economic liberty, we insist that those governments respect their citizens as responsible authors of their own lives.

When people are free, they think of themselves, in some sense, as the central causes of the particular lives they are leading. This is a familiar idea among Western and, perhaps in particular, American citizens. But, in Western countries, it is not just captains of industry or heroes of Ayn Rand novels who define themselves through their accomplishments in the economic realm. In the West, many ordinary people—middle-class parents, single moms, entry-level workers, small-scale entrepreneurs—become who they are, and express who they hope to be, by the personal choices they make regarding working, saving, and spending. These are areas in which people earn esteem from others and feel a sense of pride for the things that they do.

To fully understand the moral importance of economic liberty, we may need to widen the lens through which we view the importance of economic activity. In economic affairs, after all, it is not only the outcome that matters: the process must be considered too. Possessing some particular bundle of material goods, from this perspective, becomes *personally meaningful* if one possesses that bundle because of one's own actions and choices. Diminishing personal agency in economic affairs—no matter how lofty the social goal—drains vital blood from a person's life. When private economic freedoms are curtailed, people become less free.

None of this is to diminish the importance of the *institutional case* for economic freedom. Economic liberties may well be linked to other basic rights and liberties; they may tend to promote the creation of social wealth, to reduce government corruption, and to mitigate the dangers of concentrated political power. But, in addition, individuals, not just in the West but everywhere, have a moral right to be respected as *causes* or, as I prefer, as *responsible authors* of their own lives. Thus, the personal case for private economic liberty is worth making too.

I mentioned that the *Index of Economic Freedom* sets out and measures ten separate areas of economic freedom, a comprehensive scheme that attends to important institutional dimensions of economic liberty. To make the *personal case* for economic liberty, I shall cut up the conceptual space a bit differently, by focusing on the first-personal aspects of economic freedom.

James Nickel, a prominent philosopher of human rights, distinguishes four (partially overlapping) categories of economic liberty, all of which protect autonomy of action in economic affairs. Nickel's four categories are liberties of labor, transacting, holding, and using.[3] Regarding the economic liberty of *labor*, Nickel says, "This is the liberty to employ one's body and time in productive activity that one has chosen or accepted, and under arrangements that one has chosen or accepted." The liberty of *transacting* allows individuals to engage in free economic activity: "the freedom to manage one's economic affairs at the individual and household levels and on larger scales as well." Transacting involves the liberty to trade in the marketplace, to create things for sale, and to save and invest. It also covers the freedom of individuals and groups to start, run, and close down businesses such as factories, shops, farms, and commercial enterprises of many sorts. The economic liberty of *holding* concerns freedom in the realm of several property.

"This category covers legitimate ways of acquiring and holding productive property, using and developing property for commercial and productive purposes, and property transactions such as investing, buying, selling, trading and giving." Finally, there is a range of liberties concerning *using*: "the liberty to make use of legitimately acquired resources for consumption and production." The liberty of using protects the freedom of citizens to buy, use, and consume natural resources, consumer goods, and services. On the commercial level, this liberty protects production-related consumption (such as deciding which parts to use, or which power sources to purchase). On the domestic level, it protects a range of personal economic decision making, including questions about what to eat and drink, what to wear, what type of housing to occupy, and a wide range of services one might choose to purchase. To simplify, I will refer to these first-personal economic liberties as the liberties of *working* and *owning*.

Most legal systems include some degree of protection for each of these categories of private economic liberty. However, systems differ dramatically in the way they specify the activities that are to be protected in each category. Systems also differ in the degree of importance they assign to such protections when they conflict with other social goals and values.[4]

I will be setting out the personal case for economic liberty within a *classical liberal* framework. This is the framework pioneered by radical English thinkers such as John Lilburne and John Locke, developed in the American context by Founders such as James Madison, and defended in our day by legal scholars such as Richard Epstein and economic historians such as Deirdre McCloskey (both contributors to this volume).

Classical liberals such as Epstein and McCloskey affirm what I call a "thick" conception of economic liberty.[5] They tend to interpret each category of private economic liberty as having a wide scope. Regarding the liberties of holding (or "owning"), for example, classical liberals affirm not only the right to ownership of personal property (as guaranteed even by most socialist systems) but rights to private ownership of productive property as well. People should be free to start small businesses, join in large capital ventures with others, and generally establish economic entities of a great many kinds (including, if they wish, worker-directed cooperatives). Closely connected, classical liberals typically interpret the economic liberty of labor to include a wide freedom of individuals to negotiate personally the terms of their employment (including both wage rates and number of hours to be worked). Classical liberals interpret the economic liberty of transacting to include the right of individuals to decide for themselves how much to save for retirement or invest in health insurance, and to make decisions about many other issues of long-term financial planning.

Further, classical liberals see these wide-ranging economic liberties as being especially weighty compared to other social values. They see economic liberties as having a political status comparable to that of the other traditional liberal rights and liberties, such as those of speech and association. But classical liberals do not treat economic liberties as moral absolutes or as in any way more basic than the other fundamental rights and liberties. While important, such liberties do not trump every other social concern.

This last feature distinguishes classical liberalism from the closely related but importantly distinct tradition of *libertarianism*. By libertarians, I am thinking of historical figures such as Lysander Spooner and more recent writers such as Murray Rothbard, Robert Nozick, and Ayn Rand. Classical liberals and libertarians share an appreciation for the great institutional and personal importance of private economic liberty. But while classical liberals see economic liberties as among the weightiest rights, libertarians tend to see property rights as the weightiest rights of all, even as moral absolutes.

Unlike libertarians, classical liberals accept that even the weightiest economic liberties can sometimes be curtailed or regulated in order to preserve other foundational liberties, and sometimes to allow the pursuit of other important social purposes as well. For example, classical liberals typically do not believe that the state should enforce contracts that alienate citizens from their other basic rights and liberties (for example, an economic contract that requires a person to engage in some form of religious devotion or to enter into slavery). Second, classical liberals traditionally grant that governments have some (carefully limited) powers of eminent domain. They also recognize governments as having the power to maintain free and competitive markets by regulating or breaking up monopolies of scarce resources or by forbidding various forms of collusion and price fixing.

My thesis is that liberties of working and owning, interpreted within a wider classical liberal framework, have great personal moral value. But this thesis is controversial among citizens of the West. It is controversial not just within pockets of Marxists and socialists, but across wide swaths of people living in (and voting in) Western liberal democracies.

Classical liberals, as we have noted, celebrate the ideal of a world in which there exist large and growing privately held business enterprises, where workers typically negotiate the terms of their own employment within a free and competitive labor market, and where individuals are largely responsible for saving for their own retirement or making their own arrangements for medical care. Classical liberals, unlike strict libertarians, see this regime of private economic liberty as operating within an institutional setting in which the state provides a floor of material benefits and opportunities that protects all citizens who face special difficulties or who fall temporarily on hard times.

Still, many people recoil at this vision of a well-functioning market society. They see the world of private economic liberty as a site of injustice, of exploitation, and of vulnerability. A world of private economic liberty is itself a world that calls for correction. Thinkers such as Michael Sandel, Debra Satz, and, in particular, Steven Lukes in his contribution to this volume, warn against any expansion of the reach of the market.[6] Thus, many people *reject*, or at least are wary of, the personal case for economic liberty.

Further, as I just hinted, many critics also reject the personal case for economic liberty on what they believe to be moral grounds. If a world of personal economic liberty is said to be unjust and exploitative, then many people will rally *against* those liberties when they hear the moral call. This fact must honestly be faced. To understand this perspective, and to see how powerfully it shapes the view of many people within Western democracies, it is important to examine the historical roots of this skeptical perspective regarding the moral value of economic liberty.

From Mill, to Keynes, to Rawls

John Stuart Mill, writing in the mid-1800s, was one of the first thinkers in the liberal tradition to express ambivalence about the moral status of economic liberty. Earlier classical liberals, such as James Madison and Benjamin Constant, had seen private economic liberties as fully on a par with the civil and political rights of individuals: the right to a fair trial, freedom of expression, political participation, personal autonomy, and so on. But when Mill surveyed the traditional list of liberal liberties, however, he singled out the economic liberties for relegation to a distinctly secondary place.

Mill's official argument for treating the economic liberties in this exceptional way is based on his distinction between two spheres of human activity. In the sphere of liberty are activities that primarily concern only the individual or, if they involve other people, they do so only with the free consent and participation of those people. Mill saw this as the sphere of individual liberty.[7] The other sphere, that of coercion, concerns activities that directly affect other people. Society does have a direct interest in the activities within this latter sphere, and so the state may properly exercise coercion there to promote the common good. While Mill sees freedoms of speech and assembly, conscience and religion, and other activities central to being the author of one's own life as self-regarding activities (that is, as aspects of liberty), he insists that economic activities—seeking a job, deciding whether to save or spend the income one earns—are other-regarding, and thus not aspects of liberty properly understood. In Mill's succinct formulation, "trade is a social act."[8] Thus trade is a domain appropriately subject to social control and regulation—without any diminution of the scope of liberty—rather than being itself a domain of protected liberty.

This is a curious argument. After all, speech and assembly are acts that affect others, and in that sense they appear to be just as "social" as trade.[9] So it seems we must look deeper to understand Mill's ambivalence about the personal importance of economic liberty.

Mill's moral and political philosophy rests ultimately on a perfectionist ideal of the person. Mill sees *individuality* as capturing something close to the moral essence of personhood. Though a self-proclaimed utilitarian, Mill emphasizes that he means "utility in the largest sense, grounded on the permanent interests of man as a progressive being."[10] Chief among those interests is that of developing a life plan to suit one's character. By creating such a plan, people express their distinctive sense of what is valuable and worth doing in life. By formulating and pursuing such a plan, people develop their higher capacities of reasoning, develop intimate connections with others, and enhance their moral sensitivities. Mill saw intellectual pursuits as central to a well-lived life, but he famously claimed to be open to experimentation. So he readily acknowledged that there might be a wide range of activities and life plans in which people find meaning and develop themselves as individuals.

However, Mill did not see how activities in the economic sphere could contribute to individuality in his sense. Freedoms of thought and association are important to forming and carrying out a life worthy of a person as a progressive being. But Mill did not see economic liberties—the freedom to hold productive property, or to enter into economic contracts—as playing any central role in this process. Starting a business, holding a job, seeking a promotion, being a breadwinner for one's family, saving for the future—these are roles that economic necessity may require people to play from time to time. But none of these activities is constitutive of liberty.[11] Economic life, Mill opined, provides barren soil for the development of individuality. Progressive beings do not need economic liberty in order to "pursue their own good their own way." For Mill, economic liberties are merely instrumentally valuable: "Property is only a means to an end, not itself the end."[12]

Mill is not the only prominent political economist to dismiss the personal importance of thick economic liberty. In 1930, John Maynard Keynes wrote a remarkable essay called "Economic Possibilities for Our Grandchildren."[13] Writing at a time of economic despair, Keynes expressed long-term optimism. He predicted that within one hundred years, during the lifetimes of his own grandchildren, the economies of Western democracies such as the United States and the United Kingdom would have grown by approximately ten times. At that point, roughly 2030, Keynes suggested, Western economies would have grown *enough*. The economic problem, the problem of scarcity that has bedeviled mankind since our appearance on this planet, would at last have been solved. That is, we would have reached a point of sufficient wealth that increases in capital accumulation could, and Keynes says, *should*, cease. When this (not-too-distant) day of prosperity dawns, Keynes suggested that a great moral change would occur across our social world.

What would change when the economic problem is solved? When the day of prosperity arrives, Keynes says that the busy, industrious, purposive, economic virtues, such as taking risks and toiling, scrimping today in order to save for tomorrow, striving and sacrificing so that the lives of one's children might be better than one's own—all those "bourgeois virtues"—might at last be recognized as the ugly vices that they have always been. We needed those deluded "virtues" to get us to the stage of sufficient wealth. But once wealth arrives, the central human problem will not be how to work better. Rather, our great problem will be how best to spend the leisure time that the toils of our parents, grandparents, and great-great-grandparents have bought us.

Keynes suggests that, for the first time in human history, life will not center on economic problems at all. Instead, it will center at last on the only properly human question: how, amid the abundance of wealth, "to live, wisely, agreeably, and well." And what about those who continue to show personal concern for economic questions, clinging to the traditional values of hard work and industry, self-reliance, and personal responsibility with respect to economic issues? In these new conditions, Keynes says that such attitudes are not virtues but "morbid neuroses." Indeed, Keynes (presumably jokingly) suggests that people who exhibit those neuroses should be confined to *mental institutions.*

Similarly, though less colorfully, John Rawls, writing in 1971, produced a great liberal democratic manifesto of social justice. Rawls offers a machinery that is designed to identify a strong set of distributive principles of justice, constrained by a list of basic rights and liberties that limit the reach and power of government. Rawls's spare list of basic rights includes protections in familiar areas of human freedom such as association and speech. However, following in the tradition of Mill and Keynes, Rawls makes no special place for the economic liberties of capitalism. Rawls's own proposed list of basic rights and liberties includes only what I shall call a "thin" conception of economic liberty: a right to the ownership of personal (but not productive) property and a narrow right to freedom of occupational choice (the right to choose the type of work one does, but no right to personally negotiate the terms on which one works). In Rawls's account, therefore, the requirements of liberal justice could be satisfied even within a socialist state.

So from Mill, through Keynes, to Rawls, and on to contemporary thinkers such as Sandel and Lukes, we can trace a line of skepticism about the moral worth of private economic liberty.

The Personal Case

I disagree with this tradition of thinking. Economic liberties are valuable not *only* because of their institutional and material advantages: for example, because the protection of private economic liberty is positively correlated with lower levels of political corruption and with increases in per capita income. Though eminent scholars have sometimes looked down their noses at the familiar work-a-day virtues associated with economic liberties, many ordinary working people see the development and exercise of these virtues, in support of one's own dreams and the dreams of those one loves, as the very *core* of a free life.

When we make decisions about how much we wish to work, at what wages, and in which business sector or profession, as when we make decisions about whether to spend now or save for later, we are not making decisions that are morally trivial. Instead, through our activities in these economic aspects of our lives, we each say something important about what we value and, indeed, about who we are. Decisions about saving and spending, for example, are among the most common economic quandaries faced by individuals, and these questions regularly confront people in free societies regardless of their income level. Those questions, distinctively, require that we each think carefully about the relationship between the person we are now and the person we will become in the future. Such decisions constitute among the most distinctive forms of taking responsibility for one's own life, and doing so in light of one's own dreams, values, and character. Economic choices about spending and saving, as with other economic decisions, such as setting oneself on one course of study or on one career path rather than another, constitute a kind of passageway from childhood or late adolescence toward full adulthood. Indeed, cross-temporal thinking of that sort is closely connected to the process of becoming a unique, fully formed individual. People who are denied the chance to make such choices for themselves, or whose range of decision making in these areas is truncated by others (no matter how well meaning), will live comparatively stunted lives, lives that are in some sense less fully *adult*.

The value of each class of liberty is often best discerned by studying the complaints of people to whom those liberties have been denied. I personally first came to understand the personal importance of economic liberty through reading work by certain leaders of the feminist movement in England and the United States during the nineteenth century.

Early feminist leaders such as Voltairine De Cleyre argued against patriarchy in a way that put the personal importance of economic liberty front and center.[14] No matter how "gilded" the social cage men of that era constructed for women, no matter how abundant the material goods available within that cage, or how tender the treatment, when still denied their economic liberties, denied the chance, that is, to have some role in the *creation* and *selection* of whatever goods they were to enjoy, feminist leaders of that era insisted that a great moral wrong was being done to them. By denying women their economic liberties, men prevented those women from fully developing as free and independent adults—as moral equals in charge of their own lives. Pointing to the comforts they were being provided by their male protectors could not make up for this fact. Denied full economic liberty, women of the era had been fundamentally disrespected—their moral agency, their capacity for responsible self-authorship, objectionably stunted and denied.

Perhaps there is an insight in this feminist critique that is relevant to us today. For that early feminist defense of economic liberty might well be turned against the material and bureaucratic ambitions of some contemporary social democracies. No matter how gilded the cage of a social democracy may seem, no matter how comfortable and plentiful the social guarantees, if the cost of receiving those benefits is the violation or truncation of personal economic liberty, then there is something objectionable about this scheme. This is a world, whatever its material bounty, with corresponding moral loss. That loss is what I mean by the personal value of economic liberty.

Human Rights

The Universal Declaration of Human Rights, adopted by the United Nations in 1948, aspired to recognize "the inherent dignity and . . . the equal and inalienable rights of all members of the human family." Such recognition, the General Assembly declared, was the necessary foundation of "freedom, justice and peace in the world."

The Declaration listed many familiar liberal democratic rights and protections, including freedom from arbitrary arrest and detention (article 9), the right to a fair and public trial (10), as well as rights to freedom of conscience and religion (18), opinion and expression (19), assembly and association (20), and political liberties, in the form of participation in democratic processes (21).

But the Declaration was famously tepid in its defense of private economic liberty. Article 17 declared that "Everyone has the right to own property alone as well as in association with others." But this formulation omitted any declaration of the right of persons privately to own productive property (whether that private ownership be individual or in association with others). Article 23 declared that everyone has the right to "free choice of employment." But this right to occupation choice omits any declaration about the liberty interest that individuals have in personally determining the conditions under which they might perform that chosen work. Indeed, the Declaration's exposition of the liberties of working is explicitly narrowed by Article 13, which avers that people have a right to movement merely "within the borders of each state," and the right to emigrate from and return to his or her own country only. This formulation omits any declaration that people have a right to move *between* countries. In sum, the Declaration affirms only what I have called a thin conception of private economic liberty.

Of course, while considered "thin" in terms of its recognition of private economic liberties, there are rival ideological perspectives from which the Declaration might be counted as thick in its defense of economic liberty. In the preamble, it affirms that people have a right not only to be free from fear but also to be free *from want*. Article 23, which sets out only a narrow right to freedom of occupational choice, avers that people have not only a right to choose which occupation to pursue but also a right to perform that work in "just and favorable conditions," including a right to protection from unemployment and a right to "just and favorable remuneration" for that work, "supplemented, if necessary, by other means of social protection." Article 24 affirms leisure, including paid holidays, as basic rights. Article 25 goes further, declaring that everyone has a right to "a standard of living adequate for the health and well-being . . . including food, clothing, housing and medical care and necessary social services." So the Declaration, while limiting the scope of the formal or negative economic liberties it recognizes, also declares various substantive or positive economic interests as basic rights.

I do not need to rehearse the reasons of *realpolitik* that led to this framing of the UN Declaration in the middle of the Cold War. But the tension we find in the Declaration is a product of more than a tension between communist and capitalist ideals of human living-together. The Declaration reflects a tension and a bias regarding the cogency of the normative possibilities with democracy itself. This bias is very much alive within the avowedly capitalist democracies of our time.

For in 1948, as today, the personal case for economic liberty is standardly conceived as being ineluctably in tension with another set of moral ideals, the ideal of material justice. The personal case for private economic liberty is pitted *against* a concern for fairness or social justice. And so, according to the normative theories of democracy that we have inherited, citizens everywhere face a set of stark and unhappy political choices: capitalism *or* democracy, classical liberalism *or* left liberalism, private economic liberty *or* freedom from want.

In *Free Market Fairness* and other work, I have been seeking ways to break this deadlock.[15] One way to do this is to hold tight to the personal case for economic liberty, and then to bring back the institutional case for economic liberty, but to do so in a way that affirms the moral requirement that the institutional benefits of private economic liberty must include citizens of all classes, genders, and races, including people working at the bottom of the existing pay scale.

If we consistently find a positive correlation between economic liberty and important social goods such as economic growth and rising per capita income, then the program of economic liberty might itself be defended on grounds of social justice. If that message can be communicated to our fellow citizens, then a *democratic* case for economic liberty might be forged. This is a classical liberal defense of private economic liberty, but with a foundational twist: it situates a liberty-based defense of private economic liberty within a broader commitment to social justice.

If we attend to the full index of economic liberties, their personal value as well as their capacity to create wealth that might be enjoyed by all, we may find ourselves aiming for a social ideal of both social abundance and personal freedom. This would allow for a richer and more attractive account of the resources available for the identification of basic human rights. Democracy *and* capitalism. Economic liberty *and* social justice. Free markets *and* fairness. By making this fuller case for economic liberty, perhaps, citizens of democratic polities, East and West, do not have to choose after all.

Notes

1. Terry Miller, Kim R. Holmes, and Edwin J. Feulner, *2013 Index of Economic Freedom: Promoting Economic Opportunity and Prosperity,* http://www.heritage.org/index/pdf/2013/book/index_2013.pdf (accessed July 3, 2017), 1.

2. For details, see the *Index of Economic Freedom* and its methodology, heritage.org/index 2013.

3. James Nickel, "Economic Liberties," in *The Idea of a Political Liberalism: Essays on Rawls,* ed. Victoria Davis and Clark Wolf (Lanham, Md.: Rowman and Littlefield, 2000), 155–76.

4. A classic discussion is Anthony Honoré, "Ownership," in *Oxford Essays in Jurisprudence,* ed. A. G. Guest (London: Oxford University Press, 1960), 108.

5. John Tomasi, *Free Market Fairness* (Princeton, N.J.: Princeton University Press, 2012).

6. See, respectively, Michael J. Sandel, *What Money Can't Buy* (New York: Farrar, Straus and Giroux, 2014); Debra Satz, *Why Some Things Should Not Be for Sale: The Moral Limits of Markets* (New York: Oxford University Press, 2010); and Steven Lukes,

"'Getting and Spending, We Lay Waste Our Powers': On the Expanding Reach of the Market," this volume.

7. Mill describes this as "a sphere of action in which society, as distinguished from the individual, has, if any, only an indirect interest; comprehending all that portion of a person's life and conduct which affects only himself, or if it also affects others, only with their free, voluntary, and undeceived consent and participation." John Stuart Mill, *On Liberty*, http://www.econlib.org/library/Mill/mlLbty.html, chap. 1, sec. 12.

8. John Stuart Mill, *Principles of Political Economy* (Amherst, N.Y.: Prometheus Books, 2004) [hereafter: *PPE*], II.ii.

9. Daniel Jacobson, "Mill on Liberty, Speech, and the Free Society," *Philosophy & Public Affairs* 20, no. 3 (2000): 293–95.

10. Mill, *On Liberty*, chap. 1, sec. 11.

11. Jacobson comments, "Since the life of a capitalist does not necessarily violate the rights of others, it constitutes a permissible way of life. While this means that capitalism cannot be prohibited, it does not follow that 'capitalist acts between consenting adults'—to borrow a phrase from Robert Nozick—are within the sphere of liberty." "Mill on Liberty, Speech, and the Free Society," 295.

12. Mill, *PPE*, II.ii, sec. 4. The next sentence reads: "Like all other proprietary rights, and even in a greater degree than most, the power of bequest may be so exercised as to conflict with the permanent interests of the human race."

13. John Maynard Keynes, "Economic Possibilities for Our Grandchildren," 1930, http://www.econ.yale.edu/smith/econ116a/keynes1.pdf (accessed November 2010), 6.

14. Wendy McElroy, *Individualist Feminism of the Nineteenth Century: Collected Writings and Biographical Profiles* (Jefferson, N.C.: McFarland, 2001).

15. Tomasi, *Free Market Fairness*; Symposium on *Free Market Fairness*, in *Bleeding Heart Libertarians* (Summer 2012) (esp. replies to Samuel Freeman and Elizabeth Anderson); John Tomasi, "Market Democracy and Meaningful Work: A Reply to Critics," *Res Publica* 21, no. 4 (2015): 443–60.

Bibliography

Honoré, Anthony. "Ownership." In *Oxford Essays in Jurisprudence*, edited by A. G. Guest, 107–47. London: Oxford University Press, 1960.

Jacobson, Daniel. "Mill on Liberty, Speech, and the Free Society." *Philosophy & Public Affairs* 20, no. 3 (2000): 276–309.

Keynes, John Maynard. "Economic Possibilities for Our Grandchildren." 1930. http://www.econ.yale.edu/smith/econ116a/keynes1 (accessed July 2010).

McElroy, Wendy. *Individualist Feminism of the Nineteenth Century: Collected Writings and Biographical Profiles*. Jefferson, N.C.: McFarland, 2001.

Mill, John Stuart. *Principles of Political Economy.* Amherst, N.Y.: Prometheus Books, 2004.

———. *On Liberty.* London: Longman, Roberts, and Green, 1869. http://www.econlib .org/library/Mill/mlLbty (accessed July 2010).

Miller, Terry, Kim R. Holmes, and Edwin J. Feulner. *2013 Index of Economic Freedom: Promoting Economic Opportunity and Prosperity.* http://www.heritage.org/index /pdf/2013/book/index_2013.pdf (accessed July 3, 2017).

Nickel, James. "Economic Liberties." In *The Idea of a Political Liberalism: Essays on Rawls,* edited by Victoria Davis and Clark Wolf, 155–76. Lanham, Md.: Rowman and Littlefield, 2000.

Sandel, Michael J. *What Money Can't Buy.* New York: Farrar, Straus and Giroux, 2014.

Satz, Debra. *Why Some Things Should Not Be for Sale: The Moral Limits of Markets.* New York: Oxford University Press, 2010.

Tomasi, John. *Free Market Fairness.* Princeton, N.J.: Princeton University Press, 2012.

———. "Market Democracy and Meaningful Work: A Reply to Critics." *Res Publica* 21, no. 4 (2015): 443–60.

CHAPTER 3

Smart Consequentialism: Kantian Moral Theory and the (Qualified) Defense of Capitalism

Richard A. Epstein

Introduction: The What and the Why of Capitalism

The purpose of this chapter is to offer a defense of what is broadly understood to be a capitalist economy, which for these purposes is well enough defined as "an economic and political system in which a country's trade and industry are controlled by private owners for profit, rather than by the state."[1] The grounds of this defense shall be overtly consequentialist, but with this twist: I shall insist that, even though many writers purport to find ways to evaluate these systems in deontological terms, these so-called backward justifications ultimately resolve themselves into consequentialist arguments. The simple starting point for all analysis is that market capitalism cannot survive if force and fraud are allowed free sway, and that they must be controlled to make long-term investment possible. No standard deontological theory—especially Kantian theory—can justify this simple proposition in an acceptable way; rather, deontology can only succeed if it is reinterpreted, against the wishes of Kant, its leading expositor, in an explicitly consequentialist fashion. The stakes here are enormous: if notions of obligation are construed too narrowly, all sorts of dangerous behaviors can go without sanction. If they are construed too broadly, all sorts of legitimate competitive behaviors can be destroyed by a set of restrictive practices, in both domestic and foreign markets. The efforts to intuit the right institutional arrangements by deontic strategies, most notably by those in the Kantian tradition (which need not and do not embrace all elements of Kant's thought), often lead to just these conceptual breakdowns.[2]

I have come to this position after a longish journey that started from the exact opposite premise: that all small-government arguments had to begin with some intuitive definition of individual autonomy that was largely divorced from calculations about overall social welfare.[3] That conclusion rested on two complementary grounds. The first was that it seemed impossible to me then to devise any method to evaluate the social consequences of any legal rules, given the huge numbers of individuals that they had to govern. The second was that the results that were reached in individual cases seemed to closely track the common law, which had worked so well for so long in so many different contexts. Why then abandon a workable intuitive approach for an unworkable theoretical framework?

It is important to understand why this approach appeared to work and why it broke down. The key element has to do with the selection of legal issues for discussion. As was common in legal analysis for at least the last half century, the major disputes under examination arose from litigation between two people. In this setting the dominant purpose was to find out the right solution exclusively from the ex post perspective. Little explicit attention was paid to the incentive effects of the rule on future transactions, including transactions that often involved unrelated parties. The plaintiff sued for breach of contract or for an injury to his person or property. The defendant often responded by showing that the plaintiff had not kept her own promises or had violated the rules of the road in ways that contributed to the accident. The resolution of these cases in a two-party universe managed to track the fault of both people, and it was hard to see why any effort to introduce third-party consequences could lead to better results than the ones already obtained.

The challenge was to understand how well these results generalized from two parties to when additional persons were added into the equation. In one sense, that process worked very well. If the plaintiff had acquired contract rights from a third party, the correct mode of analysis broke down the transaction into three parts: the original deal between the promisor and the promisee, the subsequent deal for the acquisition of the rights between the assignor and the assignee, and the ultimate suit between the assignee and the original promisor. On the tort side, similar issues could arise when two or more individuals committed actions that hurt a third. The process of breakdown and reassembly worked well without any overt consideration of larger social phenomena.

Yet as my own studies progressed, the limits of this approach became far clearer. It was not possible to think of property rules solely in terms of the individual right to exclude, when complex rights in water, oil and gas, the radio spectrum, and the Internet were at issue.[4] Nor did the simple paradigms cover the difficulties with protecting information contained in patents, copyrights, trademarks, trade secrets, and data sets. It was not possible to think about torts solely in terms of damage to person or property when there was urgent concern over the dissipation of common-pool assets like fish and game, or the pollution of public air and water. It was not possible to understand how to operate a bankruptcy system without understanding the collective action problems that arose when multiple creditors pursued single debtors. Nor could one, using the bilateral common-law mode of analysis, figure out the optimal governance structures for corporations or partnerships, let alone those complex political structures that require systems of taxation for revenue collection and public expenditure. Even in the area of ordinary business arrangements, it was not possible to think about the antitrust law solely in terms of private transactions, for many claims entail systematic adverse effects on third parties via the creation of cartels and monopoly. In all these critical cases, it did not work to hold that people should just keep their promises, because all antitrust violators were more than happy to do that. And it did not help to think of torts as solely dealing with the protection of private property when so many valuable assets lay in the public realm.

The more global approach that builds these externalities of private conduct into the ground floor of a functioning legal system became a real focal point of the overall analysis.[5] At one point, the new cases seemed to overwhelm the old rule. The phenomenon is most pronounced in connection with the rules that stand in the closest arrangement to capitalism, as rules on taxation, regulation, and trade surely do. At all points, the purpose of the analysis is to *solve* particular disputes as they arise in the context of ordinary and social life. At this point, it is at major variance with so much of modern philosophy, which is concerned less with legal interactions as such than with a priori accounts of duties to one's self and with psychological accounts of the relationship of individual goodwill to the morality of given actions.[6] Neither of these issues has ever made a dent in standard legal analysis of natural law concepts, even though the same words are used on just this topic by eminent philosophers of natural law.

How then to take these new complications into account? One possibility was to jettison the old system and to start afresh with a different set of rules— assuming that one could articulate what they were. But in the end the better approach was to build on the initial corrective-justice system, so useful in resolving small number disputes, by adding layers of complexity when circumstances required it. The overall approach is not vacuous, given the small number of core principles that formed the basis of the common and (one must never forget) the Roman law. These rules have proved robust even after the full range of external effects is included.

So here is how this overall program evolved. The first question to ask about any private solution between A and B is to convert it into a proposition that relates to overall social welfare by dealing with the externalities, both positive and negative, that it creates. The happy conclusion here is that the common-law rules of property, tort, and contract prove relatively robust over a large portion of their original domain. The explanation is this: with these two- or few-party disputes, no outsider is systematically implicated in their application. The parties have virtually identical positions, so that the impact on one is similar to the impact on all. At this point a good approximation of the externality, positive or negative, is just n (the number of people) multiplied by the effect on any one of them. It follows therefore that for most contract transactions, a mutual gain between the parties results in increased opportunities for third persons, so that positive externalities dominate the system. Indeed, the benefit helps explain why it is critical to have public subsidies for legal enforcement: providing the security that incentivizes voluntary transactions is the only way to secure those external gains. Likewise, in the domain of torts the prohibition on force and fraud between private parties also generates external gains, which again explains why public enforcement of these norms increases its overall positive effect on human well-being. Contracts are positive-sum games; torts are negative-sum games. The enforcement of the first and the suppression of the second produce social as well as private gains, at least as a first approximation.

Yet by the same token, this initial libertarian-like move does not necessarily exhaust the gains from social intervention. The previously noted complex systems all involve cases where some deviation from the common-law rules can either stop an externality (e.g., systematic welfare losses from cartel or monopoly) or create an externality (e.g., more intellectual property through the protection of patents and copyrights): more than the common law can generate. So at this point there is the universal test that each modification of the initial common-law baseline has to meet: it must show that the new system produces a Pareto improvement over the old one, such that at least one person is left better off and no one is left worse off after these changes are made. Indeed, in many cases with the change of general rules, we can even go further and create a system that produces pro rata gains for all, eliminating the competition over surplus by using a uniform rule that benefits all equally.

The number of these potential modifications in the law is quite large. Yet *none* of them, if accepted, can be treated as reaching the final resting point. Instead, each new legal tweak forms a new baseline that may in turn be subject to further adjustments, provided they meet the old test of Pareto improvements, now relative to this new baseline. So antitrust enforcement may be relaxed to induce much-needed cooperation in network industries, and the copyright law can be subject to the fair use exception. There is no artificial or a priori way to limit the candidates for exception from the preexisting rules, and no reason to think that the set of potentially valuable changes is static over time. (Technological change can necessitate new rules; for instance, airplane overflight can only take place with some relaxation of the *ad coelum* rule that used to dominate real property law.) The system is thus dynamic and principled at the same time. But without a consequentialist base, the entire enterprise would be doomed from the start, because no one could decide which property right transformations are required.

Given these qualifications, one should then return to the standard definition of capitalism to see what it captures and, more important, what it misses. Again, capitalism is "an economic and political system in which a country's trade and industry are controlled by private owners for profit, rather than by the state."[7] Reference to private owners acting for profit rightly directs our attention to the unexceptionable proposition that investors are entitled to a reasonable rate of return on investment. But this definition, as with others like it, tends to downplay the role that private labor—entrepreneurial, managerial, and manual—and government activity play in a well-structured economy. It makes it appear that other factors of production are subordinate to capital. On the positive side, it means that the system of voluntary exchange for goods and services should be run by private parties. But the definition is equally important for what it misses. Even on the private side, it ignores the role of charitable institutions for education, medical research, religion, and the assistance of the poor. These clearly do not fall into the conventional definition of "trade or industry," but they are areas in which voluntarism works well. And the definition misses all the places from antitrust law to common-pool problems where new property systems are required. These are part of a capitalist system only in the sense that capitalism categorically rejects the approaches of its more interventionist rivals, such as socialism or progressivism, that start with powerful government ownership or regulation of the means of production, even in ordinary markets for services and goods, where the mixed system works. The purpose of this chapter is to examine the moral foundations of this capitalist system as outlined above, and to do so from two perspectives that should be, but often are not, part and parcel of moral discourse on this topic. The exercise here will take place with only a tiny slice of its potentially endless application. But it does so in areas where Kantian-like arguments are thought to have their greatest sway.

The first purpose of this chapter, then, is to expand on the initial point that consequentialist arguments, rightly understood, are essential to the moral apparatus used to evaluate the desirability of capitalism and two of its constituent elements: the institutions of private property and voluntary contract. Indeed, I will go further and assert, in a way that is certain to cause umbrage among many moralists (both pro- and anti-capitalism), that the *only* way in which to understand capitalism is in terms of its overall social utility measured not in the aggregate, but by the Pareto and Kaldor-Hicks standards that construct collective social indices out of individual preferences, without seeking to sum the utilities of one person, in some cardinalist fashion with those of all others.

These two definitions are familiar enough not to require extensive elaboration. A Pareto improvement makes at least one person better off and no person worse off. A Kaldor-Hicks improvement produces gains such that the winners could make compensatory payments to the losers in ways that would still leave themselves better off, even if the payments are only hypothetical. In this world, all externalities are eliminated in theory because everyone has his or her place in the social utility function. Both systems are therefore comprehensive. One common feature is that all permissible moves expand the overall social pie, even if they differ in their distributional effects. Put otherwise, neither system tolerates negative-sum games. The political economy of operating under the two systems also differs in how coalitions will behave, but I leave those public choice questions to another day. The use of either of these measuring rods essentially preserves the central role that each person in the community plays in the overall social calculus, because at no point is any person forced to take a status inferior to that accorded to any other person. That point is straightforward for the Pareto system. It is more controversial under Kaldor-Hicks, where some do win and some lose. But from the ex ante perspective no one knows which role he or she will occupy, so that future expectations are necessarily positive. And in both systems, each person counts for one and only one, and each person has a distinctive role to play in the organization of overall social interactions.

For these purposes, both formulations are the appropriate rule of analysis because they each take into account the welfare of *all* citizens, and thus immunize versions of market capitalism deriving from them against the charge that they are simply efforts of the privileged to stack the deck in their favor, which often travels under the rubric of "possessive individualism."[8] The choice between these two formulas matters, of course.[9] The great disadvantage of the Kaldor-Hicks rule is that hypothetical compensation does not help the party who is left worse off, no matter how perverse those distributional consequences, so that in general the correct approach is to start with the Pareto formula, which is kept in place except in those few transactions that satisfy two conditions: first, the net gains from the proposed change in legal regimes must be enormous; second, it must be practically impossible to organize a sensible set of compensation payments to losers at anything less than prohibitive cost.

It is also important to state briefly how these two tests relate to the Rawlsian approach of organizing social arrangements from behind a veil of ignorance.[10] In principle, that approach could lead to similar results because individuals behind the veil have to consider the welfare of everyone throughout the social order in order to figure out how to maximize their own welfare once the veil is lifted. But Rawls does not supply us with the needed tools for making those judgments, and unfortunately tends to overrate the importance of risk aversion in ordinary social affairs, a defect that can only be resolved by resorting to either the Pareto or Kaldor-Hicks models. More concretely, Rawls, like most philosophers, does not take into account the transaction costs associated with putting the correct institutional arrangements into play, even though these are critical for getting the right trade-offs in institutional design.

Once this last task is done, I shall then show how these social measures map onto the conventional account of Kantian universalism in ways that capture the essential force of his argument without falling into the unswerving absolutism, be it of autonomy, property, or duty, that all too often plagues Kantian thought. In speaking of a Kantian approach, I do not necessarily mean Kant's philosophy alone.[11] The term also covers other philosophers who are deeply suspicious of, if not hostile to, consequentialist arguments, and who seek to ground morality in some primary and necessary principles that do not lose their force in a world of empirical facts that lacks the necessary uniformity for categorical judgments. I hope to demonstrate why these moral arguments, however great their ingenuity, cannot help in solving the sorts of problems that have captured the attention of serious lawyers, especially in the natural law tradition from ancient times.[12]

The enormous literature that seeks to explicate Kantian notions works given the presumption that the only thing that matters is the moral judgment of right and wrong. But that hopelessly blinkered view ignores all questions of whether the same rules should apply to civil or criminal liability, and shows not the slightest interest in whether our institutions should be designed to stop various wrongs before they occur or to wait until after the harm has taken place. As such, any system of Kantian ethics, standing alone, is so impoverished that it cannot explain how the morality of any individual or collective dispute ties in with a commitment to capitalism, socialism, or anything else. The profundity of the discourse barely conceals the poverty of its specific results.

The chief source of this difficulty is the widespread unwillingness to see how serious judges and lawyers have developed their theories of responsibility. It is that approach that I urge resistant readers to consider here. Within this explicitly legal framework, I shall first address the morality of capitalism by looking at ordinary private disputes, which cover both contracts that are enforced *and* those that are regarded as illegal and unenforceable. The purpose of this exercise is to dispel the notion that any form of market order will necessarily ignore systematic negative externalities and to show how the overall system is put together in a way that properly identifies those voluntary arrangements that should and should not be enforced. Indeed, unless a decent law governs the commission of fraud, markets will disappear because people will know in advance that they cannot rely on the promises and cooperation of others, which is of course an explicit consequentialist justification. But making the point in the general way will not do the job without some more granular investigation of the respective roles of lying and of the sanctity of promises in the overall legal system. It is critical for markets to show how voluntary exchanges, suitably understood and enforced, create desirable outcomes measured under the criterion set out above.

Thereafter, in the second section, I shall explain what I perceive to be the strengths and weaknesses of the Kantian account of the duties of benevolence. Questions of benevolence have long been a great challenge to any legal system. In general, the view has been that these obligations are not enforceable by direct legal action, for there is no obvious way to pair up any particular benevolent actor with any designated recipient. Instead, the usual response in these areas is to think of "imperfect obligations" of beneficence, where it is understood that these obligations bind as a matter of conscience and social convention but not as a matter of positive law. And the source of that obligation stems from two sorts. In individual cases of rescue or assistance, it arises from the necessity of the moment. But in systemic cases of poverty and bad luck, it arises from the perceived need to take steps to aid those less fortunate than ourselves.

The third section then explores how Kantian morality deals with the big-picture issues of public control over the entire legal system. Kantian moral theories do not explain how individual disputes fit within the larger social welfare functions where negative and positive externalities have to be systematically addressed. By the same token, his moral absolutism leads him astray even in the small-number conflicts that do fall within his zone of interest. I look at the larger landscape first and then turn to the smaller portraits. Needless to say, I can only touch a fraction of the issues mentioned earlier in the broad outline of the introduction.

Smart Consequentialism in Ordinary Private Disputes

A Framework of Presumptions

The previous analysis looked at the role of Kantian and consequentialist theories from the vantage point of large social perspectives. But Kant's failure, shared by most Kantians, to understand the search for Pareto improvements leads to his well-known absolutism in two-party situations, an absolutism that in no way is or should be required by his overall moral theory. The most general point here is that every time Kant uses the term "absolute," or worse, "absolute necessity," he steers the analysis in the wrong direction. The point becomes evident by the use of ordinary language—and I mean ordinary language in every language—in which discussions of moral behavior are couched not in terms of absolutes but in terms of presumptions. The presumption is the standard tool by which people try to escape two serious impediments to thinking about the cases that come before them. The first is the vice that Kant deplored, namely, the formless nature of moral judgments in a world in which case determinations were left unguided by general principles transcending the particular. The second is the vice that Kant committed, which is to assume that all presumptions were irrebuttable, so that once the basic facts are determined no constellation of additional facts or circumstances can lead to an alteration of the basic judgment.

It is, however, not necessary to succumb to the weaknesses of ad hoc justifications in order to avoid the Procrustean bed of absolute rules. Thus common language speaks constantly of reasons why a particular rule does not apply. Some of these involve justifications for conduct, and others involve excuses. With regard to the first, deliberate actions inflicting harm (remember, it is not possible to justify an accidental harm, even if it may be excused) that are prima facie wrongful can become proper, say in the case of self-defense or consent. These defenses are themselves defeasible. The privilege of self-defense does not allow the use of excessive force, and the consent to harm in the context of a hazardous activity or sport is put to one side if induced by fraud or duress. Similarly, a charge of murder may be deflected by the excuse of insanity or perhaps duress by third persons. My purpose here is not to develop all stages of these various decision trees,[13] but simply to draw attention to their general structure.

These excuses operate in some ways like justifications in that they undercut the prima facie case. But it would be wrong to think that they had the same valence. If I am justly using force to defend myself from a third party's attack, any person who comes to my aid is entitled to a similar defense if he or she inflicts harm on my assailant. But if I am gripped by insanity and attack another person, a third person who assists me is guilty of a crime, even though the insanity excuse may let me off the hook. But if I again attempt the same attack a second time after recovery from a bout of insanity, I would be guilty of a crime. In contrast, a party who is justified in the one case is justified if the identical circumstances should arise thereafter. We need both excuses and justifications as classes of defense, and this is but one instance of many where the durability of ordinary language bears silent testimony to the basic distinctions it embodies—a lesson that too many skeptics forget in too many contexts.

This basic argument can be put into explicit consequentialist terms.[14] The initial challenge is to put some order into moral life. But we recognize that we cannot use a sweeping facile formulation to resolve all outstanding challenges at a single bound, so we start small and build out. The initial presumption is that all individuals are allowed to do what they will. The logic of this position is that we know that one person has profited from this kind of arrangement, which, *ceteris paribus*, is an improvement over the prior state of affairs where no one is allowed to do anything. But this presumption in favor of liberty cannot survive unmodified if other individuals are harmed in the process. At that point the question is how to take that harm into account. A careless Millian could use the harm principle to negate virtually every action done by one person on the ground that it necessarily hurts another. But to take that position is to make the mistake of ignoring the principle of *damnum absque injuria* and treating all forms of competitive injury as actionable. Thus, one backs off from that position, so that the harm principle covers only force and fraud, just as the libertarian and Kantian would have it.

At this point, however, it becomes silly to claim that every use of force or fraud necessarily requires condemnation, so the office of the doctrines of justification and excuse is to back off from this conception in those cases where the long-term social benefits from the use of force or fraud—think self-defense—justify the deviation from the prima facie case. Further iterations allow for further refinements. With each step, the hope is that the systematic social gains make these incremental adjustments universalizable. But with each additional positive step, the potential gains from the next iteration get smaller, until the equities are so close that the proper rule becomes much more difficult to determine. But the consolation is that the further we go down any particular branch of the decision tree, the lower the likelihood that the choice of decision rule will matter in any particular case. At some point, therefore, the final choice of rule will depend on conflicting inferences from various facts and circumstances in ways that offend every Kantian fiber. Nonetheless, any sound social system requires constant trade-offs at the margin, and these are inconsistent with any invocation of Kantian absolutes. Put simply, there is no social system that runs without a bit of wobble. The drag generated in the toughest but least frequent situations only confirms the commonsense view that in trials, whether before a judge or jury, there are always some cases that could come out either way. The moral theory can never negate the factual uncertainty, so, ironically, the same consequentialist logic that works with the macro questions works with the micro questions as well. Below, I explain how the basic point plays out with fraud and promise keeping, both of which are high on the list of Kantian duties.

Fraud

One constant refrain in Kantian writing is the categorical duty to refrain from the commission of fraudulent acts. On this point, Kant spurns the wisdom of everyday life, and moves instead to a more ethereal plane by insisting,

> Everyone must admit that if a law is to have moral force, i.e., to be the basis of an obligation, it must carry with it absolute necessity; that, for example, the precept, "Thou shalt not lie," is not valid for men alone, as if other rational beings had no need to observe it; and so with all the other moral laws properly so called; that, therefore, the basis of obligation must not be sought in the nature of man, or in the circumstances in the world in which he is placed, but *a priori* simply in the conception of pure reason.[15]

This whole approach jumps head first into an intellectual morass. What Kantian philosophers refuse to grasp is that there are no transcendental a priori moral truths that exist independent of the welfare of the community that is regulated, except in some ethereal universe where everybody uniformly respects the freedom, dignity, and autonomy of others, at which point there would no place for any law to deal with coercion or fraud at all. For these purposes, I am quite happy to acknowledge that other rational beings know the importance of lying in interactions with their rivals, and the risk of lying to their allies. The need for deception and cooperation exists among all social animals. Kant may have compared uneducated people to cattle (Vieh). But it is dangerous to underestimate the sophistication of animals. Many animals—think of predator and prey relationships—know instinctively how to communicate and, when necessary, deceive.[16] Cognitively advanced language skills are not necessary to practice dissimulation or to fake an attack in one direction before striking from another. Higher-level cognition is overrated for decisions made in the here and now, such as the decision either to cooperate or to deceive. Those who cannot read these signals, like people with acute autism, are at a huge social disadvantage.[17]

Yet let us see what to make of the absolute precept, "Thou shalt not lie," which is supposed to be the result of pure reason. Unfortunately, things just don't work out that way, because the method of presumptions and justifications applies to this realm of human discourse as it does everywhere else. In most instances, people communicate with people with whom they hope to cooperate, as they are bound by a common interest, often within families or businesses. In these settings, they typically wish to convey their own inner sentiments in order to achieve the synergies that come from cooperation. So they develop modes of sincerity and other bonding mechanisms (guarantees, admissions, releases, and even hostages) to defuse the possibility that their overtures will be rejected as lies when in fact they are not intended to deceive. Note the explicit contrast: the lie is the effort to take advantage of another, but it need not succeed. Ordinary language captures the point: one *lies to* another person, but only if the lie is successful *deceives* the target. Truthful communication is encouraged in the standard case because it facilitates win-win transactions. And where there are repeat dealings, the likelihood of truth telling increases, because the one-time gain from a lie is often less to the liar than the gain from a long-term policy of honesty.

Yet in some settings it pays for a person to lie. The potential liar calculates the gains from succeeding and the losses from being exposed as a liar. Both probabilities, along with the severity of the deception, matter. But the ordinary liar does not take into account the welfare of the target because the target does not fit into the liar's utility function—or, as Kantians would say, the target is now treated as an object of exploitation. To be sure, the victim may well adopt a protective stance (which would not be necessary were all people truthful), which, even if generally effective, is in at least some fraction of cases overcome. The moral and legal response to lying is generally hostile because the presumption is that any lie (if it has its intended effect, as it sometimes will) always generates a win-lose situation, where the gains to the liar are likely to be far smaller than the losses suffered by the target. Put another way, people are most likely to lie in those cases where they know that they cannot buy goods for an acceptable price, or obtain personal relationships if they tell the truth.

It is therefore perfectly clear that lying is a strong prima facie wrong. Historically, the traditional remedy for serious fraud was the private right of action brought by the individual who relied to her detriment on the fraudulent statement of another.[18] In modern times, the need to nip fraud in the bud has resulted in efforts to punish false statements without proof of individual injury on the simple ground that if these lies are broadly disseminated, fraud is sure to occur, even if the causal connections on the matter are obscure.[19] The phrase "justified fraud" is jarring to the ear. But the proposition that deception is sometimes justified is as much a part of the conventional wisdom as is justified force, as in the case of self-defense. For these purposes, however, the key question is *which* justifications are allowed for the commission of fraud, and it is here that the Kantian position goes astray.

The most famous Kantian illustration of the issue involves the parent lying to an intruder about the whereabouts of the intended target. That absolute obligation applies, as best as one can tell, even to a mother who seeks to protect her children from an intruder who intends to kill them.[20] Oddly enough, it appears that Kant does not condemn someone who chooses to remain silent. But that concession is minimal and formal. It does not cover the response, "I don't know," if the party does know. Nor is it of any help in cases where the intruder will find the target anyhow if not thrown off the track.

The modern equivalent involves the teachers who lied to Adam Lanza, the Newtown killer, who demanded to know where the pupils had been hidden. Does anyone think that some absolute duty to tell the truth applies to this heinous situation? Quite the opposite: the common view, and surely the correct one, is that any person who did voluntarily tell the truth under those circumstances committed a grievous moral and legal wrong that should result in public excoriation on the one hand and criminal sanctions on the other. If force may be used in the defense of these children, surely deception is equally justified, if not more so, because it does not in and of itself involve death or physical injury to the assailant, or the prospect of collateral harm to third persons.

The question arises, what do Kantian ethics have to add to this analysis? The short answer is nothing. It is widely accepted, even by devoted Kantians, that Kant's austere rationales ring hollow. Modern Kantians therefore struggle to find ingenious ways of salvaging his position. One of the best known is the effort of the noted Kantian scholar, Christine Korsgaard, to put a friendlier face on the Kantian position.[21] But in my view her effort wholly fails to resurrect his position. She starts with Kant's example of a servant, who under the instruction of his master tells a visitor that the master is not home, which in turn allows the master to escape and thereafter commit a crime.[22] Kant tries to deal with the issues in this case by making the obvious point that the master is guilty for the false statement of the servant. Those who act through another act for themselves, as the Romans used to say. But as to the servant, the discussion gets muddy. Kant starts with the odd formulation that the servant "violated a duty to himself by lying,"[23] which is a complete nonstarter for either criminal or civil liability, as duties in the law run to other people, not to oneself. It is also critical to know whether the servant knew of the nefarious purpose of his master, because he would not bear either criminal or civil liability if he thought that the master wanted to avoid a boring visitor by sneaking out to drink a pint at the pub. And it is surely correct under standard theories of complicity that the servant is indeed responsible for the ultimate loss if his deliberate lie was made in order to facilitate the master's action: his actions were intended to aid, and did aid, the criminal result. So we don't need Kant to get the right answer.

The more difficult case arises where one fails to lie to protect innocent persons, as in the Newtown scenario already mentioned. Korsgaard quotes the insufficient Kantian response that telling the truth might not be so bad; after all, the victim may have slipped out, so that no harm will occur.[24] But in these cases it is always the ex ante perspective that counts, and there is surely a duty to lie if the odds are overwhelming that the crime will be consummated unless the killer is thrown off the scent. Korsgaard notes that lies will never work if they are universally practiced.[25] But in so doing, she misses the point that these lies will always be disregarded if people never tell the truth. If a party tells the truth sometimes but not always, then the murderer can be thrown off the trail, and so too if the lie contains novel elements that make the alternative account more plausible. In any event, surely anyone should try to lie if he or she thinks that it is likely to do more harm than good, so that the ability to invent low-probability scenarios where telling the truth does better than telling a lie has nothing to do with the situation.

It is therefore clear where Korsgaard goes astray. She is reduced to saying that lying is always bad in some *ideal* universe, which is trivially true because in that universe there is no reason to lie at all. And she is surely correct when she notes that the use of coercion and deception are prima facie wrongs, which indeed they are, and for good consequentialist reasons.[26] It is indeed the case that if you lie to a person by telling him to drink soup that you know contains poison, you have furnished a cause of death for which liability has been established since Roman times under the Lex Aquilia, on the simple ground that actions of the victim taken in ignorance of the true state of affairs do not sever the causal connection to the original wrong.[27] But in her entire essay, Korsgaard never once mentions the critical notion of justifications that help sort out the various tangles. You are justified in lying to prevent a person from killing either yourself or a stranger. Doctors have been held justified in lying to a patient of limited competence if such lies improve the prospective outcome for treatment, and even here, it is usually necessary to speak the truth to the patient's guardian. Indeed, this particular example highlights the point that consequentialist justifications for lying may include probabilistic calculations, so Kant's servant might quite reasonably anticipate that lying to the murderer at the door will permit the master to escape in nine cases out of ten. Therefore, Kant's concern that the servant's lie could perhaps result in "the murderer [meeting the fleeing master] as he went away"[28] seems quite out of touch with the expected value of lies formed in defense of another. The occasional adverse outcome permitted by consequentialist theory hardly justifies on a priori grounds a set of moral practices that consistently results in greater harms. The constant Kantian effort to put all the weight of the law of fraud on noncontextual grounds ignores all these practical issues of implementation. If one can use force to deter aggression, so much more for the use of fraud. Lying in defense of self and third persons constitutes a strong ex ante Pareto and Kaldor-Hicks improvement. The rule is easily generalizable by the same approach that creates the right to individual autonomy or self-control in the first place.

The catalogue of justified lies can be expanded to other cases. One example comes from the securities industry. Normally, it is wrongful for a person to tout a stock by falsely announcing that it has attributes that lead buyers to overvalue it. Thus, if the stock is in fact worth $50 and the buyer is deceived into thinking it is worth $60, the seller will be able to sell at $55, thereby shortchanging the buyer. The entire cycle of wealth creation is thus undermined by that transaction. Nonetheless all deliberate misrepresentations do not necessarily distort market activity. One common situation involves a firm that is in active negotiations to sell its shares to an outside bidder. The success of this transaction depends in large measure on the ability of the acquiring corporation to purchase shares at current market prices before the announcement goes public, which requires all parties working on the transaction to be sworn to secrecy. Hence the officers of either corporation have to lie in response to a reporter's question of whether a corporate takeover is imminent. To answer yes is to kill the deal. To fudge the answer will be construed as a tacit admission of ongoing negotiations. Nonetheless, in a muddy opinion, the Supreme Court has refused to categorically allow these statements, even if the corporate officers are not engaged in any insider trading.[29] But to do so reduces the likelihood of a successful deal that benefits all shareholders. Justifying this lie advances overall social welfare, and thus meets the test of Kantian generality.

The question of justified fraud arises in other contexts. It would, for example, be rather odd to ask people to play poker without allowing them to bluff, so that fraud over the table is now built into the rules, which do not allow a player to sneak a peek at anyone else's cards. The first lie makes the game possible. The second destroys it. More generally, participants in conventional business negotiations are not required to state their reservation price to the other side, but each can ask or offer what they see fit. But they cannot make false statements about the condition of the firm or its business prospects. Indeed, in some cases, so-called big boy letters are exchanged, whereby each party says that it is willing to proceed notwithstanding that it might have been deceived somewhere earlier in the chain of negotiations. These letters are best understood as global settlements of fraud claims that remove the uncertainty of dealing with these disputes when the transaction is either ongoing or completed.[30]

Justified fraud in the form of "white lies" commonly arises with many low-level social interactions, where the truth will only hurt a friend whom you don't invite to a particular dinner party. Similarly, everyone accepts that people are allowed to put on makeup to cover facial blemishes, to dye their hair so that it does not look gray, or to wear long-sleeved sweaters to conceal bruises or tattoos on their arms. The basic logic in all these cases is that there is no way to protect these zones of privacy if one has to reveal the practices used to keep the matters private. At the same time, however, the social conventions are sharply reversed when the concealment is used to secure not privacy and self-respect, but pecuniary gain from a trading partner. For example, in the insurance context, there is a profound asymmetry surrounding knowledge about the scope and materiality of the risk for a potential insured. To overcome that asymmetry, it is commonplace for insurers in unregulated markets to demand detailed information about risk from their potential insureds before writing coverage policies and before setting premiums or benefits. In these cases, no widespread social convention insulates false statements from condemnation because the effort is no longer merely to protect the scope of one's private life, but also to gain financial advantage from a potential business partner. One of the dangers of current health-care laws is that they allow for concealment of this information, which induces huge uncertainty and cross-subsidy into a system that has in effect sanctioned fraud by authorizing concealment of relevant information. Of course, the company that knows that some, but not which, of its customers bear large risks can raise its prices across the board, but in so doing it forfeits some honest customers who do not find the purchase worthwhile at the higher price. When the primary goal is redistribution, it is no longer possible to act on honest information, which in effect prevents low-risk (and high-income) people from obtaining a better deal on their insurance. The Kantian position does nothing to advance the claims for redistribution, which is one of its important if neglected virtues.

More generally, in working through this maze the law tends to honor "reasonable expectations," a proposition that is often attacked as circular on the ground that only after the rules are stated can the expectations become clear. But that criticism misses how ordinary social interactions work when no regulations command or forbid particular types of conduct. Think of a set of random pairings as part of an n-party game, where n is very large. The set of reasonable expectations are those which, when consistently followed, tend to produce in reciprocal fashion the largest net gains to all parties over time. The high frequency and the reversal of roles tends to lead to a convergence that helps advance this overall improvement, which can be altered in the same way that it forms. Here too there is nothing about a theory of pure reason that should disparage the only form of guidance for social interactions. That Kant virtually never talks about custom is his problem, not ours. Social context matters, and if people cannot read the cues, they cannot flourish.

Contractual Duties

The previous discussion of fraud and assumption of risk naturally leads to a discussion of the role of promises in the law of contract. Promises, like fraud, critically structure how ordinary people interact with each other to achieve some common goal or purpose, which works to their mutual advantage, as they define it. It is therefore important to get some sense as to how and when these various promises should be enforced. The question here is in tension with the Kantian project, which in plumbing the foundations of moral authority puts all matters of public enforcement to one side. Imposing sanctions is never costless, but involves both private and public expenses. Accordingly, the question must be asked whether the gains from enforcement, both in the individual case and in the long haul, justify the expense. With most social engagements, social sanctions suffice; we should never underestimate the force of gossip and casual chatter in enforcing a shared social norm. Legal response is decidedly the exception and not the rule.

Nonetheless, once the size of the overall stakes of any given transaction increases, the addition of legal sanctions now helps stabilize relations by increasing the likelihood of performance or compromise. But in some fraction of cases, the informal mechanisms fail, so that enforcement becomes a norm. In dealing with this question, the central issue is what the payoff is for any form of Kantian absolutism. One way in which Kant goes astray is his insistence that a binding set of obligations involves a joinder of wills of the two parties. Under this subjective theory of contract, the risk of misspoken words can fall on the party who hears them, not on the one who speaks them; the costs of error fall not on the party who makes the mistake but on the one victimized by it. One consequence of that result is to increase the rate of error (given that its costs are in part externalized), which in turn leads to a reduction in the security of transactions, which in turn works to the disadvantage of all parties by reducing the potential gains from exchange. Accordingly, the usual view is that the objective theory of contract prevails in order to lower the error rate in question. To be sure, there are some cases where the mistake on one side is known to the other party, who is then not allowed, as the expression goes, to "snap up" an offer he knows is too good to be true. The entire interplay of objective and subjective rules thus meets the categorical imperative of minimizing two kinds of error. In addition, it also promotes the Kantian ideal, because the key to successful negotiation lies in having subjective intentions and their objective manifestations properly aligned. The point of this objective is consistent, I think, with any sensible view on business relationships and thus supports the morality of capitalism as the institution by which it is commonly known.

There is a second sense in which the Kantian views on promising should be regarded as seriously incomplete. In line with the Kantian view of the absolute obligation never to lie is the Kantian claim that there is likewise an absolute duty to keep promises. Once again, a smart presumption becomes a dumb absolute that undercuts common morality and social stability. Initially, there is clearly much good sense in supporting as an initial *presumption* the moral worth of promises, because promising is the institution that facilitates cooperation and allows people to share the gains from trade and exchange. The basic proposition at the very least is that courts should enforce those promises that the parties think should create legal relations, which is the background norm with respect to all business transactions and few purely social ones. For these purposes, I will not address the many difficulties in fleshing out all the operative features of a mature system of contract law, for my objective is only to note that the universal enforcement of all seriously made promises is a Kantian pipedream when tested against the vast set of social conventions that surround the practice of promising. The obvious counterexamples of Kantian absolutism include promises that are induced by duress, deception, or concealment, all of which are wrongful under a Kantian system. It seems beyond sense to say that the appropriate resolution in these cases is to enforce the legal promise on the one hand, and then to allow the party who is coerced or deceived to recover in a separate lawsuit the same money that was paid. The integration of the two forms of contract is expressed in legal terms by noting that the two promises are dependent,[31] such that the wrongful conduct in inducement offers a prima facie defense to the wrongful conduct in question, which again shows how the logic of justification and abuse carries over from one substantive area of law to another.

The same coordination question arises when two or more promises are in play at the same time. I am aware of no discussion in the Kantian or moral theory that tackles this problem head on. Yet disputes over sequential performance arise frequently in ordinary life. Nor do I see any way in which the tools of Kantian absolutism can help resolve any of these problems. In contrast, in this context the consequentialist approach that seeks to minimize error costs offers a roadmap through the swamp that should satisfy all people regardless of their philosophical orientation.

On this point, an instructive place to start is with the useful formulation of the problem by Edwin Patterson,[32] which is in line with Lord Kelvin's basic observation about the importance of knowing what is to be minimized or maximized. The normative element takes over, so that the question is what set of legal arrangements will in effect achieve the Paretian end in question. In the case of the law of conditions, that question boils down to the following proposition. The rules of engagement between the parties are intended to *minimize the credit risk* between the parties; that is, the expected probability of default by either or both parties, multiplied by the actual level of harm in question.

This simple case illustrates the basic problem. Party A promises to buy goods from Party B for $100. Nothing is said about the sequence of performance. A now wishes to enforce B's promise to deliver the goods that were sold. But note the difficulties. If B is forced to deliver before A pays him, it is quite likely that he will have to sue for the money, which A may not have. Yet if A is forced to pay for the goods before they are delivered, B may never follow through on his side of this bargain. This assurance problem is one reason why Hobbes said that a state is needed to oversee bargains.[33] But lawsuits are expensive and imperfect relative to the institution of self-help, which in this instance requires that A tender (that is, present for immediate delivery) the money before he is allowed to bring a suit for nondelivery. Likewise, B must tender the goods before he can maintain a suit for nonpayment. In effect, the rule that enforces concurrent performance operates as a dominant background norm.

Nonsimultaneous exchanges raise still greater coordination problems. The most famous example is *Kingston v. Preston*,[34] where it was held by the great commercial judge, Lord Mansfield, that the seller of a business on credit did not have to deliver it lock, stock, and barrel unless the buyer of the business first perfected a security interest in the property at hand. The dependent conditions clearly reduced the appropriate credit risk. In construction and employment contracts, payment takes just a moment, but work on a construction contract or an employment relationship takes a long time to perform. In these situations, the temporal risk of mismatched performance cannot be avoided. In most labor situations, the risk of default by the worker is greater than that of the employer (who is generally subject to stronger reputational sanctions and often to locational immobility), so that if the performance is deemed "entire," all the work must be done before any of the payment is made. That solution, however, pushes too much of the risk onto the employee, so that wages are commonly paid weekly or monthly in order to keep the risks to two sides in rough alignment over the life of the agreement. The situation with construction contracts is still more complex, because work must be inspected before payment is made. Consequently, a complex schedule of progress payments is generally tailored to the specific case by negotiation precisely because the background norms are too weak to solve the problem. In general, the larger the stakes, the more intensive the investment in contractual infrastructure needed to reduce the credit risk to acceptable proportions. Thus, when rules dealing with sequence are no longer sufficient, they are replaced with stronger, more expensive devices, such as creation of escrow accounts with trusted and bonded third parties to simultaneously control the bilateral risks of nonperformance.

The role of implied terms intended to minimize credit risk is pervasive throughout the law of contract, and these terms often bind precisely because the cost of drafting express terms might be more than the project is worth. In many cases, the use of standard-form contracts reduces that cost and creates a much-desired uniformity among customers of a large firm. There is no space to address these issues here, but the takeaway remains important. Thinking about promises in Kantian terms does not give the slightest clue as to how these problems should be faced as a matter of either law or practice. The systematic consequentialist accounts provide a useful start in that direction and do so in a way that supports the morality of capitalism but not the grand Kantian maxim about the universalization of general rules. It is critical to remember that presumptive rules dominate those absolute ones that only invite confusion and dissimulation. I cannot understand why a set of legal rules that seeks at every point to advance human welfare would be dismissed as immoral. On the other hand, I see every sign of danger in legal rules that block the road to success with ill-conceived regulatory and taxing initiatives.

Smart Consequentialism and Beneficence

The last point that must be briefly considered in this account is the role of beneficence in human affairs. In some cases, bilateral transactions have a component of beneficence, as when one person hires another person because he or she hopes to train them for greater opportunities. A wide range of internships and special programs may well have that character. But there are also situations where the question is whether one person should gratuitously provide out of his or her own resources to assist others in need. The Kantian who examines these questions from a moral perspective does not have to worry about whether these duties of beneficence should be enforceable or not. No promise is legally enforceable in that sense. But it is commonly asked whether gifts should be made to charity or whether easy rescues should be effectuated, to which the answer generally is yes. The simple observation about the enormity of the gain on one side and the trifling loss on the other leads all thoughtful people to think that some of such activities are required.

But it hardly follows that any such generalized activity should be enforceable, for here the risks outweigh the benefits. The number of potential recipients of private benevolence is huge, and there is no collective social mechanism that pairs up a particular person of means with a person in need. To this rule, there is, I think, an important exception in those cases where a party motivated by benevolence makes an explicit promise to pay certain sums to another in recognition of the work that he has done—in the most famous case of this sort, by the father of an emancipated son to an innkeeper who had gratuitously cared for the son until his death.[35] But when that explicit promise was not made, the standard legal solution was to insist that obligations of beneficence are "imperfect" in the sense that everyone should engage in them, but no one should be legally bound to do so. In any well-functioning society, the set of moral sentiments and social sanctions combine to produce high levels of support, especially in good times when individuals are not pressed to meet their own familial obligations. It is to Kant's great credit on this point that he takes just the same view as the classical liberal moralist, also by invoking the language of imperfect duties.[36]

In dealing with these situations, it is important to think of two kinds of situations. In the first, a party wants to make a large charitable gift to, say, a hospital. The usual view is that the party can choose to give it to a Protestant, Jewish, or Roman Catholic cause without having to explain that position to others. That is the correct view because donors normally want to make an impact, so that once the early gifts are made certain, others are likely to fill in the gaps in the social safety net by making their gifts where they are likely to do the most good. Any effort to direct the terms and conditions of the gift are likely to cause more harm than good. It is no accident that the level of benevolence at the height of laissez-faire was very great. Leaving things alone has a huge payoff.

The situation is perhaps otherwise when immediate action is needed to save a person in distress, where there is no luxury of having other people fill in the gaps. In this case, it is tempting to want to make the duties enforceable in cases where the losses are enormous, as in the situation of a traveler who passed by a needy person whom he could easily help, where the law usually refuses to intervene.[37] Moralists can, I think, argue with some force that some imperfect obligations are more important than others, such that giving a dime to a poor child does not excuse refusing to rescue a person in mortal danger.[38] But it would be a great mistake to cash out those obligations in terms of legal enforcement, backed by damages. Indeed, the various proposals to allow an action in tort against the party who does not rescue have been widely and uniformly rejected, even by people who accept that the moral duty may run to particular individuals in given settings. The same is true even if there is a supposed moral duty of reciprocal rescue.[39] Given the different positions and patterns of behavior, such obligations are much too unlikely to produce Pareto improvements. There is too much uncertainty over whether such risk exists and how it arose, and there is a real sense that it is dangerous to force the issue when the real social problem is death, not from failure to rescue, but from foolish efforts to rescue by parties who are not in a position to do so.[40]

Moralists may try to abstract away from these enforcement issues, but lawyers thinking about how to put together a legal system cannot. So, ironically, in these cases the high willingness to rescue offers a good reason not to make it a legal duty. Conversely, the fact that 99.999 percent of the population would never commit murder does not eliminate the need for legal sanctions against the 0.001 percent that do. With benevolence one can look to the top of the social distribution. With murder it is only the bottom tail that counts. The grounds for the distinction between perfect and imperfect obligation turn out to be very solid indeed.

Smart Consequentialism at the Social Level

Thus far I have addressed consequentialism in its various forms in connection with small-number disputes. But it is perfectly proper to ask whether, and if so how, these insights transfer into larger discussions of overall social welfare. That topic was also part of the overall Kantian agenda, where it instantiates itself in his two major account of the categorical imperative. First: "Act only on that maxim by which you can at the same time will that it should become a universal law."[41] Second: "Act in such a way that you always treat humanity, whether in your person or in any other person, always at the same time as an end, never merely as a means."[42] The clear point of these and other similar maxims is that a person should not regard other individuals as though they were the mere instruments of his will, but instead must treat others' rights as equal with his or her own.

Analytically, however, it hardly follows from this proposition that no person is allowed to act in his or her self-interest, if it turns out that other people acting in the same fashion, and subject to the same constraints, will result in overall social improvements of the sort that follow when self-interested traders act in a competitive market. But by the same token, this maxim produces different results in those cases in which traders on the same side of the market collude to raise the price and lower the quantities of goods that they have for sale. More specifically, the Kantian imperative technically permits every trade to form cartels, but obviously this universalization of monopolies does not produce any long-term social improvements. In fact, each additional cartel diminishes overall social utility—just as the ones before it did—so that the appropriate response by the Kantian standard is that which is dictated by the standard principles of welfare economics. Neither Kaldor-Hicks nor Paretian standards tolerate negative-sum games that only compound losses when their practices are universally imitated.

This simple point can be generalized by the following argument. Suppose that there are two social organizations, the first of which leaves everyone at least as well off as in the second one, where at least one person is better off. What reason is there to prefer the second arrangement over the first? Is there any moral reason to impose a loss on one person that does not create an equal (or greater) gain for a second? Some people might want to respond to this by noting that the increase of the welfare of one person could itself be a harm to the second, so that it is by definition impossible ever to find an arrangement in which the naïve condition set out above can be satisfied. But it is dangerous business indeed to allow those veto preferences to work themselves into the social equation, because the same logic could apply to an arrangement that leaves everyone else out in equal proportion so long as one nag thinks that his utility is necessarily hampered by the gains obtained by others. The correct procedure therefore says that it is a Pareto improvement of sorts to ignore all the negative sentiments that one individual has toward the well-being of another, lest multiple individual outbursts of anger lock everyone into the worst of all possible situations.

This overall notion is closely mirrored in standard legal theory by the old notion of *damnum absque iniuria*, which translated means that certain classes of harm have to be excluded from moral consideration lest they wreck our entire system of social arrangements. The modern version of this notion comes from standard economics, which says that it is appropriate to ignore "pecuniary" externalities while taking into account real externalities. For example, common-law judges have long recognized that businesses may freely improve their own operations, even if doing so results in clientele losses to competitors.[43] These phrases do not have any obvious cognates in ordinary English, and indeed they sometimes sound a bit like double-talk. The key point here is that the correct result will never be reached in these cases if one looks only at the interactions between the two parties, where one wins and one loses, whether we consider competition or pollution. But from a social perspective, competition is a positive-sum game from which all parties benefit in the ex ante position. By the same standard, as noted, cartelization is not. For these purposes, moreover, the traditional tort of nuisance that is always in play with standard pollutants is decidedly negative-sum, which is why it has always been regarded with deep hostility—even when practiced by individuals claiming that their ventures will produce huge social gains— if only due to the fear that repetition of like conduct by others will compound the difficulties.[44] But this problem of compounded harm has no proper analogy in the case of competition, because the more rapid the cycle of trade, the higher the level of overall social welfare. The only way, therefore, to distinguish between two types of harms suffered among neighbors is through the lens of overall social welfare, a deeply consequentialist notion.

A consistent Kantian, rightly advised, should adopt this identical position under his own standard of universalization. Kant was surely no stranger to economic thought, and the following passage from the *Groundwork to the Metaphysics of Morals* takes a leaf out of the work of Adam Smith: "All professions, handicrafts, and arts have made progress by the division of labour. That is to say, one person can accomplish something most perfectly and easily if he confines himself to a particular job that differs significantly from other jobs in the treatment it requires."[45] This passage is simply an earlier formulation of the general proposition that specialization leads to gains from trade benefits all comers, just as the consequentialist would have it. The maxim "engage in trade" is easily generalized to cover all persons. The other propositions fall within the same category. Thus the actions of an aggressive competitor who offers better goods at lower prices can be universalized as consistent with the Kantian ideal, but the actions of the monopolist and the polluter cannot. To be sure, I am not aware of any of Kant's writings that address these issues in just this form, which is not surprising, since the intellectual apparatus needed to put these conceptions into play only had systematic exposition in the twentieth century, in connection not only with Pareto, Kaldor, and Hicks, but also with the pioneers of the marginalist revolution, including Stanley Jevons, Carl Menger, Leon Walras, and Alfred Marshall. So the question here is not what Kant thought about these issues but whether he could, if presented with this information, have denied the force of this consequentialist reformulation of his views, even though they do not rest on any a priori question of necessary truth or an absolutist conception of duty to which Kant expressed such loyalty.

There are of course some ragged edges in these arguments, because the standard measures of social welfare do not care which party gets what portion of the gain so long as no one is left worse off. But the indeterminate allocation of the gain permits a lot of political jockeying over those relative shares, which arises in connection with various exaction games that are now part and parcel of the American political landscape.[46] In these cases, majoritarian sentiments often dominate in general elections, but specialized interest groups can exert enormous influence on specific pieces of legislation. Both of these shrink the pie, so that even if the bottom echelons win the political struggles, they experience overall rates of economic decline, which is the picture in the United States over the last decade, and especially the years between the banking crisis in 2008 and the end of the Obama presidency in 2017. Accordingly, there is much appeal to an ideal of equal improvement in social arrangements, often expressed in the notion that all social gains should be shared pro rata (whether by person or in proportion to capital investment is a separate question) across all individuals. This intuitive notion of (Kantian) fairness has powerful consequentialist roots that should never be forgotten. The simple Pareto rule is that in a two-party world, the activities of the political order are usefully confined to the world of gains. Any consistent northeast movement satisfies the test, which means that in any real-world setting there is a risk that people staying in the northeast quadrant can reduce overall gain by seeking to redirect social wealth in their own direction. A social response that lets people in a competitive market set their own prices keeps the state out of the business of reallocating social surplus in ways that lead to rent dissipation. This hands-off approach to the private division of gain is not obtainable in administering any government program of taxation and regulation, so now some collective solution has to be devised to eliminate rent dissipation. In this context, the commonsense view of pro rata allocation specifies a unique division of the gain, which again blocks the various lobbying intrigues intended to increase the size of the individual slice while inevitably reducing the overall size of the pie. In the end, this relentless downward vector reduces overall rates of growth and social welfare.

To many people, this question of political intrigue might sound like an esoteric problem, but in fact it cuts to the core of modern politics, which is illustrated all too well by the so-called exaction game routinely used by government in exercise of its permitting powers. From a general point of view, the practice of preapproving new, major construction projects cannot be regarded as illegitimate. Many harms are irreversible once committed, yet it is often impossible for a putative victim to know in advance that he or she stands in the line of fire. A victim who does have such information should be entitled to obtain an injunction, at least in the case where the harms in question are imminent. It is possible to enjoin the form of conduct that creates obligations of compensation (consistent with the Kantian view) for the completed harm, which typically covers death, bodily injury, and property damage. There is of course always the risk that this form of anticipatory prohibition can prevent actions, which, if allowed to run their course, would not have generated any losses to strangers. But in the face of necessary uncertainty, there is, I believe, no determined non- or anti-consequentialist who has a better program than the one suggested by economic theory: *minimize the expected value or weighted sum of the two types of errors.* Type I error is letting a project go forward that should stop. Type II is stopping a project that should be allowed to go forward. The same test can apply to building permits, environmental harm, and new drug releases.

It is impossible to reduce both kinds of error to zero unless we presuppose a level of knowledge and a level of resources that can never be obtained in a world defined by scarcity. It would be obtuse under any theory to demand the impossible. Yet at the same time it would be foolish to tolerate unnecessarily high loss rates. It follows therefore that under conditions of uncertainty, *loss minimization becomes the new categorical imperative,* one that can be universalized across all persons, as a kind of a necessary truth that rests on the contingent nature of human activities. This approach again carries over into the moral sciences the maxim that Lord Kelvin recommended for serious work in the physical sciences: know what it is that you are seeking to maximize (or minimize) and then solve the problem with that objective in mind. In the physical sciences, it is generally the case that this means maximizing rate flows or minimizing leakage. In the social context, the normative dimension takes over, so that now the new categorical imperative is to minimize the expected sum of two kinds of error—false positives and false negatives.

In some situations, a corner solution might be appropriate, so that one kind of error is controlled and the other is let by. But more often the solution is interior, so that the two kinds of error are traded off against each other, taking into account their probability and severity. In the easy cases, subjective utilities can be used because some choices can be resolved in ways that leave both sides better off by their own rights: these are Pareto improvements.

In some instances there are rules of thumb that work, which becomes clear in the legal discussion of permitting conditions later on in this chapter.[47] But oftentimes the tradeoffs are much more difficult to make, and could easily require reducing subjective preferences to some common utility metric that involves what is commonly called in legal jargon a "balancing of interests," which is indeed a staple in dealing with everything from trading off privacy with national security, or economic activity with pollution control. Making these observations is not a criticism that is unique to Kantian theory. The same objection applies to libertarians who also tend to look at completed harms, and thus ignore the uncertainties that always arise in dealing with prospective ones. In fact, the correspondence between those two approaches is noticeable because both adopt categorical rules that do not and cannot carry the day in these situations.

The use of these metrics should not be understood as being an "open sesame" to any kind of government regulation. The exaction problem arises precisely because the form of injunctive relief is not shaped by the desire to minimize the sum of two kinds of error.[48] Instead, the purpose is to extract some portion of the gain from parties seeking permits by holding them up for reasons unrelated to the occurrence of any future kind of harm. The game goes like this.[49] The landowner wishes to build a new home by the sea. The state government wants a lateral easement that would allow members of the public to pass to and fro across his land (that is, above the mean high water mark that marks the delineation between common and private property). The easement would cost $100,000 to purchase in a voluntary private transaction, but its value to the public, as determined by the City, is $75,000. Given the option to exercise a purchase option, the local citizenry will, if their institutions are properly aligned, decline to make a purchase that has a net cost to them of $25,000. That is the right social result, even for a Kantian, because no one wants to generalize any action that, if repeated, generates continuing social losses.

The owner's need for the building permit gives the city an opportunity to acquire that easement for *nothing* by the simple expedient of bundling the demand for the easement as a condition of permit approval. The permit approval to the owner is the right to put up a big house instead of a little one, and it is worth $500,000 for the owner to do this. If given the choice of taking the bundle or not, he takes the bundle and improves his private position by $400,000 (after accounting for the loss of the easement). But the acquisition of the easement still does not make sense, given that a net social loss of

$25,000 remains. The bundling conceals the losses, which is why proper procedure requires the government to separate the two transactions (i.e., permitting and exercising eminent domain) in order to reach the right results in both operations.

The point can be put in Kantian terms, because it is manifest that this procedure allows the government to reduce the individual property owner so as to become solely a means to a collective end. The case is no better than if the government demanded $25,000 for permit approval. The practice does not improve with repetition. So it thus follows that the discretion a state needs to decide how to minimize two forms of uncertainty should not be a cloak under which it imposes restrictions on permits not related to the execution of its legitimate social functions. Once again, I see no way in which the Kantian could be able to reject this conclusion. Yet by the same token, standard Kantians do not have in their arsenal the tools that would allow them to derive the results from their first-preferred set of first principles. The consequentialist approach thus works well here, and supplies far firmer foundations for the central institutions of capitalism than any other, typically deontic theory that is based on bare intuition.

Conclusion

The basic purpose of this chapter is to explain why the system loosely described as capitalist meets moral standards from either Kantian or utilitarian premises. The inclusion of utilitarian premises is necessary because, when push comes to shove, the dogmatic nature of the Kantian duties cannot survive rational reflection in light of the manifold counterintuitive results they generate. The basic prohibitions against using force, lying, and breaking promises are all good starting points. But the further one moves from the core cases, the harder it is to defend the absolutism that systematically denies Pareto improvements from each new baseline. The point here manifests itself in discrete ways in each of the three areas—private disputes, beneficence, and major social regulations—addressed here.

First, a consequentialist approach decisively demonstrates why and how absolute duties are untenable in dealing with the use of force, with lying, and with breaking promises. The basic structure of any language always allows for excuses and justifications. The point in all these cases is that, while the initial Kantian injunctions are good starting points, there are systematic social improvements—all part of a Paretian framework—from allowing certain well-recognized defenses based on such critical notions as self-defense and consent. The theory allows for the incorporation of social norms and customary practices that are unwisely excluded from the Kantian framework. In addition, by its insistence on the minimization of error costs, the Kantian moral theory systematically ignores how legal and social rules should handle pervasive uncertainty in daily activities.

Second, on matters of beneficence, Kant is, I think, clearly right on the moral ground, but the limitations of his theory, and of much moral philosophy, are that it gives little guidance on what to do within a legal system, where it becomes imperative to explain why certain duties are subject to legal sanctions and others are not.

Third, the general measures of social welfare developed by economists meet the standard of universalizability. There is no one who should not seek to amass his or her fortune by introducing newer products and lower prices. When imitated by all, the results of competitive activity are benevolent in ways they are not when cartelization and other activities condemned by the antitrust laws are adopted.

Full-throated consequentialism is far better able to handle these three different constellations of issues. In virtually every situation it outperforms Kantian theories, and in so doing lends enormous support for the institution of capitalism.

Notes

My thanks to Thomas Coyle and Mikayla Consalvo, NYU Law School, class of 2015, for their helpful comments on an earlier draft of this chapter, and to Bijan Aboutarabi and John Tienken, University of Chicago Law School, class of 2018, and Philip Cooper, University of Chicago Law School, class of 2017, for their helpful comments on a later revision of the essay. I should also like to thank an anonymous referee for helpful suggestions and a list of relevant sources for review.

1. *Concise Oxford English Dictionary*, 10th ed. (Oxford: Oxford University Press, 2002), 207.

2. The point is made explicitly in Allen W. Wood, *Kantian Ethics* (Cambridge: Cambridge University Press, 2008), 1.

3. For my two early papers on this point, see Richard A. Epstein, "A Theory of Strict Liability," *Journal of Legal Studies* 2, no. 1 (1973): 151–204; Richard A. Epstein, "Defenses and Subsequent Pleas in a System of Strict Liability," *Journal of Legal Studies* 3,

no. 1 (1974): 165–215. The particular results in those papers are still, I believe, largely correct, notwithstanding changes in methodological approach.

4. See, e.g., Richard A. Epstein, "Property Rights in Water, Spectrum, and Minerals," *University of Colorado Law Review* 86, no. 2 (2015): 389–429.

5. Although the intellectual pressures were building up earlier than the time of these papers' publication, my two papers that reflect this change are Richard A. Epstein, "Possession as the Root of Title," *Georgia Law Review* 13 (1979): 1221–43; Richard A. Epstein, "Nuisance Law: Corrective Justice and Its Utilitarian Constraints," *Journal of Legal Studies* 8, no. 1 (1979): 49–102.

6. Consider such a representative view from Kant:

[S]o with all the other moral laws [in addition to the proposition "Thou shalt not lie"] properly so called; that, therefore, the basis of obligation must not be sought in the nature of man, or in the circumstances in the world in which he is placed, but *a priori* simply in the conception of pure reason. . . . [Therefore obligations] should be determined solely from *a priori* principles without any empirical motives, and which we might call a pure will, but volition in general, with all the actions and conditions which belong to it in this general signification.

Immanuel Kant, *Groundwork for the Metaphysics of Morals*, ed. Arnulf Zweig, trans. Arnulf Zweig and Thomas E. Hill Jr. (Oxford: Oxford University Press, 2002), 222. Such sentiments as these are noble, perhaps, but ultimately dogmatic and even perverse.

7. *Concise Oxford English Dictionary*, 207.

8. The point receives its most influential expression in C. B. Macpherson, *The Political Theory of Possessive Individualism: From Hobbes to Locke* (Oxford: Oxford University Press, 1962). Macpherson was an avowed socialist.

9. I discuss this point at length in Richard A. Epstein, "From Natural Law to Social Welfare: Theoretical Principles and Practical Applications," *Iowa Law Review* 100 (2015): 1743–72. Perhaps the best illustration is with the uncompensated transformation of water rights from the riparian systems suitable for gentle English rivers to the prior appropriation system needed for the Colorado River. The key decision is *Coffin v. Left Hand Ditch Co.*, 6 Colo. 443, 449 (1992), which justified this radical (and needed) transformation of property rights on grounds of "imperative necessity."

10. John Rawls, *A Theory of Justice* (Cambridge, Mass.: Harvard University Press, 1971).

11. See Wood, *Kantian Ethics*, 1.

12. For one illustration, see G. W. F. Hegel, *The Scientific Ways of Treating Natural Law, Its Place in Moral Philosophy, and Its Relation to the Positive Sciences of Law*, trans. T. M. Knox (1803; Philadelphia: University of Pennsylvania Press, 1975), which from the few excerpts I have read never closes in on key questions such as who bears the risk of loss for goods of one person that are held in the possession of another under a contract

of bailment, which is a major question throughout classical law. See, for explication, Christine M. Korsgaard, "Kant's Formula of Universal Law," *Pacific Philosophical Quarterly* 66, no. 1–2 (1985): 24–47. Korsgaard concludes rightly that in the normal case goods deposited with a bailee must be returned to their owner, but without any appreciation of the immense difficulties that can arise in the explication of this branch of the law. For some of the complexities, see, for instance, Oliver Wendell Holmes Jr., *The Common Law* (London: Macmillan, 1881), "Lecture 5: The Bailee at Common Law," http://www.gutenberg.org/files/2449/2449-h/2449-h.htm#link2H_4_0005.

13. For a youthful attempt in this direction, see Richard A. Epstein, "Pleadings and Presumptions," *University of Chicago Law Review* 40 (1973): 556–82. For its substantive elaboration, see Epstein, "A Theory of Strict Liability"; Epstein, "Defenses and Subsequent Pleas in a System of Strict Liability"; Richard A. Epstein, "Intentional Harms," *Journal of Legal Studies* 4, no. 2 (1975): 391–442.

14. I discuss this point under the heading of moral Incrementalism in Richard A. Epstein, *Skepticism and Freedom: A Modern Case for Classical Liberalism* (Chicago: University of Chicago Press, 2003), 84–107.

15. Kant, *Groundwork for the Metaphysics of Morals*, 222.

16. Immanuel Kant, *What Is Enlightenment?* (1783), in Immanuel Kant, *Political Writings*, ed. H. S. Reiss, trans. H. B. Nisbet (Cambridge: Cambridge University Press, 1991).

17. For those who doubt the point, see the movie *Temple Grandin* (2010), in which Temple's mother and aunt spend time teaching her to read faces, so as to know the mental state behind a smile and a frown, and thousands of other expressions in between.

18. For an early version of the rule, see *Pasley v. Freeman*, 100 Eng. Rep. 450 (K.B. 1789).

19. For an illustration of where lies in some cases have adverse consequences that are hard to track, *see United States v. Alvarez*, 567 U.S. 709 (2012), where a divided Court struck down a statute that was intended to protect against deception but could not identify its individual targets. In my view those are just the cases where direct regulation is appropriate, given the difficulty of maintaining any private right of action. See Richard A. Epstein, "The Supreme Court's Other Bogus Ruling," *Defining Ideas*, July 10, 2012, http://www.hoover.org/research/supreme-courts-other-bogus-ruling.

20. See Immanuel Kant, "On a Supposed Right to Lie Because of Philanthropic Concerns," in Immanuel Kant, *Ethical Philosophy*, ed. Warner A. Wick, trans. James W. Ellington (Indianapolis: Hackett, 1983), 162–66.

21. Christine M. Korsgaard, "The Right to Lie: Kant on Dealing with Evil," *Philosophy & Public Affairs* 15, no. 4 (1986): 325–49.

22. Ibid., 326.

23. Ibid.

24. Ibid., 329.

25. Ibid., 328–30.

26. Ibid., 327, 333.

27. Justinian. *The Digest of Justinian, Vol. 1*, bk. 9, title 9, pr. & 1. Edited by Alan Watson (Philadelphia: University of Pennsylvania Press, 2009).

28. Korsgaard, "The Right to Lie," 326.

29. See *Basic Inc. v. Levinson*, 485 U.S. 224 (1988).

30. *Pharos Capital Partners L.P. v. Deloitte & Touche*, No. 12-4381 (6th Cir. Oct. 23, 2013).

31. *Kingston v. Preston*, 99 Eng. Rep. 437 (K.B. 1773).

32. "The policy of the law, here as in the tendency to construct concurrent conditions, is to minimize credit risks." Edwin Patterson, "Constructive Conditions in Contracts," *Columbia Law Review* 42 (1942): 918.

33. "[T]he validity of covenants begins not but with the constitution of a civil power, sufficient to compel men to keep them." Thomas Hobbes, *Leviathan*, ed. Michael Oakeshott (New York: Collier, 1962), 114.

34. 99 Eng. Rep. 437 (K.B. 1773).

35. *Mills v. Wyman*, 20 Mass. 207 (1825).

36. For a nineteenth-century account, see Joseph Story, "Imperfect Obligations," in *Encyclopedia Americana* (1844; repr., Clark, N.J.: Lawbook Exchange, 2006), 123. He writes: "We call those rights *perfect*, which are determinate, and which may be asserted by force, or in civil society by the operation of law; and *imperfect,* those which are indeterminate and vague, and which may not be asserted by force or by law, but are obligatory only upon the conscience of the parties." The latter cover "gratitude for favors bestowed on others, or to charity, if he is in want, or to the affection of others, even if he is truly deserving of it." For an analysis of the Kantian position, see Karen Stohr, "Kantian Benevolence and the Problem of Obligatory Aid," *Journal of Moral Philosophy* 8, no. 1 (Feb. 2011): 45–67.

37. For discussion, see James Barr Ames, "Law and Morals," *Harvard Law Review* 22 (1908): 97–113. For my response, see Epstein, "A Theory of Strict Liability," 198–200.

38. Brad Hooker, *Ideal Code, Real World* (Oxford: Oxford University Press, 2000), 161.

39. See Barbara Herman, "Mutual Aid and Respect for Persons," *Ethics* 94, no. 4 (1984): 577–602.

40. See David Hyman, "Rescue Without Law: An Empirical Perspective on the Duty to Rescue," *Texas Law Review* 84 (2006): 712.

41. Kant, *Groundwork for the Metaphysics of Morals*, 222.

42. Ibid., 230.

43. See *Keeble v. Hickeringill*, 103 Eng. Rep. 1127 (Q.B. 1707): "This is like the case [where] [o]ne schoolmaster set[] up a new school to the damage of an ancient school, and thereby the scholars [were] allured from the old school to come to his new. []The action there was held not to lie[]."

44. See, for instance, *Strobel v. Kerr Salt Co.*, 58 N.E. 142, 146 (NY 1900): "Relaxation of legal liabilities and remission of legal duties to meet the current needs of great business organizations, in one direction, would logically be followed by the same relaxation and remission, on the same grounds, in all other directions. One invasion of individual right would follow another, and it might be only a question of time when, under the operations of even a single colliery, a whole countryside would be depopulated."

45. Kant, *Groundwork for the Metaphysics of Morals*, 190. See also Adam Smith, *An Inquiry into the Nature and Causes of the Wealth of Nations* (1776; repr., New York: Modern Library, 2000).

46. For my book-length treatment of the problem of cooperative surplus from positive-sum projects, see Richard A. Epstein, *Bargaining with the State* (Princeton, N.J.: Princeton University Press, 1993).

47. See *Nollan v. California Coastal Commission*, 483 U.S. 825 (1987), and accompanying text.

48. For my recent account, see Richard A. Epstein, "The Bundling Problem in Takings Law: Where the Exaction Process Goes off the Rails," *Brigham-Kanner Property Rights Conference Journal* 4 (2015): 133–50.

49. This is a simplified version of *Nollan v. California Coastal Commission*.

Bibliography

Ames, James Barr. "Law and Morals." *Harvard Law Review* 22 (1908): 97–113.

Epstein, Richard A. *Bargaining with the State*. Princeton, N.J.: Princeton University Press, 1993.

———. "The Bundling Problem in Takings Law: Where the Exaction Process Goes off the Rails." *Brigham-Kanner Property Rights Conference Journal* 4 (2015): 133–50.

———. "Defenses and Subsequent Pleas in a System of Strict Liability." *Journal of Legal Studies* 3, no. 1 (1974): 165–215.

———. "From Natural Law to Social Welfare: Theoretical Principles and Practical Applications." *Iowa Law Review* 100 (2015): 1743–72.

———. "Intentional Harms." *Journal of Legal Studies* 4, no. 2 (1975): 391–442.

———. "Nuisance Law: Corrective Justice and Its Utilitarian Constraints." *Journal of Legal Studies* 8, no. 1 (1979): 49–102.

———. "Pleadings and Presumptions." *University of Chicago Law Review* 40 (1973): 556–82.

———. "Possession as the Root of Title." *Georgia Law Review* 13 (1979): 1221–43.

———. "Property Rights in Water, Spectrum, and Minerals." *University of Colorado Law Review* 86, no. 2 (2015): 389–429.

——. *Skepticism and Freedom: A Modern Case for Classical Liberalism*. Chicago: University of Chicago Press, 2003.

——. "The Supreme Court's Other Bogus Ruling." *Defining Ideas*, July 10, 2012. http://www.hoover.org/research/supreme-courts-other-bogus-ruling.

——. "A Theory of Strict Liability." *Journal of Legal Studies* 2, no. 1 (1973): 151–204.

Hegel, G. W. F. *The Scientific Ways of Treating Natural Law, Its Place in Moral Philosophy, and Its Relation to the Positive Sciences of Law*. Translated by T. M. Knox. 1803. Philadelphia: University of Pennsylvania Press, 1975.

Herman, Barbara. "Mutual Aid and Respect for Persons." *Ethics* 94, no. 4 (1984): 577–602.

Hobbes, Thomas. *Leviathan*. Ed. Michael Oakeshott. New York: Collier, 1962.

Holmes, Oliver Wendell, Jr. *The Common Law*. London: Macmillan, 1881.

Hooker, Brad. *Ideal Code, Real World*. Oxford: Oxford University Press, 2000.

Hyman, David. "Rescue Without Law: An Empirical Perspective on the Duty to Rescue." *Texas Law Review* 84 (2006): 653–737.

Justinian. *The Digest of Justinian: Volume 1*. Edited by Alan Watson. Philadelphia: University of Pennsylvania Press, 2009.

Kant, Immanuel. *Ethical Philosophy*. Edited by Warner A. Wick. Translated by James W. Ellington. Indianapolis: Hackett, 1983.

——. *Groundwork for the Metaphysics of Morals*. Edited by Arnulf Zweig. Translated by Arnulf Zweig and Thomas E. Hill Jr. Oxford: Oxford University Press, 2002.

——. *Political Writings*. Edited by H. S. Reiss. Translated by H. B. Nisbet. Cambridge: Cambridge University Press, 1991.

Korsgaard, Christine M. "Kant's Formula of Universal Law." *Pacific Philosophical Quarterly* 66, no. 1–2 (1985): 24–47.

——. "The Right to Lie: Kant on Dealing with Evil." *Philosophy & Public Affairs* 15, no. 4 (1986): 325–49.

Macpherson, C. B. *The Political Theory of Possessive Individualism: From Hobbes to Locke*. Oxford: Oxford University Press, 1962.

Patterson, Edwin. "Constructive Conditions in Contracts." *Columbia Law Review* 42 (1942): 903–54.

Rawls, John. *A Theory of Justice*. Cambridge, Mass.: Harvard University Press, 1971.

Smith, Adam. *An Inquiry into the Nature and Causes of the Wealth of Nations*. 1776. Repr., New York: Modern Library, 2000.

Stohr, Karen. "Kantian Benevolence and the Problem of Obligatory Aid." *Journal of Moral Philosophy* 8, no. 1 (Feb. 2011): 45–67.

Story, Joseph. *Encyclopedia Americana*. 1844. Repr., Clark, N.J.: Lawbook Exchange, 2006.

Wood, Allen W. *Kantian Ethics*. Cambridge: Cambridge University Press, 2008.

CHAPTER 4

"Getting and Spending, We Lay Waste Our Powers": On the Expanding Reach of the Market

Steven Lukes

The world of the market—of "getting and spending"—is ever more with us and also within us, where "us" means more and more people across the globe. More and more of us see market relations and activities involving buying, selling, and investing as normal and natural. Jean Drèze and Amartya Sen write in their recent book on India that in "recent years, market phobia has subsided greatly in India, and while that is useful, it is important not to be gripped by the market mania of wanting to marketize everything that can be handed over to the market."[1] My assumption in this chapter will be that each of these pathologies results from an exclusive, one-sided view of the relation (to quote Milton Friedman for the first and last time) between capitalism and freedom.

Wordsworth's thought that "the world is too much with us," that, as the market expands, we thereby "lay waste our powers" and "have given our hearts away"[2] is, of course, a familiar theme of the Romantics, taken up by Coleridge, claiming that the "true seat and sources" of the "existing distress" are to be found in the "Overbalance of the commercial spirit,"[3] and by the deeply conservative Carlyle, lamenting Victorian society's ruthless commercialism and destruction of communal bonds and the "dismal science" of political economy. Five years before the *Communist Manifesto*, Carlyle had written of "the brutish godforgetting Profit-and-Loss Philosophy" and protested that "Cash-payment is not the sole nexus of man with man,"[4] which, in turn, Marx and Engels vividly described as spreading across the globe, drowning its inhabitants in "the icy water of egotistical calculation."[5]

The basic, underlying theme is, of course, an ancient one, reaching back to the biblical declaration of the impossibility of serving both God and mammon and the episode of Jesus cleansing the Temple by expelling the money changers, and across the centuries in denunciations of avarice and of usury within Christianity, with parallels in other religious traditions. What Romanticism supplied was a new specificity and relevance to the times, in response to the onset of the Industrial Revolution and the rise of capitalism. Here were the beginnings of a conflict of views that is still with us and on which I want to focus attention by asking what is in dispute at the core of it.

In a famous and luminous essay that displays his characteristic deep simplicity and elegance of thought, Albert Hirschman discussed what he called "rival views of market society." Hirschman identified four such views. The first was the *doux commerce thesis*, expounded by Smith, Montesquieu, Sir James Steuart, Condorcet, and Paine, and becoming conventional wisdom by the mid-eighteenth century. In this view, "a society where the market assumes a central position for the satisfaction of human wants will not only produce considerable new wealth because of the division of labor and consequent technical progress, but will generate as a product, or external economy, a more 'polished' human type—more honest, reliable, orderly, and disciplined, as well as more friendly and helpful, ever ready to find solutions to conflicts and a middle ground for opposed opinions." Thus commerce and industry encourage the virtues of "industriousness and assiduity, . . . frugality, punctuality, and, most important perhaps for the functioning of market society, probity."[6]

The second view was the *self-destruction thesis*: that markets, rather than generating requisite dispositions, tend to deplete or erode them, that the market "undermines the moral values that are its own essential underpinnings."[7] Hirschman quotes Fred Hirsch, asserting that as "individual behavior has been increasingly directed to individual advantage, habits and instincts based on communal attitudes and objectives have lost out," and "the individualistic, rationalistic basis of the market undermines religious support."[8] He might have cited countless others, such as Richard Titmuss,[9] generalizing from his claim that buying and selling blood crowds out altruism. In consequence, there are various versions of capitalism's eventual demise, some Marxist in inspiration, as with the Frankfurt School, others more Weberian, as in Schumpeter. And here he might also have cited Karl Polanyi, according to whom the great harm that what Polanyi called "the market system" did was to unravel social bonds. The Great Transformation consisted in the disembedding of the economy, in the world-transforming project of building a self-regulating market economy, in which the three factors of production—labor, land, and money—were treated as ordinary commodities and subjected to market exchange. These were, Polanyi thought, "fictitious commodities," and their marketization led to the destruction of livelihoods, habitats, and communities and thus to countermovements of social protection, leading to political stalemate and ultimately fascism and the Second World War.[10]

The third and fourth views were similarly symmetrical. According to the *feudal shackles thesis*, directly contradicting the self-destruction thesis, the problem with capitalism was not its corrosive power but its weakness: "a number of societies that have been penetrated by capitalism are criticized and considered to be in trouble because this penetration has been too partial, timid, and halfhearted, with substantial elements of the previous social order being left intact."[11] This view was propounded first by Marx himself and later by Lukács, reflecting on Germany's alleged backwardness, and by Gramsci on Italy's supposed failure to complete the bourgeois revolution, then by neo-Marxist analysts of the dependent countries of the capitalist periphery, especially in Latin America, and eventually generalized, by Arno Mayer and others, to capitalist societies everywhere, including England and France. The *feudal blessings thesis* celebrates, instead of deploring, the virtues of a feudal past, viewed as "the indispensable seedbed of both Western democracy and capitalism." The blessings in this fourth view are, when absent, a source of difficulties and a curse in disguise, as exemplified in the exceptionalism of the United States, where, in Tocqueville's famous words, Americans were "born equal, instead of becoming so." For there, according to Louis Hartz (as Hirschman interprets him), the very lack of feudal remnants resulted in a lack of ideological diversity and thus the absence of an authentic conservative tradition, the weaknesses of socialist movements, and so "the protracted sterility of liberal political thought itself," the "tyranny of the majority," and "colossal liberal absolutism." Hence the failure to consolidate the New Deal reforms and welfare state schemes into "a new economic order or ideology."[12]

Having constructed this impressive *tableau idéologique*, Hirschman then continues, with his characteristic subtlety, to suggest that these apparent contradictions do not mean mutual incompatibility. He argues, in particular, that precapitalist forms and values often "hamper the full development of capitalism while also bequeathing something precious to it" and, addressing the *doux commerce* and self-destruction theses, that "the moral basis of capitalist society" should be seen as "being constantly depleted and replenished at the same time." Concerning social cohesion, Hirschman writes, "the constant practice of commercial transactions generates feelings of trust, empathy for others, and similar *doux* feelings," and yet it is also true that "such practice permeates all spheres of life with the element of calculation and of instrumental reason."[13]

Enlightening as they are, Hirschman's rival views are packages, combinations of elements that propose alternative accounts of how markets function and of the vulnerabilities and prospects of market societies. Moreover, any one version of each of them makes a normative assumption about such prospects: about what is to be hoped for and what is to be feared. What I want to do here is to narrow the focus by concentrating on one of the elements, indeed the central element, present in these alternative accounts of markets: namely, the activities of buying, selling, and investing. How are we to conceive of these practices and the disposition to engage in them? Are they manifestations of freedom or of a growing subjection? What exactly does the rivalry of views in this case amount to? Do they exclude one another or do the alternative views, as Hirschman's last quotation suggests, pick out aspects of what occurs that are mutually compatible? Or are they only sometimes compatible, and if so when? And what is the role of facts, of evidence of actual social and economic arrangements, in answering these questions?

What, then, are the alternative views? Let us begin with the concept of individuals in pursuit of their interests. Here, once more, Hirschman is of help. Arising initially at the time of the Renaissance to signify the drive for self-preservation and self-aggrandizement, the concept of "interest" stabilized in the eighteenth century to signify self-centeredness and the rational calculation of material costs and benefits, and more specifically moneymaking and "the methodical pursuit and accumulation of private wealth."[14] That was clearly how Mandeville and Hume thought of interests, and it was Adam Smith's understanding in his encomium of the butcher, brewer, and baker pursuing their interests rather than exercising their benevolence. It is what James Mill meant when he extended it to the science of politics (to be succeeded by political scientists down to the rational choice enthusiasts of the present time), and it has been the staple assumption of mainstream classical and neoclassical economics to this day. The scope of what counts as the interests pursued expands, of course, beyond money and wealth, but retains a materialist emphasis, and there is always the danger of becoming, as Macaulay noted in criticism of Mill, tautologous: of meaning "only that men, if they can, will do as they choose . . . it is . . . idle to attribute any importance to a proposition which, when interpreted, means only that a man had rather do what he had rather do."[15] The concept of interest also expanded to incorporate the idea of long-term or enlightened self-interest, but all the while retaining the self-referential, prudential, instrumental, strategic focus on the securing of one's (usually material) advantages in a complex and competitive world of scarcity. Thus, as applied to market behavior, individuals' rational pursuit of their interests, which economists came to describe, supposedly more neutrally, as choices that exhibit "revealed preferences," maximizing utility under constraints, was, and continues to be, seen as manifesting their freedom. So, one view is that the exercise of economic freedom, thus understood, is to be promoted, perhaps maximized, and defended against its many critics and enemies.

There are several versions of the contrary view. These are different ways of putting the exercise of economic freedom into question: because it jeopardizes other values, because it does actual harm, or because it is merely a means to other, higher, more worthy values. We have already met the denunciation of market behavior and its enthusiasts by Coleridge and Carlyle, echoing Burke's lament at the rise of "sophisters, oeconomists and calculators"—a line of critique that survives in both conservative and communitarian thinking today. Markets upset hierarchies and can undermine solidarity.

*   *   *

As we also saw, this kind of critique was taken up by the young Marx (and survives alongside the later focus on exploitation, which became central), notably in the early manuscript on "money" (a "disruptive power for the individual and for social bonds"[16]) and in the *Manifesto*, which describes the bourgeoisie as "creating a world after its own image" in which "all that is solid melts into air," converting previously honored professionals ("the physician, the lawyer, the priest, the poet, the man of science") into paid wage-laborers and resolving "personal worth into exchange value."[17] Marx here gave vivid expression to the burgeoning theme of *commodification*—the complex idea that monetary exchange engenders a kind of corruption, which, Marx clearly believed, debases or distorts the value of the good or service being exchanged. He also clearly believed that this in turn generates a kind of contagion, impairing or degrading otherwise well-functioning and potentially flourishing activities and relationships.

In her book *Contested Commodities*, Margaret Radin has most helpfully given us a useful breakdown of what appear to be the component elements of commodification. Goods and services, she suggests are commodified when they exhibit

(1) objectification—treating persons and things instrumentally, as manipulable at will;

(2) fungibility—when they are fully interchangeable with no effect on their value to the holder;

(3) commensurability—when their values can be arrayed as a function of one continuous variable or can be linearly ranked;

(4) money equivalence—where the continuous variable in terms of which they can be ranked is monetary value.[18]

What exactly was it, one wonders, apart from their fundamental critique of exploitation, that was at the heart of Marx's and Engels's critique of bourgeois market relations? What is the harm that they do? Was it the dominance of instrumental attitudes, treating people as means, not ends? Was it indifference, the willingness to substitute workers for one another, without concern for the manifold differences among them and the complexities of their several lives? Was it the readiness to compare the incomparable, reducing the rich variety of human value perspectives to ranking on a single scale? Or was it specifically the ranking in terms of money, setting a price on everyone and everything?

However that may be, this theme has been richly developed, above all by Georg Simmel, who wrote that the "modern mind has become more and more a calculating one" and of the essence of the "blasé attitude" distinctive of modern metropolitan life as "an indifference towards the distinctions between things." The money economy, Simmel wrote, has "filled the daily life of so many people with weighing, calculating, enumerating and the reduction of qualitative values to quantitative terms. Because of the character of calculability which money has, there has come into the relationships of the elements of life a precision and a degree of certainty in the definition of the equalities and the inequalities and an unambiguousness in agreements and arrangements, just as externally this arrangement has been brought about through the general diffusion of pocket watches."[19] (Compare the *doux commerce* view's praise for the market's encouragement of the virtue of punctuality.)

*   *   *

The theme of commodification raises two important questions concerning the moral limits of markets. First, which goods and services and which kinds of interpersonal relations should be off-limits to markets—to buying, selling, and investing—even if markets were to work well? And second, assuming that some should, on what grounds should they be so shielded? Two recent books have addressed these questions in interestingly different ways. Michael Sandel's *What Money Can't Buy* proposes an open-ended, heterogeneous list of examples (from queue jumping and bribing kids to get good grades to trading immigration rights and the terrorism futures market) and advances the argument that the harm marketing a good or service does is to degrade it; that is, to treat it according to a lower mode of valuation than is appropriate to it. To describe what is disquieting about this, Sandel writes, "We need the vocabulary of corruption and degradation."[20] We need, he writes, a public debate about the meaning and purpose of goods and the values that should govern them. One problem here is that there are rival views, rather than what Michael Walzer calls "shared understandings,"[21] about the meaning of many particular goods and of human flourishing and, more important, there is only a tenuous connection in many cases between the meaning we give to a good and its distribution by a market. (Thus Bibles are bought and sold, as were indulgences in the Middle Ages.) It is often quite unclear why buying and selling such goods and services damages them, and, if so, how. Moreover, returning to Radin's distinctions, one can ask: are there not many contexts, especially in modern urban living, in which instrumental relationships—seeing the world in anonymous and commensurable terms and, indeed, often in monetary terms—are much to be valued? Indeed, are instrumental relationships not sometimes the essential precondition for and counterpoint to mutual relationships in more intimate settings?

*   *   *

In this connection, the work of the sociologist Viviana Zelizer is pertinent. Much of it concerns the ways in which, in a Hirschman-like manner, the worlds of interpersonal relations and commercial activity interact. Intimacy, she writes, "is certainly an area that separate spheres/hostile worlds proponents have been especially keen to protect from economic activity. Critics, moralists and social scientists at large have frequently thought not only that money corrupts, but more generally that economic rationality and the sentiments attached to intimate relations rest on fundamentally contradictory principles. To mix both, they argue, brings trouble." By contrast, Zelizer argues, "people constantly mingle their most intimate relations with economic activities, including monetary payments; households, for instance, are hotbeds of economic interaction. Instead of menacing alien intrusions, economic transactions repeatedly serve to create, define, sustain and challenge our multiple intimate relations."[22] On the other hand, there are areas of life (Walzer calls them "spheres of justice") where the increasing prevalence of marketing and marketizing seems harmful. Consider so-called Baumol goods. The economist William Baumol argued that there are services "in which the human touch is crucial, and are thus resistant to labor productivity growth"; they resist standardization because "treatment must be tailored to the individual case" and "quality is, or is at least believed to be, inescapably correlated with the amount of human labor devoted to their production."[23] Baumol's original examples were the performing arts, but he then extended them to other services, such as teaching, doctoring, and policing. But, as Colin Leys has argued, in the medical field, for example, capitalism involves a relentless pressure to "wean customers from services onto consuming material goods and providing the labor component themselves," consigning any small residue to high-end markets, or leaving them to (increasingly) beleaguered state provision.[24] Hence the growing consumption of drugs and painkillers, the speeding up of consultations, and the very fragmentation of medical services. The U.S. health-care system strikes me as exemplifying in an acute form the corruption of medical service provision by the prevalence of market incentives that lead physicians to see their medical practice as a revenue stream.[25]

Interestingly, the other recent book about the moral limits of markets deals with this very question. I refer to Debra Satz's *Why Some Things Should Not Be for Sale*. She rejects the corruption argument (more or less on the grounds adduced above) and advances instead the argument that some markets are noxious when they jeopardize the value of equality: that is, when they undermine the conditions that people need if they are to relate as equals, as citizens with equal standing or status. In such cases the underlying conditions of the market agents can be highly unequal, as when some are seriously lacking in agency or knowledge, or some are significantly more vulnerable than others. The examples she takes, which are different from Sandel's, are markets in women's reproductive labor, in women's sexual labor (prostitution), in child labor, in involuntary slavery, and in organ transplants, human kidneys in particular.

This interesting argument is not, I think, an argument about intrinsic harm. It is not an argument about the damage that the marketizing of goods and services does to the good itself; rather, it is an argument in terms of what she calls "contextual reasons." That is to say, given the world as it is and the world as it is likely to be, the marketing is damaging and harmful to equality. The example that she gives is prostitution. She argues about prostitution that, given currently prevailing beliefs and attitudes, this market perpetuates status inequality between men and women. Prostitution, she writes, is "a theatre of inequality because it displays for us a practice in which women are seen as servants of men's desires and it shapes and influences the ways in which women as a whole are seen."[26] Stigma surrounds the practice and is reinforced by it. In a different culture perhaps things could be otherwise, but she doubts this very seriously. She criticizes feminists who argue that prostitutes can function as sex therapists fulfilling a legitimate social need, as well as providing a source of social experiment and alternative conceptions of sexuality and gender. She writes that such "feminists have minimized the cultural stereotypes that surround prostitution and exaggerated their own power to shape the practice. Prostitution, like pornography, is not easily separated from the larger surrounding culture that marginalizes, stereotypes and stigmatizes women. . . . I think we need to look carefully at what men and women actually learn in prostitution and I doubt that ethnographic studies of prostitution would support the claim that prostitution adds to women's dignity or empowerment."[27] She thinks—and this is the point about contextual reasons—that the powerful intuition that prostitution is intrinsically degrading is bound up with well-entrenched views of male gender identity and women's sexual role in the context of that identity. Prostitution is connected to stigma, unequal status, and thus injustice, operating through beliefs and attitudes that, although theoretically they could be changed so that buying and selling sex might not involve any of those harms, she does not believe they could be in the foreseeable future.

Economic liberty, I suggested, can also be put into question when it is not valued in itself but viewed instrumentally, seen as a mere transitional value, something worth having merely as a means to the attainment of higher, more worthy purposes. This view derives from John Stuart Mill, for whom there was little scope for "moral and social progress" among minds "engrossed by the art of getting on." It was most clearly expressed, in high Bloomsbury vein, by Keynes, who wrote: "The strenuous purposeful moneymakers may carry all of us along with them into the lap of economic abundance. But it will be those people, who can keep alive and cultivate into a fuller perfection the art of life itself and do not sell themselves for the means of life, who will be able to enjoy the abundance when it comes." Then, Keynes continued, "for the first time since his creation man will be faced with his real, his permanent problem—how to use his freedom from pressing economic cares, how to occupy the leisure, which science and compound interest have won for him, to live wisely and agreeably and well."[28] And this high-minded view is also to be found in John Rawls, who wrote: "What men [sic] want is meaningful work in association with others. . . . To achieve this state of things great wealth is not necessary. In fact, beyond some point it is more likely to be a positive hindrance, a meaningless distraction at best if not a temptation to indulgence and emptiness."[29] These passages are quoted in John Tomasi's book *Free Market Fairness*, which has the great virtue of posing the question before us in very contemporary terms by confronting what he calls the "high liberal" and in particular social democratic disdain for economic liberty with his preferred alternative. This, he claims, will be justifiable to all citizens, including the least advantaged, and is "the more inspiring ideal."[30] It is a conception of justice based on a "thick" conception of economic liberty, involving wide individual freedom of contract and powerful rights to the ownership of productive property on the argument that such rights are needed for the independence of citizens, freeing them from reliance on the state regarding the provision of their most basic needs. Such rights also empower citizens as consumers, that is, as adults who set long-term plans for themselves and then live and develop their own characters in light of those goals.

Wordsworth's idea was that getting and spending lays waste our powers. Tomasi's, in striking contrast, is that a social democratic state that curtails thick economic liberty in pursuit of social justice by reducing inequalities creates social conditions in which the moral powers of citizens can be exercised and developed in only a stunted way. The exercise of such liberty is the basis for esteem from fellow citizens, self-respect, and self-authorship: the wealth individuals acquire empowers them to become authors of lives truly their own. Appealing to Hayek as against Rawls, Tomasi's view is that markets, as opposed to social democracies, seek to de-politicize social life by commodifying it and are to be celebrated for doing so.[31]

I have sought to show that the defense of robust economic freedom faces several ways of putting it in question: by claiming that it jeopardizes other basic values, such as solidarity and equality, that it brings about positive harms through commodification, or that it is merely a means to enable the realization of other, more worthy human values. And I cited the comment by Drèze and Sen that this discussion can become polarized into a standoff between marketphobia and marketmania. So I want to conclude with a series of thoughts that raise the question of the extent to which it is possible to evaluate these rival views without ideological bias and by appealing to evidence that is, in turn, ideologically unbiased.

First, a comment about the prospects for economic growth, in view of the fact that both market liberals and social democrats assume that there is a prospect of continuing economic growth in the heartlands of advanced capitalism. Tomasi prefers "enthusiastically capitalist regimes that embrace economic growth as a positive ideal," arguing that growth "has changed the premises upon which the 'economic paternalism' of the early social democratic theorists was based."[32] (He calls social democracies "paternalist" presumably because they prioritize on the basis of need rather than allowing citizens to determine *for themselves* what it is they want.) But there are reasons to think that this enthusiasm for the future of growth may be both anachronistic and utopian, at least so far as the United States and perhaps other advanced industrial societies are concerned. Quite apart from ecological concerns about the cumulating consequences of growth for civilized life on the planet (that suggest the need to put up "stop signs"), there are several grounds, as Robert Gordon has argued,[33] for questioning whether the extraordinary growth generated by the Second Industrial Revolution that began in 1870 is likely to continue. That capitalist growth was of course the basis for the flourishing of social democracy in the twentieth century, especially in northern Europe during the three decades following the Second World War. Its continuance is by no means assured.

Second, turning to the debate between market liberals and social democrats, we need to ask: what is the *scope* of (defensible or justifiable) economic freedom (of buying, selling, and investing)? Economic or market liberals favor its indefinite expansion; social democrats seek to resist it and indeed aim to roll it back through decommodifying a (varying) range of currently marketized goods and services. Is the answer to be determined by whatever happens to be accepted as such; that is, by the scope of market practices in any given time and place? On that basis, its scope is continually widening. Or is it to be determined by what one can justifiably claim to be the *appropriate* scope of the market? What asking this question shows is that what counts as such economic liberty cannot be value free, for if we answer in the first way we are implicitly accepting the judgments of some particular social order about the appropriate scope of the market. And that raises the question, already touched upon, of when market relations and practices are appropriate and when they are not, and why. When, in Debra Satz's phrase, are markets noxious? And when, even more precisely, should the market component of practices (think of banking and medicine) be subject to extensive and detailed regulation and control? "The market" needs to be disaggregated into different kinds of markets and subject to evaluation of the effects of allowing their operations to go unregulated.

Third, we need, similarly, to consider the scope of market-like thinking and analysis of relations and activities that are outside the sphere of what is normally thought of as economic. To what extent is economics-style understanding of other areas of social life, from politics and administration to intimate relations and family life, illuminated by conceptualizing them using the language of incentives, costs and benefits, trade-offs, pricing, and revealed preferences? There are at least two serious problems with such approaches (as developed, for example, by Gary Becker and George Stigler). The first is that the very notion of "revealed preference" assumes the presence of some stable disposition that lies behind choices across multiple and varied situations, an assumption more plausible in some contexts, such as some markets, than in others. The second is that this way of analyzing behavior fails to distinguish between tastes and values and thus between changes of taste and autonomous, reflective changes in values.

Finally, we come to the key question of the *relevance* of factual evidence to the assessment of this evaluative question. Here Tomasi argues, helpfully, that to address the case for "free market fairness" satisfactorily, as against the "high liberal" and in particular social democratic case, the argument must be conducted at the level of "ideal theory," that is, by considering the alternative regime types "operating under maximally favorable—but still possible—historic, economic, and cultural conditions." "Possible" does not mean feasible from any particular status quo. Thus, a relatively successful single-payer national health-care system is certainly possible but not feasibly attainable in the United States today. But, so far as "possibility" is concerned, there is a large-sized problem. Tomasi suggests that "possible" means that these conditions must pass the "(admittedly ambiguous) test of sociological realism" and that they must be "compatible with the general laws of political sociology."[34] (I am not convinced that there are any such laws.) Rawls made similar suggestions, but, it must be acknowledged, I submit, that these are rather hand-waving-like provisions, given the current state of our knowledge and the divisions among social scientists on some of the key issues involved. To take one example, social scientists are certainly not in consensual agreement that, as Tomasi writes, "Whether we consider factors on the demand side—such as their arrangements for quality medical care and schooling—or if we consider factors on the supply side—such as arrangements for the creation of diverse and desirable positions—market democratic regimes can typically make a stronger claim to maximize the opportunities of the worst-off class of citizens over time."[35] Let us, however, assume this large problem solved and that we have reached some degree of consensus about the facts and so can focus on the moral issues. Advocates of "thick" economic liberty see the market activities of buying and selling goods and services and risk-taking investment as a central feature of a good life, since for "many people, commercial activity in a competitive marketplace is a deeply meaningful aspect of their lives. People express themselves, they grow up and become who they are, in part because of their independent experiences as independent participants in the cooperative venture that is economic life."[36]

Such activities, these advocates claim, minimize domination and coercion, which results from "collective decision making procedures," and enables them to secure wealth, which, in Tomasi's words, "empowers them to become authors of lives truly their own" with a "life script" that "each chooses to compose."[37]

From a "high liberal" and social democratic viewpoint, however, these claims express several *illusions*. One is this very idea of independent self-authorship, rendering those who believe it blind to the contributions of others, to the background role of institutions, laws, and norms, and to the role of luck. A second is the idea that market freedom renders market actors free from coercion and domination. This illusion springs from the very narrow conceptualization of freedom as freedom from arbitrary interference by others (as most sharply articulated by Hayek). In such a view, as Hayek clearly saw, poverty, unemployment, and, in general, being a victim of bad luck in the market cannot count as unfreedom. And a third illusion is to fail to see that the individuals, supposed in this view to be "authors of lives truly their own," are themselves deeply affected by the very markets in which they live and act. As indeed we have seen that Smith and the other advocates of the *doux commerce thesis* knew, markets shape preferences and capacities. As Satz remarks, they knew that "labor markets could function in ways that shaped their participants as submissive inferiors and dominating superiors bent on exercising their arbitrary power."[38]

In our own time, this process has taken a far more troubling turn, where citizens and patients come to see themselves as consumers and risk-takers. Michel Foucault, commenting on the ideas of Gary Becker, rightly observed as long ago as 1979 that with advent of neoliberalism the individual becomes an entrepreneurial self.[39] Thus *homo economicus* becomes an entrepreneur, an entrepreneur of himself. In consequence there develops the analysis of noneconomic behavior through a grid of economic intelligibility, and the criticism and appraisal of the action of public authorities in market terms become pervasive, including the criminal and penal justice system. What Foucault saw in Becker was the profound and widely influential insight that economics could become an "approach to human behavior."[40] "Human capital" becomes inseparable from the individual who is its bearer, and the model of *homo economics* thereby becomes broadly applicable to all of human life: to getting married, committing a crime, raising children and all the rest of life.[41] The neoliberal world, in short, has become the world of "everyday neoliberalism."[42]

At this point in our discussion, we may well have reached the place where, in Wittgenstein's famous phrase, one's spade is turned. I doubt whether the advocates of thick economic liberty and the virtues of the market can be brought to see what I have called illusions as illusions. From a social democratic perspective, their view of economic liberty looks Panglossian: the view that the world of everyday neoliberalism is the best of all possible worlds.

Notes

1. Jean Drèze and Amartya Sen, *An Uncertain Glory: India and Its Contradictions* (Princeton, N.J.: Princeton University Press, 2013), 183.

2. William Wordsworth, *The Poetical Works of Wordsworth*, ed. Thomas Hutchinson, new ed. (London: Oxford University Press, 1950), 206.

3. Samuel Taylor Coleridge, "Lay Sermon 2," in *Lay Sermons*, 3rd ed. (London: Edward Moxon, 1852), 233.

4. Thomas Carlyle, *Past and Present* (1843; repr., New York: New York University Press, 1977), 187.

5. Karl Marx and Friedrich Engels, *Manifesto of the Communist Party* (Moscow: Foreign Languages Publishing House, 1957), 51.

6. Albert O. Hirschman, *Rival Views of Market Society and Other Recent Essays* (New York: Viking, 1986), 109.

7. Ibid., 110

8. Ibid., 117–18, 143.

9. See Richard Titmuss, *The Gift Relationship: From Human Blood to Social Policy* (London: Allen & Unwin, 1970).

10. Karl Polanyi, *The Great Transformation: The Political and Economic Origins of Our Time* (Boston: Beacon Press, 1944).

11. Hirschman, *Rival Views*, 125.

12. Ibid., 133–34

13. Ibid., 139–40.

14. Ibid., 41.

15. Quoted in ibid., 48.

16. Karl Marx, *Early Writings*, trans. and ed. T. B. Bottomore (London: C. A. Watts, 1963).

17. Marx and Engels, *Manifesto of the Communist Party*.

18. Margaret Radin, *Contested Commodities: The Trouble with Trade in Sex, Children, Body Parts, and Other Things* (Cambridge, Mass.: Harvard University Press), 113.

19. Georg Simmel, "The Metropolis and Mental Life," in *Georg Simmel on Individuality and Social Forms*, ed. Donald Levine (Chicago: University of Chicago Press, 1972), 328.

20. Michael J. Sandel, *What Money Can't Buy: The Moral Limits of Markets* (New York: Farrar, Straus and Giroux, 2012), 187.

21. Michael Walzer, *Spheres of Justice: A Defense of Pluralism and Equality* (Oxford: Martin Robertson, 1983), passim.

22. Viviana Zelizer, *Economic Lives* (Princeton, N.J.: Princeton University Press, 2011), 167.

23. William Baumol, "Health Care, Education and the Cost Disease," in *Baumol's Cost Disease: The Arts and Other Victims*, ed. Ruth Towse (London: Edward Elgar, 1997), 513.

24. Colin Leys, *Market-Driven Politics: Neoliberal Democracy and the Public Interest* (London: Verso, 2001), 212.

25. See, for example, Atul Gawande, "The Cost Conundrum," *New Yorker*, June 1, 2009.

26. Debra Satz, *Why Some Things Should Not Be for Sale* (Oxford: Oxford University Press, 2010), 147.

27. Ibid., 148.

28. John Maynard Keynes, *Economic Possibilities for Our Grandchildren*, 1930, http://www.panarchy.org/keynes/possibilities.html. Quoted in John Tomasi, *Free Market Fairness* (Princeton, N.J.: Princeton University Press, 2012).

29. John Rawls, *A Theory of Justice* (Cambridge, Mass.: Harvard University Press, 1971), 180.

30. Tomasi, *Free Market Fairness*, 265.

31. For a more developed critique of Tomasi's views, see Steven Lukes, "Social Democracy and Economic Liberty," *Res Publica* 21, no. 4 (2015): 429–41.

32. Tomasi, *Free Market Fairness*, 192.

33. See Robert Gordon, *The Rise and Fall of American Growth: The U.S. Standard of Living Since the Civil War* (Princeton, N.J.: Princeton University Press, 2016).

34. Tomasi, *Free Market Fairness*, 217, 222–23.

35. Ibid.

36. Ibid., 182.

37. Ibid., 269.

38. Satz, *Why Some Things*, 5.

39. Michel Foucault, *The Birth of Biopolitics: Lectures at the Collège de France, 1978–1979*, ed. Michel Senellart, trans. Graham Burchell (New York: Picador, 2010).

40. See Gary Becker, *The Economic Approach to Human Behavior* (Chicago: University of Chicago Press, 1978).

41. Foucault, *The Birth of Biopolitics*.

42. See Philip Mirowski, *Never Let a Serious Crisis Go to Waste: How Neoliberalism Survived the Financial Meltdown* (New York: Verso, 2013).

Bibliography

Baumol, William. "Health Care, Education and the Cost Disease." In *Baumol's Cost Disease: The Arts and Other Victims*, edited by Ruth Towse, 510–21. London: Edward Elgar, 1997.

Becker, Gary. *The Economic Approach to Human Behavior*. Chicago: University of Chicago Press, 1978.

Carlyle, Thomas. *Past and Present*. 1843. Repr., New York: New York University Press, 1977.

Coleridge, Samuel Taylor. *Lay Sermons*. 3rd ed. London: Edward Moxon, 1852.

Drèze, Jean, and Amartya Sen. *An Uncertain Glory: India and Its Contradictions*. Princeton, N.J.: Princeton University Press, 2013.

Foucault, Michel. *The Birth of Biopolitics: Lectures at the Collège de France, 1978–1979*. Edited by Michel Senellart. Translated by Graham Burchell. New York: Picador, 2010.

Gawande, Atul. "The Cost Conundrum." *New Yorker*, June 1, 2009.

Gordon, Robert J. *The Rise* and *Fall of American Growth: The U.S. Standard of Living Since the Civil War*. Princeton, N.J.: Princeton University Press, 2016.

Hirschman, Albert O. *Rival Views of Market Society and Other Recent Essays*. New York: Viking, 1986.

Leys, Colin. *Market-Driven Politics: Neoliberal Democracy and the Public Interest*. London: Verso, 2001.

Lukes, Steven. "Social Democracy and Economic Liberty." *Res Publica* 21, no. 4 (2015): 429–41.

Marx, Karl. *Early Writings*. Translated and edited by T. B. Bottomore. London: C. A. Watts, 1963.

Marx, Karl, and Friedrich Engels. *Manifesto of the Communist Party*. Moscow: Foreign Languages Publishing House, 1957.

Mirowski, Philip. *Never Let a Serious Crisis Go to Waste: How Neoliberalism Survived the Financial Meltdown*. New York: Verso, 2013.

Polanyi, Karl. *The Great Transformation: The Political and Economic Origins of Our Time*. Boston: Beacon Press, 1944.

Radin, Margaret. *Contested Commodities: The Trouble with Trade in Sex, Children, Body Parts, and Other Things*. Cambridge, Mass.: Harvard University Press, 1996.

Rawls, John. *A Theory of Justice*. Cambridge, Mass.: Harvard University Press, 1971.

Sandel, Michael J. *What Money Can't Buy: The Moral Basis of Markets*. New York: Farrar, Straus, and Giroux, 2012.

Satz, Debra. *Why Some Things Should Not Be for Sale: The Moral Basis of Markets*. Oxford: Oxford University Press, 2012.

Simmel, Georg. *Georg Simmel on Individuality and Social Forms*. Edited by Donald Levine. Chicago: University of Chicago Press, 1972.

Titmuss, Richard. *The Gift Relationship: From Human Blood to Social Policy*. London: Allen and Unwin, 1970.

Tomasi, John. *Free Market Fairness*. Princeton, N.J.: Princeton University Press, 2012.

Walzer, Michael. *Spheres of Justice: A Defense of Pluralism and Equality*. Oxford: Martin Robertson, 1983.

Wordsworth, William. *The Poetical Works of Wordsworth*. Edited by Thomas Hutchinson. New ed. London: Oxford University Press, 1950.

Zelizer, Viviana. *Economic Lives: How Culture Shapes the Economy*. Princeton, N.J.: Princeton University Press, 2011.

CHAPTER 5

Five Pillars of Decent and Dynamic Societies

Robert P. George

Business is a calling, even a vocation. It is, to be sure, a way of making a living, sometimes a very good living indeed, but it is also a way of serving. In these dimensions it is like law, medicine, and the other learned professions. And the great schools of business are like the great law and medical schools. Like the other great professional schools, however, many business schools are going through something of an identity crisis. According to Rakesh Khurana, the author of an important book on the formation of business leaders, the "logic of stewardship has disappeared" from business education.[1] "Panoramic, long-term thinking," George Anders says, summing up Khurana's argument in a *Wall Street Journal* review of the book, "has given way to an almost grotesque obsession with maximizing shareholder value over increasingly brief spans."[2]

Now, I am not competent to judge whether business education in general stands guilty as charged under Khurana's indictment. If it does, then the loss of the sense of professionalism that is betokened by the situation he describes is in no way unique to business education or to business itself. The same is true in legal and medical education, and in law and medicine. But it does strike me as important that business leaders think broadly about the long-term interests of their firms, the shareholders of those firms, and the relationship between the overall social health of society, which affects the fate of business and which business itself helps to shape, and those long-term interests.

Wherever business operates, it does so in the context of a larger society. It is affected by what happens in various other dimensions of the society, and it in turn affects them. Society plainly has a large stake in the question of what goes on in business, and business, I wish to suggest, has a large stake in what goes on in the broader society. Business, in important ways, depends for its flourishing on things that business itself cannot produce. In many cases, these things are produced, if they are produced at all, by other social institutions. So business has a stake in the health, the flourishing of these institutions.

So far, I have been speaking very abstractly, as philosophers are inclined to do. Let me now speak a bit more concretely, in the mode of the sociologist, as it were. Any healthy society, any decent society will rest upon three pillars. The first of these is respect for the person—the individual human being—and his or her dignity. What I mean is that the formal and informal institutions of society, and the beliefs and practices of the people, are such that human beings are regarded and treated as ends in themselves and not as mere means to other ends. A person is understood to be a subject of justice and human rights, and not an object, an instrument, or a thing. Where this pillar is missing or badly eroded, the human being is generally regarded as a cog in the larger social wheel whose flourishing may legitimately be sacrificed for the sake of the collectivity. In its most extreme modern forms, the individual is reduced by totalitarian regimes to the status of an instrumentality to serve the ends of the fascist state or the future communist utopia. Where liberal regimes are in place but have gone awry, it is usually because a reigning utilitarian ethic results in the reduction of the human person to a means rather than an end to which other things—including the systems and institutions of law, education, and the economy—are means. In cultures in which religious fanaticism has taken hold, the dignity of the individual is typically sacrificed for the sake of theological ideas and goals. By contrast, where a healthy liberal ethos is in place, it supports the dignity of the human person by giving witness to fundamental human rights and civil liberties; and where a healthy religious life flourishes, faith provides a grounding for the dignity and inviolability of the human person by, for example, proposing an understanding of each and every member of the human family, even those of different faiths or professing no particular faith, as persons made in the image and likeness of God or bearing a divine spark that is evident in the human powers of reason and freedom of the will. In its full flower, the first pillar of a decent society is present when a society in its institutional commitments and social practices manifests the conviction that human beings as such possess a profound, inherent, and equal dignity, one that in no way varies according to such factors as race, sex, ethnicity, alienage, age, size, stage of development, or condition of dependency.

The second pillar of any decent society is the institution of the family.[3] It is indispensable. The marriage-based family is the original and best department of health, education, and welfare.[4] Although no family is perfect, no institution excels the healthy family in its capacity to transmit to each new generation the understandings and traits of character—the virtues—upon which the success of every other institution of society, from law and government to educational institutions and business firms, vitally depends. Where families fail to form, or where the breakdown of families is rampant, the effective transmission of the virtues of honesty, civility, self-restraint, concern for the welfare of others, justice, compassion, and personal responsibility are imperiled. Without these virtues, respect for the dignity of the human person, the first pillar of a decent society, will be undermined and sooner or later lost, for even the most laudable formal institutions cannot uphold respect for human dignity where the virtues that make that respect a reality and give it vitality in actual social practices have vanished. Respect for the dignity of the human being requires more than formally sound institutions; it requires a cultural ethos in which people act from conviction to treat each other as human beings should be treated—with respect, civility, justice, and compassion. The best legal and political institutions ever devised are of little value where selfishness, contempt for others, dishonesty, injustice, and other types of immorality and irresponsibility flourish. Indeed, the effective working of governmental institutions themselves depends upon most people most of the time obeying the law out of a sense of moral obligation, and not merely out of fear of detection and punishment for law-breaking. And perhaps it goes without saying that the success of business depends on there being reasonably virtuous, trustworthy, law-abiding, promise-keeping people to serve as workers and managers, lenders, regulators, and payers of bills for goods and services provided by business firms.

Of course, the third pillar of any decent society is a fair and effective system of law and government.[5] This is necessary not only because none of us is perfectly virtuous all the time, and almost every society will include at least some people who will be deterred from wrongdoing, if at all, only by the threat of punishment. More important even than that, contemporary philosophers of law tell us, is the function of law in coordinating human behavior for the sake of achieving common goals—the common good—especially in dealing with the complexities of modern life. Even if all of us were perfectly virtuous all of the time, we would still need a system of laws (considered as a scheme of authoritatively stipulated coordination norms) to accomplish many of our common ends, whether in economic life or in just transporting ourselves from place to place on the streets and highways. Of course, the success of business firms and the economy as a whole depends vitally on a fair and effective system and set of institutions for the administration of justice. We need judges who are skilled in the craft of law and free of corruption. We need to be able to rely on courts to settle disputes, including disputes between (or among) parties who are both (or all) in good faith; and if we are to be confident in entering into contracts and other types of agreements by which business is actually done, we need to know that they will be enforced, and enforced in a timely manner. Indeed, the knowledge that they will be enforced is sufficient most of the time to ensure that courts will not actually be called on to enforce them. A sociological fact of which we can be certain is this: where there is no reliable system of the administration of justice—no confidence that the courts will hold people to their obligations under the law—business will not flourish, and everyone in the society will suffer.

A society can, in my opinion, be a decent one even if it is not a dynamic one. A society will be a decent one, even if lacking in dynamism, where the three pillars I mentioned are in good shape and are functioning in a mutually supportive way (as they will do if each is, in fact, in a healthy condition). Now, some people believe that a truly decent society cannot be a dynamic one. Dynamism, they believe, entails forms of instability that tend to undermine the pillars of a decent society. So there have been people, such as some of the so-called Southern Agrarians in the United States, who opposed not only industrialism but the very idea of a commercial society, fearing that commercial economies inevitably produce consumerist and acquisitive materialist attitudes that corrode the foundations of decency.[6] And there have been groups, such as some of the Amish communities in the United States and Canada, who reject education for their children beyond what is necessary to master reading, writing, and arithmetic, on the ground that higher education leads to worldliness and apostasy and undermines religious faith and moral virtue.[7] So there is a question in the minds of some as to whether a decent society can be a dynamic one. My own view is that, though a decent society need not be a dynamic one (I have great respect for the decency of Amish societies, for example), I believe that dynamism need not erode decency. A dynamic society need not be one in which consumerism and materialism become rife and moral and spiritual values disappear. Indeed, dynamism can play a positive moral role and, I would venture to say, almost certainly will play such a role where what makes dynamism possible is sufficient to sustain dynamism over the long term. Now, that is, I realize, a rather cryptic comment, so let me hasten to explain what I mean. And to do that, I will have to offer some thoughts on what in fact makes social dynamism possible.

The two pillars of social dynamism are, first, institutions of research and education in which the frontiers of knowledge across a wide range of fields in the humanities, social sciences, and natural sciences are pushed back, and through which knowledge beyond the minimum is transmitted to students and disseminated to the public at large; and, second, business firms and institutions associated with such firms and supporting them or managed in ways that are at least in some respects patterned on their principles, by which wealth is generated, distributed, and preserved.

We can think of universities, for example, and business firms, together with respect for the dignity of the human person, the institution of the family, and the system of law and government, as the five pillars of decent and dynamic societies. These last two pillars are dependent in various ways for their well-being on the well-being of the others, and they can help to support the others in turn. At the same time, of course, there is no point in pretending that ideologies and practices hostile and damaging to the pillars of a decent society cannot manifest themselves in higher education and in business. If and when this happens, these institutions do indeed become engines of the erosion of social values on which they themselves depend, not only for their own integrity, but for their long-term survival. Business, for example, really does have a stake, as I've suggested, in the flourishing of the family, just as it has a stake in the integrity and health of the system of law and government by which contracts are enforced and fair competition is maintained.

It is all too easy to take any and all of the pillars of decent and dynamic societies for granted. So it is important to remember that each of them has come under attack historically from different angles and forces. I have already mentioned the way that the dignity of the individual human person has been attacked or compromised in different cultures by such things as fascist and communist totalitarianism, utilitarianism, and religious fanaticism. But we could easily identify other forces that have attacked or undermined the dignity of persons, and we could equally easily identify and examine ideologies and forces that have threatened and weakened the other pillars of decent and dynamic societies. Operating from within universities, persons and movements hostile to one or the other of these pillars, usually preaching or acting in the name of high ideals of one sort or another, have gone on the attack. Attacks on business and the very idea of the market economy and economic freedom coming from the academic world are, of course, well known. Students are sometimes taught to hold business, and especially businessmen, in contempt as heartless exploiters driven by greed. In my own days as a student, these attacks were often made explicitly in the name of Marxism. One notices less of that in the aftermath of the collapse of the Soviet empire, but the attacks themselves have abated little. Similarly, attacks on the family, and particularly on the institution of marriage on which the family is built, are common in the academy. The line here is that the family, at least as traditionally constituted and understood, is a patriarchal and exploitative institution that oppresses women and imposes on people forms of sexual restraint that are psychologically damaging and inhibiting of the free expression of their personality.[8] I believe that there is a real threat to the family here—one that must be taken seriously. The defense of marriage and the family in the public debate, including the debate within the formal institutions of academia, is critical. The reality is that the rise of ideologies hostile to marriage and the family has had a measurable social impact, and its costs are counted in ruined relationships, damaged lives, and all that follows from these personal catastrophes in the social sphere. In many western nations, families are often failing to form and marriage is coming to be regarded as an optional "life-style choice"—one among various optional ways of conducting relationships and having and rearing children. Out-of-wedlock birthrates are very high, with the negative consequences of this particular phenomenon being borne less by the affluent than by those in the poorest and most vulnerable sectors of society. In 1965, the Harvard sociologist and later U.S. senator Daniel Patrick Moynihan shocked Americans by reporting findings that the out-of-wedlock birth rate among African Americans in the United States had reached 25 percent.[9] He warned that the phenomenon of boys and girls being raised in circumstances of fatherlessness in poorer communities would result in social pathologies that would cause severe harm to those most in need of the supports of solid family life. His predictions were all too quickly verified. The widespread failure of family formation portended disastrous social consequences of delinquency, despair, drug abuse, and crime and incarceration. A snowball effect resulted in the further growth of the out-of-wedlock birth rate. It is now over 70 percent among African Americans. It is worth noting, by the way, that at the time of Moynihan's report, the out-of-wedlock birth rate for the United States population as a whole was about 6 percent. Today, that rate is well above 40 percent.

You will have no trouble surmising the consequences for business of these developments. And they are only a small part of the larger story. The breakdown of the marriage culture, though worse in some places than in others, has meant very widespread divorce, as well as failures of families to form in the first place. And we now know that divorce in most cases really does harm children in ways that are susceptible of measurement across large numbers of cases. That does not necessarily mean that civil divorce should never be permitted by law, but it does mean that where the judgment of prudence is that divorce should be lawful in certain circumstances or for certain reasons, law and policy governing marital dissolution and the care of children should be shaped in such a way as to minimize the negative impact on the marriage culture and to give priority to the interests of children. We sought to do this in the United States, but then made a terrible error in the 1970s by replacing "fault" divorce in many jurisdictions with "no-fault" and indeed unilateral divorce that enabled someone guilty of no wrongdoing to be divorced by a spouse against his or her will. It seemed for various reasons at the time to be a good idea, one that would make marital dissolution less acrimonious and expensive, and thus serve the interests of families and the civil justice system. What advocates of the change did not foresee was its impact on the public's understanding of the marital commitment and, thus, on the marriage culture and the rate of divorce.

I cannot comment at length on the situation in the European nations. I can report, however, that many family scholars there and here in the United States are observing with particular interest the relationship between social and legal changes pertaining to marriage and the family, on the one hand, and the decline of birth rates to the point of near demographic collapse on the other. There are fascinating and important issues here, issues of obvious social and economic significance that deserve rigorous sociological study.

As an advocate of dynamic societies, I believe in the market economy and the free enterprise system. I particularly value the social mobility that economic dynamism makes possible. At the same time, I am not a supporter of the laissez-faire doctrine embraced by strict libertarians. I believe that law and government do have important and, indeed, indispensable roles to play in regulating enterprises for the sake of protecting public health, safety, and morals, preventing exploitation and abuse, and promoting fair competitive circumstances of exchange. But these roles are compatible, I would insist, with the ideal of limited government and the principle of subsidiarity according to which government must respect individual initiative to the extent reasonably possible and avoid violating the autonomy and usurping the authority of families, religious communities, and other institutions of civil society that play the primary role in building character and transmitting virtues. Having said that, I would warn that limited government—considered as an ideal as vital to business as to the family—cannot be maintained where the marriage culture collapses and families fail to form or easily dissolve. Where these things happen, the health, education, and welfare functions of the family will have to be undertaken by someone, or some institution, and that will sooner or later be the government. To deal with it, bureaucracies will grow, and with it the tax burden. Moreover, the growth of crime and other pathologies where family breakdown is rampant will result in the need for more extensive policing and incarceration and, again, increased taxes to pay for these government services. The long and short of it is that if we want limited government, and a level of taxation that is not unduly burdensome, we need healthy institutions of civil society, beginning with a flourishing marriage culture supporting family formation and preservation. The same is true if we shift the question to one of a responsible and capable work force. Business cannot manufacture honest, hard-working people to employ. Nor can government compel these virtues by law. Business firms, like the legal system, depend on there being many such people, but they must rely on the family, assisted by religious communities and other institutions of civil society, to produce them. So business, like law and government, really should view itself as having a stake in the health of the family. It should avoid doing anything to contribute to undermining the family, and it should do what it can where it can to strengthen the institution.

I shall close with some brief reflections on the ways in which business has historically contributed to the strength of the other pillars of decent and dynamic societies. While it is true that some business firms have been exploitative of workers, many firms have enhanced the dignity of individuals by offering challenging and decently paid jobs, providing opportunities for further useful education, either on the job or in training programs, and encouraging workers to think creatively about how to improve the quality of products and the efficiency of production. Moreover, business has made upward economic and social mobility possible for countless persons. The free enterprise system has given many people the freedom to pursue fulfilling and remunerative careers that would have been unimaginable as options for their grandparents, and provided opportunities for them to become entrepreneurs and investors. Whole societies have been made better off by economic growth produced by market economies. Of course, businesses and successful business leaders and investors have helped to relieve poverty and have advanced many good causes through their charitable giving; even where it is government rather than business supplying the money, it is business that is generating the wealth that government acquires by taxation and uses to provide a social safety net for the poor and to carry out its other functions and projects.

While some business firms, it is true, have been involved in corruption and have even stimulated it, it is also true that business has in many places been in the forefront of demanding reform of corrupt courts and governmental agencies. Business leaders have helped to shape laws and policies that are suitable for modern systems of production and exchange, and that will enable us to meet the challenges of the globalized economy.

Notwithstanding the hostility to business in some sectors of academia and the elite intellectual culture, businesses and business leaders and entrepreneurs have been instrumental in supporting education at every level, especially higher education. This is particularly true in the United States, where the tradition of alumni giving is strong and where colleges and universities depend upon it, but it is true to a not inconsiderable extent in Europe and elsewhere, too. Even where the overwhelming bulk of financial support is provided by governments, it is once again important to remember that governments obtain most of the money they spend through taxation, and taxation at the levels necessary to support modern universities is possible only as a result of the successful efforts of businesses.

So business is a pillar of decent and dynamic societies, it can and must support the other pillars, and it is, in important ways, dependent on them for its own flourishing. I hope that today many leaders of business and successful entrepreneurs and investors will turn their minds to the question of what they can contribute to the cause of upholding marriage and the family in the face of great threats. What business leaders have done in other domains let them now do in defense of this distinctively human and uniquely humanizing institution. Some will counsel that "business has no horse in this race." They will say that it is a moral, cultural, and religious question about which business people as such need not concern themselves. This is a grave mistake, one that should prompt us to recall Lenin's famous boast that "the capitalists will sell us the rope that we will hang them with." Just as the family has a stake in business, which, after all, provides employment and compensation, and which generates economic prosperity and with it social mobility, business has a stake in the family. This will be clear, I believe, if we adopt the "panoramic, long term view," and follow out (if I may borrow Professor Khurana's phrase) the logic of stewardship.

Notes

1. Rakesh Khurana, *From Higher Aims to Hired Hands: The Social Transformation of American Business Schools and the Unfulfilled Promise of Management as a Profession* (Princeton, N.J.: Princeton University Press, 2007).

2. George Anders, "Management Leaders Turn Attention to Followers," *Wall Street Journal*, December 24, 2007, https://www.wsj.com/articles/SB119844629771347563 (accessed June 21, 2017).

3. On the importance of the family and family stability for the flourishing of persons and the success of communities and societies, see, among many recent works, Robert Putnam, *Our Kids: The American Dream in Crisis* (New York: Simon and Schuster, 2016); Charles Murray, *Coming Apart: The State of White America, 1960–2010* (New York: Crown Forum, 2012); and W. Bradford Wilcox and Nicholas Wolfinger, *Soul Mates: Religion, Sex, Love, and Marriage Among African Americans and Latinos* (New York: Oxford University Press, 2016).

4. On the nature and social role of marriage as the conjugal union of husband and wife, and the problems with redefining marriage in an effort to accommodate same-sex and polyamorous (multiple partner) unions, see Sherif Girgis, Ryan T. Anderson, and Robert P. George, *What Is Marriage? Man and Woman: A Defense* (New York: Encounter Books, 2012) and Patrick Lee and Robert P. George, *Conjugal Union: What Marriage Is and Why It Matters* (New York: Cambridge University Press, 2014).

5. On the importance of law and government to social success, going quite beyond the important value of maintaining order and protecting people from predation by private actors, see John Finnis, *Natural Law and Natural Rights* (Oxford: Clarendon Press, 1980), especially chapters 9–12.

6. On the thought of the Southern Agrarians, see John Crowe Ransom et al., *I'll Take My Stand: The South and the Agrarian Tradition* (New York: Harper, 1930).

7. On the educational philosophy of the Amish, see John Andrew Hostetler, *Amish Society* (Baltimore: Johns Hopkins University Press, 1968).

8. Among countless examples, see Judith Stacey, "Good Riddance to 'the Family': A Reply to David Popenoe," *Journal of Marriage and the Family* 55, no. 3 (August 1993): 545–47; and Susan Muller Okin, *Justice, Gender, and the Family* (New York: Basic Books, 1989).

9. U.S. Department of Labor, Office of Planning and Research, *The Negro Family: The Case for National Action* (Washington, D.C.: U.S. Government Printing Office, 1965).

Bibliography

Anders, George. "Management Leaders Turn Attention to Followers." *Wall Street Journal*, December 24, 2007. https://www.wsj.com/articles/SB119844629771347563 (accessed June 21, 2017).

Finnis, John. *Natural Law and Natural Rights*. Oxford: Clarendon Press, 1980.

Girgis, Sherif, Ryan T. Anderson, and Robert P. George. *What Is Marriage? Man and Woman: A Defense*. New York: Encounter Books, 2012.

Hostetler, John Andrew. *Amish Society*. Baltimore: Johns Hopkins University Press, 1968.

Khurana, Rakesh. *From Higher Aims to Hired Hands: The Social Transformation of American Business Schools and the Unfulfilled Promise of Management as a Profession*. Princeton, N.J.: Princeton University Press, 2007.

Lee, Patrick, and Robert P. George. *Conjugal Union: What Marriage Is and Why It Matters*. New York: Cambridge University Press, 2014.

Murray, Charles. *Coming Apart: The State of White America, 1960–2010*. New York: Crown Forum, 2012.

Okin, Susan Muller. *Justice, Gender, and the Family*. New York: Basic Books, 1989.

Putnam, Robert. *Our Kids: The American Dream in Crisis*. New York: Simon and Schuster, 2016.

Ransom, John Crowe, Donald Davidson, Frank Lawrence Owsley, John Gould Fletcher, Lyle H. Lanier, Allen Tate, Andrew Nelson Lytle, Robert Penn Warren, John Donald Wade, Henry Blue Kline, and Stark Young. *I'll Take My Stand: The South and the Agrarian Tradition*. New York: Harper, 1930.

Stacey, Judith. "Good Riddance to 'the Family': A Reply to David Popenoe." *Journal of Marriage and the Family* 55, no 3 (August 1993): 545–47.

U.S. Department of Labor, Office of Planning and Research. *The Negro Family: The Case for National Action*. Washington, D.C.: U.S. Government Printing Office, 1965.

Wilcox, W. Bradford, and Nicholas Wolfinger. *Soul Mates: Religion, Sex, Love, and Marriage Among African Americans and Latinos*. New York: Oxford University Press, 2016.

CHAPTER 6

Higher Education and American Capitalism Today

Peter Augustine Lawler

Education is always somewhat determined by the practical requirements of the way of life of a particular people. Our forms of education are largely for a middle-class society full of free people who work. And so it is inevitable and beneficial that education in our country is largely guided by the morality of what's called liberal and democratic capitalism. But surely countries can be praised for also aiming higher, or sustaining forms of education that look beyond the reigning practical imperatives in the direction of the relatively timeless truths about who each of us is and what we are supposed to do. My purpose here is to begin by looking at the state of our middle-class morality today, defined as it is both by the twenty-first century's globally competitive marketplace and by a kind of libertarian securitarianism, and then to view critically the fading place of higher education in our world.

Let me begin with the takeaway exaggeration that the morality of capitalism has won. All of American life is being transformed by the imperatives of the twenty-first century's global marketplace. Our two parties, until the unexpected insurgencies of Trump and Sanders, seemed to be converging in a kind of libertarian direction.[1] The Koch brothers, we read, are "moderating" the Republican Party by purging it of its concern with social issues that are really reactionary prejudices. Silicon Valley is "moderating" the progressivism of the Democratic Party by purging it of policies that stifle growth and innovation by stripping members of our meritocracy based on productivity of their honestly earned property and money. More people than ever have access to the world, past and present, through what they can call up on their various screens. The average lifespan continues to increase, and the realm of personal freedom or autonomy, as our Supreme Court explains, continues to grow. More than ever, America is defined by a meritocracy based on productivity. Race, class, gender, sexual orientation, even the imperatives of biology (such as birth and death), and so forth mean less than ever in constraining the opportunities for free and industrious individuals.

Forces opposed to the reign of that meritocracy, such as unions, are in retreat. Unions depended on American industries' relative lack of competition from the rest of the world. Given the intensification of that competition, unions have become excessively counterproductive and unable to deliver the goods to their members. Other safety nets that ordinary people have come to depend on to cushion the influence of the rigors of the market on our lives are also atrophying. These include pensions, all kinds of tenure, government entitlements, employer and employee loyalty in general, relatively independent local communities, family, and churches. More and more, the American worker is becoming an independent contractor selling his or her flexible skills and competencies to whoever can use them at the moment. We have here, all factors considered, a multifaceted new birth of freedom, an expanded menu of individual choice, and a reduction in some ways of personal security and relational flourishing (the latter especially for ordinary Americans).[2]

One paradox about our unprecedented situation is that Americans are becoming both more and less middle class. When Alexis de Tocqueville said that ours is a middle-class democracy, he meant that almost all Americans (outside the slave states) thought of themselves as and were free beings who work.[3] To be middle class is to be free like an aristocrat to work like a slave. Well, not exactly like a slave. The American works for himself and his family and believes that everyone has the right and duty to do the same. What the aristocrat calls leisure, he calls laziness. A free middle-class country will inevitably have vast disparities of wealth, but a kind of rough equality of hope: a hope supported by the perception of some connection between talent, effort, and success and by the fact that wealth circulates rapidly and fortunes are made and lost so readily and rapidly.

America, Tocqueville noticed, was also characterized by a rough similarity of habits and opinions, and Tocqueville offended us most when he observed that there is little real diversity of thought in America. No one (outside the literary South) talks up the advantages of an aristocratic leisure class for culture; everyone has a technological (as opposed to a "purely theoretical") understanding of what science is, and everyone appreciates the utility of the family and religion. Most people apply the spirit of industry even to literature, vacations, and "free time" generally. Most people speak far too complacently about the way self-interest can explain and justify social duties.[4]

The worry is getting more common that inequality is increasing and mobility decreasing. Probably more than ever, the gap in wealth mirrors a gap in productivity between, as the deeply astute libertarian futurist Tyler Cowen has shown, a cognitive elite of maybe 15 percent that owes its wealth to being skilled and industrious in either working with "genius machines" or marketing the products of or managing the work of those who do, and the rest of the population, who are in fact becoming less productive and so less prosperous.[5] Cowen proclaims that "average is over," meaning that the middle class, in the sense of the middle management who produce and earn something in between the highly productive and the marginally productive, is withering away.[6]

The division of labor is increasingly pronounced between those who do "mental labor" and those who relatively mindlessly work off scripts devised by top management and marketing, often located in some centralized and even undisclosed location. The perfection of the division of labor plus technological development (robotization and the screen, for examples) are making many jobs in "the middle" obsolete and people who work below that middle less productive.

Consider that perhaps the most stunningly efficient workplace in America right now is the Amazon warehouse. It was somewhat less efficient not so long ago, when it employed nearly 200 employees. Productivity and reliability soared as the astute use of robots cut the actual number of persons to under twenty. Even the nicer, more homey chain restaurants such as Panera Bread are replacing cashiers with kiosks, and the geniuses in their home office in St. Louis anticipate that the more impersonal service will be quicker and more nearly error-free.

"Average is over" means, for Cowen, that many or most of those Americans who could formerly think of themselves as middle class will become "marginally productive" at best. And maverick conservatives such as Joel Kotkin, in a similar spirit, write about the "proletarianization" of the middle class.[7] Others still have noticed that some of the features of the "idiocracy" displayed in the funny dystopian movie of that name are already with us. Social critics such as Charles Murray describe the American "cognitive elite" as smarter and more sensible than ever, with excellent work habits, surprisingly stable family lives, and due attention to what the studies show about health and safety.[8] Our sophisticates may talk the 1960s talk about "Do your own thing," but few people actually live that bohemian way and are free from the prudent calculation about probabilities that makes one's being and the being of one's own more secure.

The high level of un-bohemian or un-romantic economic and familial responsibility is impressive; time and energy are lavished on both work and kids. Sure, our productive meritocrats typically have only a kid or two. But, for women especially, the scarcity of time is still more of a problem than it was for many more child-laden middle-class families of the past. Young, successful women now typically earn as much or more than their husbands, but equal investment of spouses in the lives of the kids remains more an ideal than a reality. We learn from Murray that our elite, our meritocracy based mostly on cognitive productivity, is smarter than the elites of the past. But it remains decisively middle class, and certainly less of a leisure class than the more WASPy elites with some of the manners of aristocrats of even our recent past. It is also middle class in the sense of having little of the aristocratic conviction that privileges that flow from wealth generate responsibilities to care for those less gifted or fortunate than oneself.

It might even be the case that the ties that have bound rich and poor together, from sharing a common Creator to common citizenship, are weaker than ever. Tocqueville feared that America might end up with a kind of industrial aristocracy that was more intellectually and emotionally detached from the common people than the aristocrats of old, and that the detachment would be based on the progress of division of labor.[9] This unfashionable, for conservatives and libertarians, fear seems more warranted than ever. It must be emphasized that this detachment is based upon real differences. Rich people are now smarter and thinner, while relatively poor people are fatter and dumber than ever. One class is full of people who have what it takes to flourish as productive participants in the twenty-first century's global marketplace; the other is not. And this meritocracy is actually becoming hereditary more than any other time in our history; "the best" are mating with the best primarily because they don't have much contact with anyone outside their gated communities in the super-rich zip codes and exclusive public or private schools.

Murray describes the deterioration of the work ethic among the bottom 50 percent. Others focus more on increasingly pathological families, the collapse of neighborhoods, the disappearance of the common life that was the parish or other form of religious congregation, and the failures of schools to produce graduates with the basic literacy required of almost everyone who works for him- or herself. There is, I think, a tendency for libertarian conservatives such as Murray to overrate the culture of dependency generated by the welfare state as the cause of the deterioration of middle-class habits and values. Someone might immediately add the sharp drop in the number of unionized industrial jobs. Those jobs were often full of repetitive drudgery but ennobled by the fact that their wages and benefits (not to mention their security) made it possible for a man to earn enough to raise a middle-class family. Too many think, not without reason, that the jobs available to them won't make it possible to have that kind of relational dignity. So they punt on working, and so punt on being responsible husbands and dads. The real problem, of course, is that they lack the skills and competencies required to be productive enough in an economy such as ours, and the jobs available to them pay less, because of the rigors of the market, than they used to pay.

Americans are more middle class insofar as they lack a shared elevated standard, such as the ones that have come from religion and tradition, which trumps the middle-class definition of us all as free beings who work. But they are less middle class descriptively. There is quite a "leisure gap" that separates our cognitive elite from the bottom half of our population.[10] The former work harder than ever; they are, in fact, workaholics with (when you add caring for kids) very little leisure time. Not only that, they stressfully perceive themselves as working harder or having less "free time" than they really do. Meanwhile, many ordinary people (mostly men), increasingly detached from meaningful work and responsible family life, have more free time than ever, too much of which they fill with activities that don't deserve to be called leisure or even recreation. For them, the screen is mostly a diversion filled with sports, games, and, sadly, porn. The hollowing out of the middle class and the atrophying of the experience of common citizenship described here are at the foundation of both Trump and Sanders campaigns. My best guess is that neither—even the embattled and clueless President Trump—will have an enduring effect on the evolution described.

It is probably more true than ever, in any case, that we lack the cultivated leisure class that values "the best that has been thought and said" (as well as painted and sung) for its own sake and has endless amounts of time to attend to the nuances of excellence. And, someone might say, although none of our prominent political leaders do, that our biggest social issue is cultivating those with the leisure, earned or given, made possible by high technology to aid as many Americans as possible in rising far above merely middle-class life. As most experts understand it, however, our biggest social problem is how to get more and more Americans the skills, competencies, and habits required to flourish, or at least make it, in the twenty-first century's competitive marketplace. The problem, maybe somewhat overstated, is that too many don't even have what's required to be proletarian cogs in a machine, to be reliably, if marginally, productive. And so all the educational experts say that we have to work harder to transform all of education around the requirements of the competitive marketplace; even our colleges have to become much more intentional in making graduates competent.

Libertarian Securitarianism

And so, from one view, Americans today are characterized by a relentlessly restless individualism. Contrary to Tocqueville's predictions about soft despotism,[11] they have not surrendered concern for their personal futures. Prudent calculations about health and safety have caused the members of our cognitive elite to live longer, and those same calculations have caused them typically to have only one or two kids. That means, the experts say, that the harsh demographic realities alone mean that our entitlements as currently configured have to be trimmed to be sustainable. And so, on this front, it would appear that the good news is that, despite Tocqueville's prediction, the road to serfdom can never get to serfdom. Our relentless obsession about the future even mainstreamed the hopes of our Silicon Valley billionaires that "transhumanism"—or the overcoming of personal contingency and death—is the likely outcome of our so far rather indefinite technological progress. According to Peter Thiel, for example, we should no longer divert ourselves from being fatalistic about our own personal extinction, but rather attend to the science of nutrition as the key to staying alive until the coming of the Singularity.[12] So many libertarian Americans focus their time and treasure on perfecting personal security.

It is easy to wonder, as Bertrand de Jouvenel first did, whether it is possible to be both a "libertarian" and a "securitarian," and certainly the brand "libertarian securitarian" does seem like an oxymoron.[13] It is true that the conclusion that the road to serfdom never gets to serfdom can be contradicted by our increasing obsession with personal security, beginning with health and safety, which is producing progressively more intrusive government regulations. That self-obsession, however, is primarily characteristic of members of our cognitive elite. It should not be confused, of course, with the revolutionary envy of the many, and the regulations it generates do not aim at economic redistribution. It is really the opposite of a class-based form of animation. Sophisticated Americans feel their personal contingency more than ever, and they spend more time than ever fending off personal extinction. They are often "libertarian" on all matters of personal morality, and even the free market, but puritanically moralistic and highly regulatory on the health-and-safety front. The same campuses that allow students to do what they please when it comes to sex (as long as it's safe and consensual, of course) are banning smoking everywhere.

The techno-goal is to subordinate erotic longing to rational control, to keep it from being risky business or the source of dangerous liaisons. So sex, from this view, in the name of "relational autonomy," is being freed up for individual enjoyment from repressive cultural or relational restraints. From another view, it is driven more by securitarian concerns than ever. Libertarians, especially among the young, are not so good at seeing the connection between the liberationist "hook-up" culture not only tolerated but affirmed by our colleges and the somewhat justified securitarian concerns about "the culture of rape" that might be flourishing on some of our campuses. That connection is, nonetheless, really there. Our campuses are both more libertarian and more securitarian than ever. Students and consumer-sensitive administrators demand a campus that's one big "safe space" where students feel perfectly comfortable doing what they please, without fear of violence or even being criticized, as they define who they are as autonomous beings.[14]

Higher Education Today

Let's turn the focus to what this emerging victory of libertarian-securitarian brand of capitalism means for higher education. It has always been the case that higher education has been about preparing people for what the branders now call "lifelong learning." From the traditional perspective we're given by Aristotle's *Nicomachean Ethics*, work is for leisure, and leisure is for contemplation, for thinking about who you are and what you're supposed to do. So lifelong learners take pleasure in cultivating their souls or educating their minds by reading the best books that are written for that purpose, including philosophy, theology, novels, poetry, plays, and so forth. And that pleasure can be about moving from reading to listening and looking, to music, art, film, and so forth. From this view, making money is easy, but knowing what to do with it is hard, because the latter depends on the cultivation that allows a person to take pleasure in what is intrinsically worthy for rational and virtuous beings such as ourselves.

Contemplation here doesn't mean theoretical physics or metaphysics, which are, as it were, purely mental activities and so not for men and women of action. It means more like reflecting on the practice of the virtues that make life worth living. The Southerners who are self-consciously Stoic (like George Washington or the fictional Atticus Finch of *To Kill a Mockingbird*) were Aristotelian in their focus on the virtues of generosity and magnanimity as being characteristics of any rational person.[15] So liberal education is about being able to rule yourself and others, as those whom President Obama praised as the proud men of Morehouse do when they fearlessly return to their local communities with the intention of assuming positions of responsibility.[16] Lifelong learning is intertwined with a life of taking responsibility for what you cannot help but know about yourself and others in the place where you live. That means, of course, that worthwhile work is for love and virtue, and not the other way around.

Today, however, lifelong learning seems to mean mainly having the flexibility to pick up new skills and competencies in response to techno-development and the changing needs of employers. So one reason among many that employer-based health care makes no any sense is that it artificially limits the worker's option to move on, and, more important, the employer's option to push him or her out the door. And it also, of course, keeps the employer from feeling guilty when downsizing those who have become marginally productive. In an increasingly disruptive and innovative global marketplace, those without the flexibility that comes from being comfortable working with machines and thinking abstractly (or unparticularly or impersonally) just have not been prepared for today's world of work. In the meritocracy increasingly based on cognitive productivity, being unable to abstract yourself from yourself and your attachments to take on new roles and contexts guarantees that you'll be left behind.[17] There's much good, of course, in being an independent contractor or out there on your own, but at the price of being displaced. The "how" of generating power, more than ever, works against the "why" provided by the secure relational context in which most people find personal significance. The new understanding of lifelong learning presupposes being stuck with being displaced.

This capitalist morality—this morality of productive displacement—can, Tocqueville reminds us, also be called middle-class morality. All human beings, from one view, are middle class, stuck between the other animals and God. We're beasts with angels in us, and it is the angel who teaches the beast how to satisfy our desires. But not only that, it is the angel who causes our desires to bloat and become more complicated and so harder to satisfy. So those stuck in the middle become increasingly defined by technology and remain restlessly dissatisfied, even in the midst of unprecedented prosperity.

Middle-class Americans are very judgmental about work. Aristocracies were poor by comparison because nobody cared or could seem to care much about money; aristocrats at least had to pretend to be above it, and servants or slaves had no hope for it. Aristocracies were poor and unjust in comparison to us, Americans know, because nobody really worked and the people who had the wealth and power didn't really earn them. Nobody has a right not to work. What aristocrats called leisure, middle-class Americans call laziness. We can pity the poor only if they are "working poor." That means middle-class education has to be for everyone, and it is education for freedom.

But that education for freedom isn't higher education, and it isn't the kind of intellectual and spiritual liberation we associate with liberal education. So Tocqueville claimed to find almost no higher education in America, and little genuine concern for the leisurely cultivation of the soul. Aristocratic education, which includes metaphysics, theology, literature, and theoretical physics, is the proud and seemingly sterile cultivation of the mind or soul. Democratic education, which is pretty much exclusively practical or technological, is oriented around the security and pleasures of bodies. The democratic claim might seem vulgarly materialistic, but it is also based on the truthful insight that nobody is too good to work. The truth is that all human beings have interests or rights and real freedom; real self-knowledge comes from acknowledging that egalitarian fact. Liberal education, from this view, is based on the illusion that some of us are more, and some of us are less, than all of us really are.

Still, as Tocqueville observes, middle-class education produces merely middle-class "brains." It prevents us from being all that we might be. Democracy is capable of turning even art and literature into industries, and of transforming language in such an insistently technical direction that the words that correspond to what's true about metaphysics and theology simply disappear. Tocqueville's biggest objection to middle-class America might be that there's no class of people with the leisure to take the education of the soul seriously, no class with the high opinion that the purpose of the human being is to know the truth for its own sake. His objection, from another view, is that Americans don't have a high enough opinion of themselves as beings with singular destinies that take us far beyond the confines of their interested concerns of the material world.[18]

This democratic skepticism reduces all real education to acquiring the techno-vocational competencies required to obtain money and power. That skepticism, Tocqueville claims, aims to obliterate all real intellectual diversity in our country. There is an unprecedented diversity of interests, and that's the diversity the celebrated *Federalist* 10 deployed to protect minorities in our country from being tyrannized over by an overbearing majority. But that diversity is grounded in a deeper uniformity that understands people pretty much as beings with interests and rights and nothing more. As we see more than ever today, diversity in one sense is at war with diversity in the moral, intellectual, and religious sense. Tocqueville saw remnants of alternative ways of life in America, but he predicted their extinction in the face of middle-class universality.

Tocqueville's Exaggeration as Today's Emerging Truth

Tocqueville's claim that there was almost no higher education in America was clearly an exaggeration. It is also one that clearly seems out of date. We have a huge and diverse array of colleges and universities, and they all think of themselves as providing higher education. But by higher education Tocqueville really did mean theoretical science and the leisurely, meticulous reading of the "great books" in their original languages, with the same sort of attention to high-minded enjoyment of art and music. How much of that is going on in our colleges and universities? Well, some, and maybe even more than Tocqueville seemed to suggest, but less and less with every passing day. The takeaway point to be made to students is that if it is about textbooks, PowerPoint, collaborative teamwork, civic engagement (as beneficial as that can be), service learning, and all that, it is not higher education.

Fewer and fewer of our colleges market themselves as offering liberal education. And others that stick with the "liberal arts" brand (because it's classy) are emptying themselves of liberal arts substance. "General education"

or the core curriculum at most colleges is becoming smaller and more optional. The main way traditional courses in the humanities are justified is in
their ability to aid in acquiring the skills and competencies required to
flourish in the competitive marketplace. It goes without saying that taking
courses in history, literature, and philosophy aren't obviously the only or
even the most efficient ways of acquiring those skills. Liberal education as
an end in itself has become an optional luxury these days, and one that
doesn't add the value required to justify the high cost of college. But "critical
thinking" and analytical reasoning do, because of their obvious benefits in a
high-tech world dominated by a cognitive elite: a cognitive elite that prides
itself not on its wisdom, but on its productivity. Our elite, despite its unprecedented wealth, remains middle class in the conviction that free beings are
all about work.

The most penetrating and effective criticisms of our colleges and universities tend to be from a libertarian or middle-class point of view. College, the
critics say, has become ridiculously expensive and irrelevant. It has become
a "bubble" in two senses.[19] As in the case of the housing bubble, costs are expanding rapidly while quality is getting shoddier.

College is also a "bubble" insofar as it insulates students from the increasingly tough imperatives of the marketplace. It is an artificial environment
not unlike that inhabited by the "bubble boy" on the legendary Seinfeld episode, one that can't be justified as fit for people who can and must eventually
survive in the real world. One result of college costing so much is that students are treated like consumers—or not even future producers. And so
campus life is all about privileges without corresponding responsibilities.

The combination of bubbles means, of course, that students are paying a
lot for degrees that won't pay off. Lots of students leave colleges with big debt
and no prospects of becoming prosperous enough to easily make the monthly
payments. Our colleges are charging students ridiculous rates not to prepare
them effectively to be free beings who work. It is just a matter of time until,
just as the housing bubble did, these bubbles burst.

It is amazing how much the critics of our higher education agree and how
pervasive their influence is. Consider this. The election between Obama and
Romney could be understood to have been between two kinds of American
corporate capitalist oligarchs. Obama had the support of Silicon Valley, while
Romney had the support of more old-school corporate giants such as the
Koch brothers and the DeVos family that runs Amway (and now the Department of Education). But the two sides of this struggle agree that what's

wrong with American education is the bubbles, and that the bubbles have to be burst in a techno-vocational, more efficient, and productive direction. Also agreeing are various foundations, the consultants and experts that surround the Harvard Business School, accrediting associations, and academic and government bureaucrats, such as those, following the powerfully intrusive lead of Bill Gates, who came up with the incredibly mediocre or relentlessly middle-class national Common Core. The cutting edge thinkers in this mode are mostly libertarian economists and various state public policy institutes, often facilitated by Republican governors, but, when it comes to the future of higher education, they don't think any differently from their Silicon Valley counterparts such as Gates.

These critics believe they're outing higher education in America as the shameful project of decadent aristocrats called professors. Their lives are full of privileges without the corresponding responsibilities. The truth is that the privileges have become indefensible. Tocqueville, in his classic account of the causes of the French Revolution—*The Old Regime and the French Revolution*—explains that the eighteenth-century French aristocrats retained privileges that only made sense when aristocrats wielded actual political power. So these privileged men came to use their leisure to engage in irresponsible "literary politics" or to talk up revolutionary theories without any real thought concerning their likely practical consequences. They set the stage for the radical disruption that was the revolution.[20] Our professors, their critics say, are "tenured radicals"[21] who preach their theories without having to be concerned with the consequences of self-indulgent teaching on their students' real futures. The result will be revolution, but not the kind they desire. Today's disruptive educational transformation will consign them and their "humanities" to the place in the trash can of educational history they richly deserve.

Disruptive Innovation Versus Higher Education

When the critics, beginning with Clayton Christensen,[22] write of disrupting higher education, they mean to apply to higher education a process that transforms various techno-industrial sectors in the competitive marketplace of twenty-first-century capitalism. It is the tendency of capitalism to drive prices down by responding to the consumers' views of what their real needs are. Colleges, just like any other industry, will survive insofar as they disrupt themselves to drive costs down, disposing ruthlessly or at least with eyes wide open of the irrelevant bells and whistles that bubbled tuitions up for reasons irrelevant to the real demands of the market. It is the good-enough colleges that have a real future, the colleges that give students exactly what they really need and want at the lowest possible price.

Some conservatives say that the main cost-control issue in American higher education today is tenured faculty who do not teach enough. It would be better if their lazy self-indulgence could be better controlled by more accountable administrators. Tenure, from this view, is a kind of union, and "faculty governance" is collective bargaining.[23] It would be better if administrators could be empowered by the "right-to-fire" situation found in our more entrepreneurial states. What the union-taming governor wants, he doesn't understand, the administrators have already been achieving. In the industrial world, the war against unions is suddenly becoming more aggressive and more effective because unions can't deliver the goods anyway, given the dynamic realities of the twenty-first century's globally competitive marketplace. The same is true of the war against tenure. Tenure is withering away, and astute administrators know better than to launch a frontal assault that would result in really bad public relations and many unnecessary casualties.

The truth is that the number of tenured faculty is rapidly diminishing as a percentage—the tenured and those on a "tenure track" now are a still fairly unoppressed and, I admit, often fairly clueless minority—of the "instructional workforce." There are doubtless good reasons why, at some places, tenured and tenure-track faculty should teach more. It would be better if more students had their "personal touch," just as it would be better if they graded their students' papers themselves at research institutions. But, given how cheap adjuncts are, it is a big mistake to believe that tenured professors taking on an additional class or two would be significant savings. It's often even the case that administrators would rather they not teach more.

At some places at least, the situation seems to be that the administrations are buying off tenured faculty with low teaching loads and various research perks.[24] That incentivizes them to be compliant with the transfer of instruction to adjuncts and other temporary faculty. It also allows them to accept the emptying out of the content of "general education" as requirements focused on the content and methods of the academic disciplines—such as history, literature, and philosophy—are replaced by those based on abstract and empty (or content-free) competencies.

Tenured and tenure-track faculty often come from highly specialized research programs where, even in history and literature, the tendency is to know more and more about less and less. There are also allegedly cutting-edge approaches, such as neuroscience, "digital humanities," rational-choice theory, and so forth, that take the researcher away from being attentive to the content that's been the core of undergraduate instruction. And then there is the pretense of "undergraduate research" (which originated in and makes a lot more sense in the hard sciences), that it is best for students to bypass the bookish acquisition of content about perennial fundamental human issues and questions and get right down to making some cutting-edge marginal contribution.

All in all, it is often not so hard to convince specialists to surrender concern for merely general education, or at least to convince them that the imperatives of the marketplace and the increasingly intrusive accreditation process demand that the value of their disciplinary contributions be reconfigured in terms of competencies. That way, they are led to believe, they will be able to hang on to their curricular "turf." The study of history (or philosophy or whatever) can be justified, after all, as deploying the skills of critical thinking, effective communication, and so forth. One problem, of course, is that those skills can be acquired more easily in other ways, ways not saddled with all that historical or philosophical content.[25]

And when the disciplines of liberal education are displaced by competencies, institutions tend to surrender the content-based distinctiveness that formed most of their educational mission. Even Notre Dame may be about to surrender its requirement of courses in philosophy and theology for all students for competency-based goals. What distinguishes or ought to distinguish Notre Dame is the seriousness by which it treats philosophy and theology as disciplines indispensable for all highly literate Catholic men and women, not primarily by its provision of a Catholic lifestyle.[26]

As institutions surrender their liberal arts substance (while sometimes retaining their classy liberal arts brand), they become pretty much identical in terms of their educational goals.[27] Lists of competencies always seem to me vague and rather random, but they still seem to turn out about the same everywhere. Their measurability usually depends on multiple-choice questions and the sham exactitude of points distributed on rubrics. And in general the data get a veneer of objectivity through the intention to aim at sometimes stunningly low and only seemingly solid goals. It is easy to mock the earnest redundancy of the competency phrases themselves. "Critical thinking"—well, if it wasn't critical, it wouldn't be thinking. "Effective communication"—well, if it wasn't effective, it wouldn't be communication.

In any case, the thought being surrendered is that the dignity of thinking and communicating must have something to do with what is being thought or communicated. It is just not true that the same methods of thought and communication can be applied in all circumstances. Thinking about what or who is a man or woman is very different from figuring out how to rotate your tires or even maximize your productivity. Communicating information is different from "winning friends and influencing people" (or persuasion and manipulation) and from communicating the truth through irony or humor or esoteric indirection—through the parables of the Bible or the dialogues of Plato. The forms of communication that distinguish the great or even good books that provide most of the content of liberal education elude measurable outcomes, and it is not immediately obvious that they have much value in the marketplace. Actually, the kind of insight they provide can be invaluable in marketing, as anyone who has watched an episode of *Mad Men* or read one of those eerie, philosophical, uncannily effective pitches of Don Draper knows. But the administrators would reply, "Well, sure, that Don's a genius, but he's so damn unreliable. We don't want professors like that!"

As the low but seemingly solid goal of competency becomes about the same everywhere, the delivery of education can become less personal or quirky and standardized according to quantitatively validated best practices. Courses can become more scripted, and then delivery can be increasingly open to the use of the screen.[28] So the "intellectual labor" of college administrators—whose numbers are "bloating" and whose perks (at the highest level) are coming to resemble those of corporate CEOs—is directed, and in much the same way as in other sectors of the economy. What is going on, for example, in the Amazon warehouse or in large chains such as Panera Bread, is occurring on our campuses. The idea of "competency" being enforced by the accrediting agencies—basically run by administrators and following a "class-based" administrative agenda—serves the goal of disciplining instruction through measurable outcomes and then displacing actual instructors, as much as possible, by education delivered on the screen.

As colleges become more identical in their competency-based curriculum, the question that obsesses a college president is how to make his or her institution distinctively attractive in the intensely competitive marketplace for the increasingly scarce resource of the student. There is an increased sensitivity to the student as consumer. One result is the amenities arms race. Typically, these innovations are the product of administrative initiatives in which "shared governance" does not come into play.

The excellent libertarian scholar Glenn Reynolds is so disgusted by such developments that his modest proposal is for campuses to be honest and market themselves as luxury cruises.[29] That means spend, and spend more, on the amenities and cut, and cut more, the cost of actual education by reducing the ranks of career faculty and replacing them with various forms of online instruction and MOOCs (Massive Open Online Courses). No college or university, so far, is going quite that far. But many are pretty far down that road. And even the small colleges that talk up the presence of real faculty have begun to describe these as worthy agents and advocates for students— in a way, just another amenity offered to the discerning consumer.

Add to the amenities arms race all the increasingly intrusive and usually stupidly counterproductive compliance requirements of the federal government and accreditation agencies and politically correct administrative initiatives having nothing to do with education, and it is easy to see where most of the so-called bubble in college tuition really comes from. It is not faculty compensation or the cost of instruction in general that is going up much more quickly than the rate of inflation.

Well, you might say, putting the focus on competencies must at least have the advantage of banishing some politically correct blathering from the classroom. Exactly the opposite is true. It institutionalizes political correctness. Some competencies are always attitudinal, about sensitivity to diversity and all that. Students learn that sensitivity is displayed through having not only correct opinions, but the right kind of enthusiasm about them. In the discipline of philosophy, for example, justice is viewed as a question, one to which there is genuine diversity of thoughtful answers. In the era of the competency, the question of justice has been answered, and all that is left is to be engaged in the right way in promulgating the final solution. So the world of the competency mixes techno-enthusiasm with dogmatic social liberalism on the justice front.[30]

Well, a remaining limit to freedom is doing what's required to be productive, and today's political correctness facilitates that single limit by devaluing bohemian, "solidarity," place-based, and faith-based standards that used to clearly rank higher than autonomy and productivity. And the imperative of productivity does not smack students in the face until after they graduate. As paying customers on campus, they are consumers, not producers.

Even if it is claimed that they have mastered this or that competency, the truth is that being or becoming competent on campus is a lifestyle option.

From Competency to Literacy?

Those few conservative reformers who genuinely want our career liberal arts professors in the classrooms filled with as many students as possible have a noble goal. If their reform is seriously personal—or, as we say these days, reform conservatism—then they should oppose every effort of our administrators to displace respected professors with proletarianized adjuncts. The reformers should also work as well as to reduce, as far as possible, the place of competency and the screen in figuring out the kind of general education—the kind of content-driven literacy—that is part of genuinely higher education. Respected professors, it turns out, as we conservatives should understand, are part of the indispensable content of higher education. The genuinely personal and relational point of view, let me add, is what the anticommunist thinkers Solzhenitsyn and Havel called the genuinely dissident point of view. It is the point of view that resists the reductionist excesses of both capitalism and communism—both consumerism and ideological terror—on behalf of "living in the truth" about who each of us is.

For now, we dissident faculty are about resisting standardization and surveillance of all kinds, whether it be from the government or the foundation or the accrediting agency. Because it is impossible to dispense with "branding" altogether in our digital world, we want to replace the idea of competency with that of literacy. And we do so with the real job market in mind. It turns out the main complaint of employers today is not that graduates lack this or that fairly minimalist techno-competency that could, after all, readily be learned on the job. It is that they don't have the level of literacy, the good habits, the sense of personal responsibility, and the fine manners that we used to be able to count on most college grads—or even most high school grads—having.

A question that bothers educators more than it should is, "Is liberal education about learning content or acquiring a method of thinking?" For me, it is undeniable that content is prior to method. You can't think well without knowing what to think with.

The argument for content is typically framed around the need for literacy. Surely every American citizen needs to possess civic literacy. That means having knowledge of the key moments and documents of our long and book-ish political tradition of liberty, as well as knowledge of how our form of government actually functions. From this view, civic literacy is prior to the often touted method of "civic engagement." To take part in our political process responsibly, citizens need to be informed or not just about shooting the bull over alleged outrages.

It would be easy to add here, of course, economic literacy, given how dependent our country now is and has always been in some measure on the global competitive marketplace. And, of course, technological literacy. Nobody really thinks economic productivity and technological progress are good for their own sakes. The "how" of money and power is for the "why" of properly human purposes. Still, there is no way to hope to subordinate the "how" to the "why" without understanding how the "how" works. The last thing liberal education should do, especially these days, is to facilitate the vanity that comes with having unreasonable contempt for what making money and deploying technological creativity can do for us all.

Even libertarians, who often seem to be unreservedly technophiliac cheerleaders for the unimpeded primacy of market forces, don't really think money and power are the bottom line. They don't even think money and power are merely good for satisfying "subjective preferences" and nothing more. For libertarians, typically, the bottom line is the free or sovereign individual, the being undefined by class, caste, or oppressive relational imperatives. That understanding of freedom, of course, requires a real philosophical literacy, and its defense requires real knowledge of its philosophical and theological alternatives. That understanding of freedom is also far from whimsical; it requires taking responsibility for oneself and one's own and refusing to be thoughtlessly dependent on others.

But there's even more. The purpose of modern technological efforts is to deploy smart and even genius machines to enhance human productivity to the point where most of us live in abundance with considerable leisure. Libertarians, for good reason, point to the screen as a kind of liberty that has been made available to us all. Through the screens on our smart devices, we all have access—for free—to most of the great cultural achievements of Western civilization. We also have access, of course, to all manner of mindless games and pornography. There's no way anyone could be satisfied by saying that the whole progress of Western civilization has been toward producing a kind of idiocracy where most people spend their days immersed in online games and porn—perhaps enhanced by legalized marijuana.

That means, if you think about it, that the content of education should mainly be found in books. It really makes all the difference—when it comes to both economic success and the choice of worthy leisure—whether a particular child is raised in a home animated by love of reading. We should prize no skill more than being able to attentively read a "real book," a book that's more than a source of self-indulgent entertainment or technical self-help. That skill is all about effective access to content. It's for building a huge and precise vocabulary that opens the particular person to the daylight of meaning—to living in the truth—that comes with connecting words to the way things really are.[31] That skill, after all, is the source of the freedom that comes from being able to use techno-happy talk ironically, to see, in the field of education, that "collaborative learning," "competency," and even "critical thinking" are lazily abstract ways of diverting oneself from the challenge of figuring out who an educated person really is. Being able to read with the joyful shared pleasure of discovery is, after all, what literacy really is. It also may be the only way of being able to deploy the screen with the ironic moderation that puts it in its proper or reasonably quite limited place in our lives.

Notes

1. See, for example, Thomas Edsall, "The Coming Democratic Schism," *New York Times*, July 15, 2014.

2. On all the claims about social trends made here, see my "Locke, Darwin, and the Science of Modern Virtue," in *The Science of Modern Virtue: On Descartes, Darwin, and Locke*, ed. Peter Augustine Lawler and Marc D. Guerra (DeKalb: Northern Illinois Press, 2013), 3–23; and Yuval Levin, *The Fractured Republic: Renewing America's Social Contract in the Age of Individualism* (New York: Basic Books, 2016).

3. Alexis de Tocqueville, *Democracy in America*, ed. Harvey C. Mansfield and Delba Winthrop (Chicago: University of Chicago Press, 2002).

4. See ibid., vol. 2, pt. 1.

5. Tyler Cowen, *Average Is Over: Powering America Beyond the Age of the Great Stagnation* (New York: Dutton, 2013).

6. These are the key themes of Cowen's book.

7. Joel Kotkin, *The New Class Conflict* (New York: Telos Press, 2014).

8. Charles A. Murray, *Coming Apart: The State of White America, 1960–2010* (New York: Crown Forum, 2013).

9. Tocqueville, *Democracy in America*, vol. 2, pt. 2, chap. 20.

10. Peter McCoy, "America's Leisure Gap," *Bloomberg*, July 19, 2012.

11. Tocqueville, *Democracy in America*, vol. 2, pt. 2, chap. 16, with vol. 2, pt. 4, chap. 6.

12. Peter A. Thiel and Blake Masters, *From Zero to One: Notes on Startups, or How to Build the Future* (New York: Crown Business, 2014).

13. Bertrand de Jouvenel, *On Power: The Natural History of Its Growth*, trans. J. F. Huntington (Indianapolis: Liberty Fund, 1993). Jouvenel shares Tocqueville's view that the love of liberty necessarily has an aristocratic dimension, one that transcends Hobbesian self-obsession.

14. See my "Campus Security: Reflections on Current Outrages," *Weekly Standard*, January 5, 2015.

15. Harper Lee, *To Kill a Mockingbird* (Philadelphia: Lippincott, 1960).

16. See my "President Obama and the Proud Men of Morehouse," *Philanthropy Daily*, May 22, 2013, which is a reflection on Obama's 2013 commencement address at Morehouse.

17. See Brink Lindsey, *Human Capitalism: How Economic Growth Has Made Us Smarter and More Unequal* (Princeton, N.J.: Princeton University Press, 2012).

18. Tocqueville, *Democracy in America*, vol. 2, pt. 1, chap. 10.

19. Glenn Harlan Reynolds, *The Higher Education Bubble* (New York: Encounter Books, 2012); Glenn Reynolds, *The Education Apocalypse* (New York: Encounter Books, 2014). The latter book is the best summary of the educational trends described here.

20. Alexis de Tocqueville, *The Old Regime and the French Revolution*, vol. 1, ed. François Furet and Françoise Melonio, trans. Alan S. Kahan (Chicago: University of Chicago Press, 1998), chap. 1.

21. Roger Kimball, *Tenured Radicals: How Politics Has Corrupted Our Higher Education*, 3rd ed. (Lanham, Md.: Ivan R. Dee, 2008).

22. Clayton M. Christensen and Henry J. Eyring, *The Innovative University: Changing the DNA of Higher Education from the Inside Out* (San Francisco: Jossey-Bass, 2011).

23. See, for example, Willam Voegeli, "Tenure, Kipnis and the PC University," *Minding the Campus*, June 22, 2015.

24. On all the issues discussed here about the transfer of power from faculty to administration, see Benjamin Ginsberg, *The Fall of the Faculty: The Rise of the All-Administrative University and Why It Matters* (Oxford: Oxford University Press 2013).

25. The best example of dissident thought about America is Aleksandr Solzhenitsyn, "Address to the International Academy of Philosophy in Lichtenstein (September 14, 1993)," in *The Great Lie: Classic and Recent Appraisals of Ideology*, ed. F. Flagg Taylor (Wilmington, Del.: ISI Books, 2011).

26. Francesca Ann Murphy, "Freedom Within the Disciplines," *First Things*, June 2015, https://www.firstthings.com/article/2015/06/freedom-within-the-disciplines (accessed July 10, 2017).

27. See Heather MacDonald, "Less Academics, More Narcissism," *City Journal*, July 14, 2011.

28. See Glenn Harlan Reynolds, *The New School: How the Information Age Will Save American Education from Itself* (New York: Encounter Books, 2014).

29. See my "Let's Scuttle the University as Hotel," *Minding the Campus*, March 24, 2013.

30. See my "Liberal Education as Respecting Who We Are," in *The Best Kind of College*, ed. Susan McWilliams and John E. Seery (Albany, N.Y.: SUNY Press, 2015), 125–42.

31. E. D. Hirsch, "A Wealth of Words: The Key to Increasing Upward Mobility Is Expanding Vocabulary," *City Journal*, Winter 2013; Charles A. Murray, *Real Education: Four Simple Truths for Bringing America's Schools Back to Reality* (New York: Crown Forum, 2009), chaps. 4–5.

Bibliography

Christensen, Clayton M., and Henry J. Eyring. *The Innovative University: Changing the DNA of Higher Education from the Inside* Out. San Francisco: Jossey-Bass, 2011.

Cowen, Tyler. *Average Is Over: Powering America Beyond the Age of the Great Stagnation*. New York: Dutton, 2013.

Edsall, Thomas. "The Coming Democratic Schism," *New York Times*, July 15, 2014.

Ginsberg, Benjamin. *The Fall of the Faculty: The Rise of the All-Administrative University and Why It Matters*. Oxford: Oxford University Press, 2013.

Hirsch, E. D. "A Wealth of Words: The Key to Increasing Upward Mobility Is Expanding Vocabulary." *City Journal*, Winter 2013.

de Jouvenel, Bertrand. *On Power: The Natural History of Its Growth*. Translated by J. F. Huntington. Indianapolis: Liberty Fund, 1993.

Kimball, Roger. *Tenured Radicals: How Politics Has Corrupted Our Higher Education*. 3rd ed. Lanham, Md.: Ivan R. Dee, 2008.

Kotkin, Joel. *The New Class Conflict*. New York: Telos Press, 2014.

Lawler, Peter Augustine. "Campus Security: Reflections on Current Outrages." *Weekly Standard*, January 5, 2015.

———. "Liberal Education as Respecting Who We Are." In *The Best Kind of College*, edited by Susan McWilliams and John E. Seery, 125–42. Albany, N.Y.: SUNY Press, 2015.

———. "Locke, Darwin, and the Science of Modern Virtue." In *The Science of Modern Virtue: On Descartes, Darwin, and Locke*, edited by Peter Augustine Lawler and Marc D. Guerra, 3–23. DeKalb: Northern Illinois Press, 2013.

———. "President Obama and the Proud Men of Morehouse." *Philanthropy Daily*, May 22, 2013.

Lee, Harper. *To Kill a Mockingbird*. Philadelphia: Lippincott, 1960.

Levin, Yuval. *The Fractured Republic: Renewing America's Social Contract in the Age of Individualism*. New York: Basic Books, 2016.

Lindsey, Brink. *Human Capitalism: How Economic Growth Has Made Us Smarter and More Unequal*. Princeton, N.J.: Princeton University Press, 2012.

MacDonald, Heather. "Less Academics, More Narcissism." *City Journal*, July 14, 2011.

McCoy, Peter. "America's Leisure Gap." *Bloomberg*, July 19, 2012.

Murphy, Francesca Ann. "Freedom Within the Disciplines." *First Things*, June 2015. https://www.firstthings.com/article/2015/06/freedom-within-the-disciplines (accessed July 10, 2017).

Murray, Charles A. *Coming Apart: The State of White America, 1960–2010*. New York: Crown Forum, 2013.

———. *Real Education: Four Simple Truths for Bringing America's Schools Back to Reality*. New York: Crown Forum, 2009.

Reynolds, Glenn Harlan. *The Education Apocalypse*. New York: Encounter Books, 2014.

———. *The Higher Education Bubble*. New York: Encounter Books, 2012.

———. "Let's Scuttle the University of Hotel." *Minding the Campus*, March 24, 2013.

———. *The New School: How the Information Age Will Save American Education from Itself*. New York: Encounter Books, 2014.

Solzhenitsyn, Aleksandr. "Address to the International Academy of Philosophy in Lichtenstein (September 14, 1993)." In *The Great Lie: Classic and Recent Appraisals of Ideology*, edited by F. Flagg Taylor. Wilmington, Del.: ISI Books, 2011.

Thiel, Peter A., and Blake Masters. *From Zero to One: Notes on Startups, or How to Build the Future*. New York: Crown Business, 2014.

de Tocqueville, Alexis. *Democracy in America*. Edited by Harvey C. Mansfield and Delba Winthrop. Chicago: University of Chicago Press, 2002.

———. *The Old Regime and the French Revolution*. Edited by François Furet and Françoise Melonio. Translated by Alan S. Kahan. Chicago: University of Chicago Press, 1998.

Voegeli, William. "Tenure, Kipnis and the PC University." *Minding the Campus*, June 22, 2015.

PART II

Non-Western Capitalism

CHAPTER 7

Dharma, Markets, and Indian Capitalism

Gurcharan Das

The idea that an ancient Indian concept, dharma, might offer insight into the nature of the competitive market is, on the face of it, bizarre. But this is precisely what I intend to show in this essay on attitudes toward markets during the course of development of commerce in India's economic history. Dharma is a difficult word to translate into English. Duty, goodness, justice, law, and religion have something to do with it, but they all fall short. For our purposes, however, think of dharma as doing the right thing, in both private and public life. The market system depends ultimately not on laws but on the self-restraint of individuals and trust between them. Dharma provides that restraint by offering the underlying norms of a society, creating obligations for citizens and rulers, and bringing a degree of trust and coherence to our everyday life.

At the heart of the market system is the idea of exchange between ordinary, self-interested human beings, who seek to advance their interests peacefully in the marketplace. What makes dharma more suitable for understanding these democratic exchanges is that it does not seek moral perfection, unlike popular, religious notions of western morality.[1] It is pragmatic, viewing men and women as sociable but imperfect. Dharma's world of moral ambiguity and uncertainty is far closer to our experience as ordinary human beings, and thus it lends itself especially to utility maximizing policy makers. Because it is not given by God in the form of commandments, it does not claim a monopoly on truth, the pursuit of which leads inevitably to theocracy or dictatorship or to narrow and rigid positions that define debate in these post-9/11 fundamentalist times.

Dharma places limits on buyers and sellers in the market place, and this allows strangers to trust and transact with each other. Because of a shared notion of dharma, I readily accept a check from you. In the same way, a taxi driver takes me as a passenger because he knows that the curbs of dharma will ensure he will get paid at the end of the journey. Thus, millions of transactions are conducted daily based on the same belief in the self-control of human beings in the global economy without written contracts or judges and policemen to enforce them. Dharma acts like invisible glue between transacting persons in the marketplace, allowing them to trust each other. The same glue also holds society together, bringing predictability to the uncertain lives of human beings.

If more people understood that markets are sustained by moral notions (such as dharma), capitalism and the business world would not have such a poor image. It is a mistake to believe that the market is based solely on greed and profit maximizing behaviour. The dharma texts constantly remind us that there is a right and wrong way to conduct business dealings.[2]

*   *   *

Dharma is a frustrating, almost untranslatable word, yet it has been the "central feature of Indian civilization down the centuries."[3] It derives from the Sanskrit root *dhṛ*, meaning to "sustain" or "hold up" like a foundation, and it appears sixty-four times in the first text on the Indian subcontinent, the *Rig Veda*, around 1500 BCE.[4] Although the Sanskrit word appears at times to be almost synonymous with the English word "moral"—and up to a point, it is—dharma, in fact, carries many connotations that go beyond the English word. From its original Vedic root of "holding up," it carries connotations of balance, harmony, and moral well-being, for both an individual and society. Some of these can help in deepening our understanding of the market. It is the moral law that sustains an individual, a society, and the cosmos (a bit like *maat* in ancient Egypt). At an individual level, it means "moral well-being," and was elevated to one of the four goals of the good human life in classical India, along with *artha*, "material well-being," *kama*, "sexual well-being," and *moksha*, "spiritual well-being."

When individuals behave with dharma they create trust in society and harmony in the cosmic order. "The god Indra then showers sweet rain and the seasons follow; harvests are bountiful, and the people thrive."[5] India has had a long tradition of encouraging and promoting markets. Since ancient times the merchant was a respected member of society, one of the "twice born," belonging to one of the higher castes in the social hierarchy. Merchants and bazaars, however, emerged even earlier as centers of exchange in the towns of the Indus Valley (3300–1500 BCE) or even in the Neolithic age, soon after Indians first engaged in agriculture and there was a surplus.

India historically had a weak state but a strong society, unlike China, which had a strong state and a weak society. India's history has been that of warring kingdoms and China's that of empires. Early on, dharma placed limits on the power of rulers. Unlike the Chinese emperor, who was the source and the interpreter of the law, dharma in India existed prior to the Raja or king, who was expected to "uphold dharma for the benefit of the people"; the Brahmin, not the Raja, was the interpreter of dharma; thus a "liberal" division of powers was created early in Indian history, which placed a check on state power and weakened the power of the state. Oppression generally came not from the state but from society (particularly from the Brahmins). And the answer to that oppression was a guru, like the Buddha, who came along periodically to deliver the people from the Brahmins.

*   *   *

Because the state was weak, regulation in India was generally light. An exception to this was the heavily regulated imagined state in the political economy text, the *Arthashastra*. The king's dharma, we are told in the epic, *Mahabharata*, was to nurture the productive forces in society, including the market: "The king, O Bharata, should always act in such a way towards the *vaishyas* [merchants, commoners] so that their productive powers may be enhanced. *Vaishyas* increase the strength of a kingdom, improve its agriculture, and develop its trade. A wise king levies mild taxes upon them."[6] Practical advice indeed—for otherwise, the epic goes on to suggest, *vaishyas* will shift to neighbouring kingdoms and the king will lose his tax base.

The king in India did not own the land but had a share (*bhaga*) of its produce for providing security and infrastructure to citizens. Normally the king's share was one-sixth, *shad-bhagin*, and this proportion carried into the tax levied by the state on the produce of the land as well as on other economic transactions. Thus, one-sixth, roughly 15 percent, went on to become the dharmic, or "just" tax rate in the later dharma texts. For this reason, there

was outrage among merchants and farmers when the Mughal Empire raised
the tax rate to 40 percent. (By the way, 15 percent happens to be the tax rate
of Singapore today!)

*   *   *

The authority on premodern commercial law are voluminous ancient texts
called the *Dharmashastras*. These texts laid down rules of business for merchants, traders, guilds, farmers, and individuals, and they did so in terms of
the moral ideals of dharma. In the medieval period, the views in the dharma
texts were amplified by many authors, who wrote commentaries on aspects
of commercial law as a part of a legal dharma tradition.[7]

The overwhelming concern in regulating economic activity both in the
dharma texts and in the *Arthashastra* is fairness. For example, the king's
Superintendent of Commodities "should forgo a large profit [on the sale of
commodities on his own land] if it will cause hardship to his subjects" (*Arthashastra* 2.16.6f). However, the texts acknowledge and even praise *labh*,
"profit." Vijnaneshvara, an influential medieval commentator on dharma
texts, defines business as "buying and selling for the sake of making a profit"
(*Laws of Yajnavalkya* 1.119). There is a sense that profit is a legitimate return
for risk-taking and its amount depends on the extent of the risk. With their
concern for fairness, the texts are clear that profits should not be made
through dishonest dealing: "Merchants buy and sell all sorts of commodities
in order to make a profit, but their profit goes up and down according to the
negotiated price. Therefore, a merchant should fix his prices according to
the time and place and he should never deal dishonestly, for this is ideal
path for merchants" (*Laws of Narada* 8.11–12). By dishonest dealing, the
dharma texts mean charging excessively high interest rate on loans, or paying excessively low wages to an employee, or not keeping a promise, or not
fulfilling a contract. For example, "a merchant who is unaware of the decreased or increased value of commodities may not cancel a purchase after it
is completed. If he does, he should pay a penalty of one-sixth of the purchase
price" (*Laws of Yajnavalkya* 2.258). In other words, people who buy and sell
commodities have to be aware that prices fluctuate and factor this into their
business plans.

There is an assumption in the dharma texts that merchants ought to set
their own prices and not the state (unlike the more statist *Arthashastra*). The

authors are aware that prices can go up and down, depending on supply and demand, and businessmen in a competitive market are at the mercy of a market price. The *Mahabharata* illustrates this point with the story of Tuladhara, a respected trader of spices and juices in Varanasi, who surprisingly instructs an arrogant, high Brahmin, Jajali, about dharma and on how to live. Speaking modestly, he compares his life as a merchant to a "twig borne along in a stream that randomly joins up with some other pieces of wood, and from here and there, with straw, wood and refuse, from time to time" (XII.253.35 ff).

*   *   *

There is irony here—a petty shop keeper is teaching a high caste Brahmin how to live. The worldly merchant, who presumably ought to covet wealth, is being held up as a model of behavior for a forest dwelling ascetic. Tuladhara is happy to go with the flow like a twig, suggesting, perhaps, that an honest person who is distrustful of worldly achievement is less likely to step on others' toes and be less violent. Unlike many societies, the merchant was generally well thought of India. He is often the hero in the animal and human stories of the *Panchatantra*, *Hitopadesha*, and *Kathasaritsagara*, which traveled to the West via the Arabs, some of them becoming part of *Aesop's Fables*. In them, the merchant is often a figure of sympathy but sometimes also of fun.

Right through history, merchants were constantly reminded that the constraints of dharma were meant to guide their business. Premchand Roychand, the nineteenth-century cotton king of Bombay, specifically referred to his "dharma duty" to discharge his obligations. He made a fortune in supplying long-staple cotton to the mills of Lancashire when the American Civil War broke out in the 1860s and their supply of raw cotton was cut off. When the war was over, Bombay's cotton market crashed, and with it came down the Bank of Bombay that Roychand controlled. Roychand was bankrupt, but he proudly recounted many years later that he slowly paid back the loans of his depositors and investors, beginning with widows—an act of dharma, in his eyes.[8]

The vocabulary of business law in *Dharmashastra* promotes the cultivation of many virtues.[9] The dharma texts make a distinction between *labh*, "profit," and *lobh*, "greed," and some examples of *lobh* they offer are selling

prohibited goods, mortgaging the same property more than once, and bilk-
ing a debtor by not letting him pay off his loan because "he is greedy for the
interest" (*Law of Yajnavalkya* 2.261, 2.23, 2.44).

In calling the laws applicable to business "Dharma of the Vaishya," the
dharma texts in effect mean that commerce is a religious duty of businessmen. The purpose of business is not only to make a profit but to do it with
righteousness. By giving business dealings religious significance, a business-
man who follows the rules of dharma for making loans, for paying employees, for securing partnerships gains religious merit, good *karma*. The idea of
gaining religious merit will remind some of the German sociologist Max
Weber's use of the same idea in explaining the rise of capitalism in Northern
Europe in his classic, *The Protestant Ethic and the Spirit of Capitalism*.

The big picture that emerges from an examination of dharma texts is that
there is purpose to economic activity. Hence, *artha*, "material well-being,"
was elevated by the ancients to one of the goals of life. The pursuit of money
is proper because it creates the material conditions for the pursuit of other
goals. The good life also has other goals as well, in particular, dharma, "moral
well-being," which is invariably placed higher than *artha*. When there is a
conflict between the two goals, dharma is always expected to prevail. While
artha's purpose is to make the world a better place, there is clearly a right
and a wrong way to pursue wealth.

The Dharma texts suggest that virtuous behavior can be rewarded in the
marketplace, and bad behavior punished. I have certainly found this to be
true in my personal experience. I have been a regular customer of a fruit
seller in Khan Market near my home in Delhi. One day I pointed out to the
shopkeeper that her mangoes were expensive. She claimed that these mangoes were of exceptional quality and I reluctantly bought them. I discovered
at home that they were, in fact, of poor quality. I thought she had been dishonest and I promptly punished her by shifting my allegiance to her competitor next door. Not only did she lose my custom, but I also told half a
dozen friends and neighbors. All of us shared similar stories about her behavior, and as word of mouth spread, she came to be known as a person of
low dharma, and lost market share. The market, it seems, was quick to punish bad behavior without the need for judges and policemen.

In the same vein, I have found that a purchase manager in a company has
the temptation to squeeze his supplier. If he does not treat the supplier fairly
and does not offer the vendor a fair price, his own company is likely to suffer
when the supplier delivers sub-standard components. On the other hand, the

market will also reward good behavior, say, in the case of a company that treats its employees well. The best will want to join such a firm, and with the influx of talent it will be rewarded with high performance and market share. A person or a firm that consistently behaves with dharma is rewarded in the end with a good reputation. Smart businessmen know this and work incessantly to improve their reputation. The dharma texts have a point—markets not only are efficient but can also reinforce good behavior.

Dharma has its limits, however, because every society has its crooks. Therefore, Bhishma instructs Yudhishthira in the *Mahabharata* that a ruler cannot rely purely on the self-restraint of individuals and he must enforce dharma (understood as law) with *danda*, the "rod" of the state, to punish those of low dharma. Even the most peaceful, dharmic ruler must then exercise force. The epic says that when dharma is low in a society, the dependence on *danda* or intrusive regulation rises. A society where dharma is weak suffers from pervasive corruption of public officials and ineffective public administration.

Unlike the Abrahamic religions, morality did not originate with God in Hinduism. *Atharvaveda* says that dharma began in "the old customary order" (18.3.1), a view that is not dissimilar to Plato's belief that morality originated in custom. In the classical dharma texts, no one looks to God as an authority on dharma. If God is not an authority, then who is? In his influential law book from the second century CE, Manu cited plural authorities: "The root of dharma is the entire Veda, the tradition and customs of those who know the Vedas, the conduct of virtuous people, and what is satisfactory to oneself" (2.6).

But the epic, *Mahabharata*, in its typically skeptical way, challenges Manu and questions whether the Vedas can be arbiters of true dharma: "In the opinion of the world the words of the Vedas are contradictory. How can there be scriptural authority over whether something is a true conclusion or not when such contradiction exists?" (12.34.10). The epic also wonders whether the wise can be relied upon to be authorities on dharma: "intelligence appears differently in different men. They all take delight in their own different understanding of things" (X.3.3).

If God is not the arbiter of dharma, and if the Vedas are contradictory, and if wise persons cannot agree about right and wrong, where does it leave the ordinary individual? Kulluka, who wrote a commentary in the fifteenth century on Manu's verse quoted above, declares that the "satisfaction of the mind is the only authority in cases of conflicting alternatives." The classical poet Kalidasa, who lived in the fifth century CE, was of the same view: "In matters where doubt intervenes, the [natural] inclination of the heart of the good person becomes the "authority' or the decisive factor" (I.22). In this view, dharma seems to depend more on reason rather than on blind faith. This is why it is sometimes difficult to judge right and wrong actions as the world is not black and white and comes in shades of gray.

Premodern India presents a world quite different world from "Oriental despotism," a term that the ancient Greeks used contemptuously to refer to the states of Asia and the Middle East, and particularly their enemy, the Persian Empire, where "the king owned all and everyone was his slave." By characterizing Asians in this manner, the Greeks were flattering themselves—they were contrasting their own status as free citizens versus slavish Asian states. Marx took up the idea of Oriental despotism, calling it the "Asiatic mode of production" to explain why "Asia fell asleep in history." The Asiatic mode referred in particular to the agrarian empires of ancient Egypt and China, where an absolute ruler often farmed out the right to collect tribute from peasants to a hierarchy of petty officials, and where extorting tribute from village communities became the mode of enrichment for the ruling nobility.

With a five-thousand-mile coastline, India was historically a vigorous trading power and in some periods commanded as much as a 25 percent share of world trade, according to Angus Maddison.[10] If you had stood at the famous port of Muziris in Kerala two thousand years ago, you would have seen a ship arriving laden with gold and silver. Every day a ship from the Roman Empire landed in a South Indian port, where it picked up fine Indian cottons, spices, and luxuries. But Indians did not care for what the Romans brought, and since accounts had to be settled, they were settled with gold and silver. Back home, Roman senators grumbled that their women used too many Indian luxuries, spices, and fine cottons and that two-thirds of Rome's bullion was being lost to India. Pliny the Elder in 77 CE called India a "sink of the world's precious metal" in his encyclopaedic work *Naturalis Historia*. One South Indian king even sent an embassy to Rome to discuss the empire's balance of payments problems.

Fifteen hundred years later, after the Europeans rediscovered India, the Portuguese had the same complaint: their gold and silver from South America was being drained in the trade with India. The British Parliament echoed this refrain in the seventeenth century. Indian textiles and spices changed culinary tastes and clothing habits around the world. Europeans began to wear underwear only in the seventeenth century, when they discovered soft and affordable Indian cloth brought by the East India Company. The names of luxury textiles—calico, muslin, chintz, bandana—gradually entered European languages. Bernier's compatriot Baron de Montesquieu summed up the situation in 1748: "Every nation, that ever traded with the Indies, has constantly carried bullion, and brought merchandises in return. . . . They want, therefore, nothing but our bullion."[11]

India's power has always been "soft," expressed not through military conquest but in the export of goods and ideas. The Sanskrit scholar Sheldon Pollock reminds us in *The Language of the Gods in the World of Men* that between the fourth and twelfth centuries the influence of India spread across Southeast and Central Asia. Across the vast area, Sanskrit became the language of the courts, government, and literature, much like Latin in medieval Europe. The elite in the East spoke different languages, but used Sanskrit to communicate across the border. We are not sure exactly how Indian culture traveled, but most likely it was through trade. Tamil literature describes seafaring merchants sailing to distant places like Java in search of gold. Their ships also carried Brahmin priests and Buddhist monks. The historian, Michael Wood, summed it well: "History is full of Empires of the Sword, but India alone created an Empire of the Spirit."[12]

India generally had a positive balance of trade with the world until the Industrial Revolution in nineteenth-century England, when the mills of Lancashire made handloom textiles technologically obsolete. As India was the world's leading exporter, Indian weavers suffered the most. Indian nationalists blamed their plight on trade, the East India Company, and the British Raj. But the truth is that handmade textiles could not compete with machine-made ones and handlooms died everywhere. After Independence in 1947, Indians forgot their great trading past, closed their borders in the name of a bogus idea called "import substitution," and denied themselves the prosperity that emerged in the world after the Second World War.

At the same time, a dirigiste, socialist state emerged in India, as it did in many parts of the world. In India, it was largely the result of Jawaharlal Nehru's efforts and the influence of Fabian socialism. Ironically, socialism was out of character with the historical temper of the country. Contrary to the classical Indian view that *artha* was meant to make the world a better place, and *labh*, "profit," was a legitimate goal of business, profit suddenly became a dirty word during the socialist period between 1950 and 1990. According to one of the dharma texts, "Profit is the desired and legitimate end of business" (*Naradashastra* 8.11). Contrast this statement with another one during an elegant lunch between two powerful Indians in the mid-1950s. The Indian prime minister, Jawaharlal Nehru, while lunching with an old friend at Teen Murti, denounced "profit" in a knee-jerk reaction. J. R. D. Tata, India's leading industrialist, had gently reminded Nehru that the public sector was also expected to make a profit. Nehru replied: "Jeh, profit is a dirty word. Let's not spoil our lunch talking about it." The socialist period in Indian history between 1950 and 1990 was clearly influenced by Marx's view of profit as exploitation. Not only did the government in this period delegitimize "profit," but it brought dozens of industries under price control, thereby destroying them. "License Raj" (as this period was called) was clearly an aberration to the generally liberal ethos of Indian history.

Even today, Indian socialists remain skeptical of the market and sometimes confuse *labh* (profit) and *lobh* (greed), a distinction that the dharma texts are careful to make. Socialists continue to believe that only greed motivates business. Adam Smith had clarified this distinction in the eighteenth century. Indeed, besides *The Wealth of Nations*, his other major work was *The Theory of Moral Sentiments*, which portrays economic motivation as highly complex and embedded in broader social habits and mores. He seems to distinguish between legitimate "self-interest" and illegitimate "selfishness." The former leads to a desire in ordinary persons to "better their condition." Another way to think about it is: when it rains, I carry an umbrella. It is a self-interested act—nothing selfish about it. *Lobh*, on the other hand, often harms another and leads a person to cross the line.

The socialist anomaly persisted for four long decades between 1950 and 1990, as India tried to industrialize through the agency of the state by placing the public sector at the "commanding heights" while stifling private enterprise with the worst controls in the world, which came to be notoriously called "License Raj." Not surprisingly, it failed. The Indian state did not have the capacity to manage a command economy, nor was a centralized bureaucratic state in keeping with the country's decentralized systems.

*   *   *

Facing bankruptcy, India made a U-turn in 1991 through a series of reforms that replaced socialist institutions with market-oriented ones. More than two and a half decades of capitalist growth made India one of the fastest growing economies in the world. During these years, India experienced a "golden decade" of growth from 2003 to 2012, when GDP growth averaged over 8 percent a year and lifted millions out of poverty, falsifying the old socialist prophecy that markets would impoverish the working class. The middle class also grew explosively after the economic reforms—from around 12 percent of the population to around a third—and gradually it began to change the country's rhetoric toward middle-class aspirations for a better life. True to its history and its temper, India is today rising from "below," unlike China whose success has been scripted from "above" by an amazing, technocratic state that has built extraordinary infrastructure.

Freed of the shackles of the Licence Raj, Indian entrepreneurs responded, even beyond the most optimistic hopes of the reformers. By 2010, there were more than 150 companies with a market capitalization of over a billion dollars; foreigners had invested in more than a thousand Indian companies via the stock market in the first decades after the reforms; 150 international companies had research and development centers in India—a testament to its human capital; almost 400 of the Fortune 500 companies had outsourced software development or business processes to India. Twenty-five Indian companies were globally competitive, another twenty were on their way, and a few were expected to become recognizable brands globally in the next decade. Because some sectors of the economy are unreformed, "robber barons" emerged, especially in the Congress-led government between 2010 and 2014.

The reforms after 1991 have been trying to recapture the old dharma-based social contract of society, grounded in free exchange. Most thoughtful Indians no longer believe in state ownership of the means of production and generally support the free market. They believe that the purpose of business is to lead society from poverty to prosperity. However, it is a work in progress. Too many Indians still think that reforms make the rich richer and the poor poorer. They confuse being "pro-market" with being "pro-business" and conflate capitalism with "crony capitalism."

Despite the market having generated widespread prosperity over two decades, people still distrust it and the nation continues to reform by stealth. India continues to reform furtively because no political party has bothered to explain the difference between being "pro-market" and "pro-business," leaving people with the impression that liberal reform mostly helps the rich. They do not understand that being pro-market is to believe in competition, which helps keep prices low, raises the quality of products, and leads to a "rules based capitalism" that serves everyone. To be pro-business, on the other hand, means to allow politicians and officials to retain power over licenses, which distorts the market's authority over economic decisions and leads to "crony capitalism." This confusion partially explains the timidity of reform and prevents India from performing to its potential. The market system's tendency toward inequality is visible to everyone, but reformers have not told Indians that they should be concerned more with opportunity rather than with inequality. The market system combined with an outstanding education and health system will do more to create opportunities than state ownership of production.

*   *   *

It is puzzling that India should offer astonishing religious and political freedom but fail when it comes to economic freedom. In a country where two out of five people are self-employed, it takes 42 days to start a business and the entrepreneur is a victim of endless red tape and corrupt inspectors. No wonder India ranked 119 on the global "freedom index" and 134 on "ease of doing business" in 2013. The English-speaking elite in India has grown up with a socialist bias against the market and is unaware that dharma underlies market behavior. It is skeptical about markets, grudgingly accepting after the reforms that markets may be efficient but are not moral. The market, of course, is neither moral nor immoral. Only human beings are. I have tried to point in this essay to an underlying foundation of dharma that supports the market system, which in the end allows people to cooperate with one another for the sake of mutual gain. The ability to cooperate socially is dependent on habits, norms of dharma, and institutions. The unfinished political agenda in India is to keep reforming its governance to allow markets to function in frictionless manner.

Some nations seem to possess a code word that, like a key, unlocks the secrets of the country. That word is "liberty" in America's case; *égalité*, "equality," in the case of France; for India, it is "dharma." Some of the most controversial deeds in these nations can only be understood when seen through the lens of their code word. For example, the gun lobby defends itself in the name of liberty in the United States; the "35-hour work" lobby defends itself in the name of equality in France; Hindu conservatives still justify caste inequality on the basis of "sva-dharma."

Just as America's founding fathers were obsessed with liberty, so were many of modern India's founders attached to dharma during the transfer of power from Britain. So much so that they placed the *dharmachakra*, "the wheel of dharma," in the center of the nation's flag, and the great Sanskrit scholar, P. V. Kane, referred to the Constitution as a "dharma text." For the men and women who took part in the constituent assembly in the late 1940s, nation-building was a profoundly moral project. The ideal that continues to exist in the Indian imagination is that of a ruler guided by dharma. Hence, it was common in Hindi newspapers to read the outraged headline—"Dharma has been wounded"—after each scandal broke out during the corruption ridden Congress-led government of 2009 to 2014.

Dharma is the core civilizational principle that has provided a degree of coherence to the Indian mind over the ages. As explained in this chapter, it has also given legal authority to free market exchange; it has legitimized profit; it has limited the state's power to tax arbitrarily by declaring one-sixth as the king's fair share. Most important, it has underlined the idea that there is a right and wrong way to do business. For a reader who still finds dharma a strange idea, it is worth noting that it is sometimes the unfamiliar that jolts us into remembering what we might have learned long time ago, in this case from the eighteenth-century philosophers of the Scottish Enlightenment, who had spoken about the connection between the market and morality.

Unlike the mood of diminished expectations in the West, it is an age of rising expectations in the East. History will remember this age by the rise of China and India based on the liberal economic idea of the market. But it is a work in progress. If these two countries want to become truly developed nations, China must eventually fix its politics and give political freedom to its people, and India will have to fix its institutions of governance. Otherwise, both will get stuck in what economists call the "middle income trap." Meanwhile, the rise of a third of humanity is good news in a more important sense—it proves once again that the liberal idea of free trade and multiplying connections to the global economy are pathways to lasting prosperity.

Notes

1. On the ambiguity of dharma, see Gurcharan Das, *The Difficulty of Being Good: On the Subtle Art of Dharma* (New Delhi: Penguin India, 2008). This book interrogates the Sanskrit epic *Mahabharata*, which is obsessed in finding the meaning of dharma, and concludes that dharma is "subtle"—that is, human beings are constantly placed in *dharma sankat*, "moral dilemmas," which do not lend themselves to black and white commandments. But this relativity does not imply that "anything goes." According to

sadharana-dharma, an aspect of dharma applicable to all human beings, people share universal moral intuitions, such as *ahimsa*, "not hurting others," *satya*, "truth telling." This aspect of dharma appealed to the Buddha and to Gandhi in particular, unlike *swa-dharma*, which is dharma applicable to a group or caste, such as a Brahmin's dharma.

2. Donald R. Davis Jr., *The Dharma of Business: Commercial Law in Medieval India* (New Delhi: Penguin India, 2017). This book provides a new perspective on business law in medieval and early modern India as it developed within the voluminous and multifaceted texts called the *Dharmashastras* and on medieval commentaries on these texts. The texts lay down rules for the business of merchants, traders, guilds, farmers, and individuals in terms of the complex religious, legal, and moral ideal of dharma.

3. Patrick Olivelle, ed., *Dharma: Studies in Its Semantic, Cultural and Religious History* (Delhi: Motilal Banarsidass, 2009), vii. Olivelle is perhaps the greatest scholar of the dharma texts since P. V. Kane, who wrote the masterly *History of Dharmashastra*, 5 vols. (Poona: Bhandarkar Oriental Research Institute, 1962–1975).

4. For an essay on the evolution of *Dharma* from the Rig Veda to present, see "Dharma: The Story of a Word," in Das, *The Difficulty of Being Good*, 306–11.

5. *Mahabharata*, I.58.14.

6. *Mahabharata*, XII.87.

7. The views on commerce and business can be found in the work of authors such as Vijnaneshvara, Devannabhatta, Mitra Mishra, and Chandeshvara, all of whom wrote long commentaries on aspects of commercial law as a part of legal dharma tradition.

8. Lakshmi Subramanian, *Three Merchants of Bombay* (Delhi: Penguin India, 2012).

9. Davis, *The Dharma of Business*, 74 ff., 84.

10. Angus Maddison, *Contours of the World Economy, 1–2030 AD: Essays in Macro-economic History* (Oxford: Oxford University Press, 2007), 379.

11. Montesquieu, *Spirit of the Laws*, trans. and ed. Anne M. Cohler, Basia Carolyn Miller, and Harold Samuel Stone (Cambridge: Cambridge University Press, 1989), Bk. 21, 354–55.

12. Michael Wood, *In Search of the First Civilizations* (London: BBC Books, 2005), 82.

Bibliography

Das, Gurcharan. *The Difficulty of Being Good: On the Subtle Art of Dharma*. New Delhi: Penguin India, 2008.

Davis, Donald R., Jr. *The Dharma of Business: Commercial Law in Medieval India*. New Delhi: Penguin India, 2017.

Kane, P. V. *History of Dharmashastra.* 5 vols. Poona: Bhandarkar Oriental Research Institute, 1962–1975.

Maddison, Angus. *Contours of the World Economy, 1–2030 AD: Essays in Macroeconomic History.* Oxford: Oxford University Press, 2007.

Montesquieu, *Spirit of the Laws.* Trans. and ed. Anne M. Cohler, Basia Carolyn Miller, and Harold Samuel Stone. Cambridge: Cambridge University Press, 1989.

Olivelle, Patrick, ed. *Dharma: Studies in Its Semantic, Cultural and Religious History.* Delhi: Motilal Banarsidass, 2009.

Subramanian, Lakshmi. *Three Merchants of Bombay.* Delhi: Penguin India, 2012.

Wood, Michael. *In Search of the First Civilizations.* London: BBC Books, 2005.

CHAPTER 8

The Great Enrichment Came and Comes from Ethics and Rhetoric

Deirdre Nansen McCloskey

Many people said before 1991 that India would never develop economically, that Hindu culture was hopelessly otherworldly and would always be hostile to market-tested improvement. True, some wise heads, such as professor of English literature Nirad Chaudhuri, demurred. In 1959 Chaudhuri pointed out that Christian England was actually *less* profit-oriented in its prayer for daily bread than was the daily Hindu prayer to Durga, the Mother Goddess: "give me longevity, fame, good fortune, O Goddess, give me sons, wealth, and all things desirable."[1] But most social scientists saw only vicious circles of poverty. Over the forty years after Independence, such a rhetoric of a Gandhi-cum-London-School-of-Economics socialism held the "Hindu rate of growth" to 3.2 percent per year, implying a miserable 1 percent a year per capita. Nehru wrote with satisfaction in 1962 that "the West also brings an antidote to the evils of cut-throat civilization—the principle of socialism. . . . This is not so unlike the old Brahmin idea of service."[2] Splendid.

But at last the anti-market rhetoric from the European 1930s and "the old Brahmin idea of service" faded. A capitalist, innovating rhetoric took root in India, partially upending the "License Raj." Nimish Adhia has shown that the leading Bollywood films changed their heroes from the 1950s to the 1980s from bureaucrats to businesspeople, and villains from factory owners to police, in parallel with a similar shift in the ratio of praise for market-tested improvement and supply in the editorial pages of the *Times of India*. And so the race commenced, especially after the economist Manmohan

Singh and his colleagues began in 1991 to guide economic policy, multiplying the production of goods and services at rates shockingly higher than in the days of five-year plans and corrupt regulation and socialist governments led by students of Harold Laski. Did the change from hatred to admiration of market-tested improvement and supply make possible the Singh reforms after 1991? Without some change in ideology, Singh would not in a democracy have been able to liberalize the Indian economy. By 2008 Indian national income was growing at fully 7 percent per capita (7.6 in 2005 and 2006). Birth rates fell, as they do when people get better off.

At 7.0 percent per year compounded, the very worst of Indian poverty will disappear in a generation of twenty years, because income per capita will have increased by a factor of 3.9. (Thus the Rule of 72: the years to double anything are 72 divided by the percentage growth rate.) In his projections for the year 2030, the leading student of such matters, the late Angus Maddison, came to the same conclusion.[3] Indian income, he reckoned, would be well over the level of per capita income at the purchasing power parity of Mexico in 2003—not heaven on earth, Lord knows, but a lot better than the Indian real per capita income of $2,160 on the same basis in 2003.[4]

Much of the culture didn't change after 1991 and Singh, and probably won't change much in the future. Economic growth does not need to make people European. Unlike the British, Indians in 2030 will probably still give offerings to Lakshmi and the son of Gauri, as they did in 1947 and 1991. Unlike the Germans, they will still play cricket, rather well. So not deep "culture" but sociology, rhetoric, ethics, is how people *talk* about each other.

In 1960 we didn't think it was possible. The old imperialist vision of China and India as always and anciently horribly overrun with $1-a-day starvelings is a recent back projection (with consequences during the 1960s and 1970s in the eugenic excesses of the family limitation movement and the Chinese single-child policy).[5] For most of history, a dense population, as in the lower Yangtze Valley or the lower Rhine, signaled that a place was doing comparatively well in aggregate—though sometimes not so wonderfully well for Jack or Jill at the bottom of the ruck. Around 1600, at the height of the Mughal Empire, for example, the Ganges Plain of India was rich, maybe world-beating per capita, or Europe-equaling, though in most eras its people one by one were $3- or $1-a-day poor, like all the other commoners on the planet.

But note the old number. Economic historians have discovered that until a couple of centuries ago the ordinary folk of Europe, Africa, Asia, and the rest were about equally poor, stuck from the caves to 1800 at an average $1 to $7 a day, notionally $3, pretty much regardless of where they lived. Our ancestors on average never approached the astonishing $33 worldwide average of today, and did not come remotely close to the dumbfounding $100 a day or higher that two billion or so of humankind now enjoy, and more and more every year. The change since 1800 is well labeled "The Great Enrichment."

"But in the good old days we were equal." No, we were not, not since the invention of agriculture, after which the stationary bandits called priests and aristocrats took command. And the equality that we ordinary peasants had was one of utter, terrified misery, walking through a pond with water up to our chins. It was an equality of the *two* St. Elizabeth's Day Floods in the Netherlands, of 1404 and 1421, in which whole villages disappeared overnight under the avenging sea, or of the Bengal Famine of 1943, in which a million and a half equal souls died.

"But we were happy." Well. It was a "happiness" of constant terror, of disease at all ages, of dead children, of violent hierarchy, of women enslaved and silenced, of *sati*, of 5 percent literacy. And anyway the main point of a human life is not happiness of a cat-like sort, relishing a fish dinner on a sunny window sill—nice though such pleasures are to have from time to time.[6] An income of $3 a day affords no scope for the exercise of vital powers along lines of excellence, a flourishing human life. Isaiah Berlin defined "negative freedom" as "the number of paths down which a man can walk, whether or not he chooses to do so."[7] Though Mark Twain noted that a man who *won't* read has no advantage over a man who *can't*, at least the literate one has an alternative path available if he ever wakes up to take it. At $3 in a traditional or totalitarian society, the number of paths are two only, conformity or brigandage. You would not want $3 a day, even if everyone around you had the same. When people can vote with their feet to escape it, they do. Every North Korean who can, does. The Nigerian men selling handbags on the streets of Venice (*Vu cumprà?* "Wanna buy?") have done so most courageously.

*   *   *

Not all of the uplifting to $33 a day worldwide, compared with $3 in 1800, is accounted for by the astounding recent success of China and India. Yet China's success since 1978 (from the $1 a day resulting from late Mao) and India's since 1991 (from similar wretchedness not alleviated by late Gandhi and early Nehru) do constitute a powerful anti-anti-globalization and

Friedmanite-liberalism argument. In 2013, for example, the new premier of China, Li Keqiang, no political liberal, hinted that if a new 11-square-mile free trade zone in Shanghai worked as well as we market liberals think it will, the idea would be extended to other places.[8] If the three other BRICS— Brazil, Russia, and South Africa—would adopt the liberal ideas applied with such enthusiasm by India and China, they, too, would experience China's and India's transformative rates of real per capita income growth, ranging from 5 to 10 percent per year. Such rates triple or quadruple real income per capita in a generation. (Alas, Brazil, Russia, and South Africa so far have stuck with pre-Friedman ideas such as Argentinian self-sufficiency, German labor laws, and a misunderstanding of Korea's export-led growth, and therefore drag along at well below 3 percent per year—at which a mere doubling of real income takes a quarter of a century. Such is the force of ideas, in this case mistaken ones.)

Free markets, that is, have not been bad for the poor of the world. The sole reliable good for the poor, on the contrary, has been the liberating and the honoring of market-tested improvement and supply. Private charity and public works, socialism and central planning, by contrast, have often made people worse off. Yet economic growth since 1800 has almost always made them better off, by enormous factors of increase. The enrichment of the poor, that is, has not come from charity or planning or protection or regulation or trade unions, all of which, despite their undoubted first-act popularity among our good friends on the left, merely redistribute a constant or a shrunken pie. Simple arithmetic shows why. If all profits in the American economy were forthwith handed over to the workers, the workers (including some amazingly highly paid "workers" such as sports and singing stars and big-company CEOs) would be 20 percent or so better off, right now. One time only. True, the very poor would do well with a share of Bill Gates's income, since their income is so low. But consider the bulk of the population: little better off. The 20 percent is to be compared with a rise in real wages from 1800 to the present by a *factor* of 10 or 30 or (allowing for improved quality of goods) 100, which is to say, 900 or 2,900 or 9,900 percent. If we want to make the non-bosses or the poor better off by a significant amount, 9,900 percent beats 20 percent every time. At 5 percent per year, market-tested improvement and supply goes beyond the one-time 20 percent in a scant four years, and then cumulates to a quadrupling.

My claim is that the old, *anti*-bourgeois view—the exceptions in Europe, and doubtless elsewhere such as Osaka in Japan in small doses—came early among the Italians and Catalans. Then the Bavarians, such as the Fuggers of Augsburg, the Hanseatic League, and above all the Dutch, dominated the public rhetoric of Scotland and England until the late seventeenth century, France until the middle of the eighteenth, Germany until the early nineteenth, most of Japan until the late nineteenth, and China and India until the late twentieth. The anti-bourgeois view is ancient, and in some circles it lasts even into the Bourgeois Era. We find echoes of it down to the present, in environmentalist hostility toward market solutions to CO_2 problems (a hostility now adopted, startlingly, by American Republicans and Australian Liberals, who first proposed the carbon tax), or in populist and left academic cries to bring down the CEOs and the World Trade Organization, or in the unselfcritical hatred among progressives of Walmart bringing low prices and pretty good jobs to the poor.

The poor worldwide have gotten richer. Even in the already advanced countries in recent decades, and contrary to widespread claims, there has been no complete stagnation of real incomes for ordinary folk. Real income even in rich countries has risen, if income is correctly measured to include working conditions, years of education, better health care, retirement years, and above all the rising quality of goods.

The Great Enrichment came, I say, from a unique unleashing of human creativity in a novel liberty and dignity for ordinary people—in northwestern Europe from the sixteenth century on, the liberating and honoring of market-tested improvement and supply. Karl Popper called the market-oriented novelty of the modern world the "open society," and the politico-economic theorists Douglass North, John Wallis, and Barry Weingast call it the "open-access" society.[9] The *ORDO* liberals of pre- and postwar Germany called it "a competitive order" or a "social market economy" (which, however, they believed required a highly active government to keep it from descending into cartels, as indeed it did once in Germany).[10] A society open to conversation and to entry yields a creativity that disturbs the rules of the game designed by the elites and the monopolies, rules favoring the already rich. The open economy creates numerous *nouveaux riches*, yet they themselves are soon competed against by still newer rich, to the benefit in the third act of us all. Such openness after 1800 made the economies that adopted it startlingly more productive, affording twice, three time, ten times, a hundred times more goods and services, and to the poorest.

*　*　*

A point of terminology reveals what was in fact unique about the economic world after 1800, now spreading to China and India.

Even more than "bourgeois," the word "capitalism" acquired its prominence from Marx and his followers. (It is often remarked correctly that Marx himself does not in *Das Kapital* use the word *Kapitalismus*. But he does use *kapitalische(n)* freely, so let's not quibble.) The word has led people astray. It should be replaced with the non-snappy but accurate "market-tested improvement and supply," or, if you want a single word, "improvement," understood as frenetic after 1800.

God won't tell us how to employ words. If we must use "capitalism," I propose, if God doesn't mind, that we agree to use the word to mean simply "markets, very widespread in Africa and Latin America in 1800 C.E., but not by any means unknown in China and Mesopotamia in 1800 B.C.E., and dating back, truth be known, to 100,000 B.C.E. in Mother Africa." (That, incidentally, is the way Max Weber and Fernand Braudel used the word in all their work.) "*Modern* capitalism" would then distinguish the strangely innovative and historically unique form that a market society at last took—the frenetically adopted technical and organizational *improvements* peculiar to the past couple of centuries, not the anciently routine markets, or the old class relations evident even in ancient Greece, or the accumulation of capital, which after all happened in the Old Stone Age, too, or the big size of business or the detailed division of labor, which happened in ancient China as much as in ancient Rome.

My proposed substitute for "*modern* capitalism"—"market-tested improvement at the frenetic post-1800 pace, and routine supply also governed by profit"—I admit does rather slant the case, though not in a way that violates the scientific evidence. An increase in the per person ability from 1800 to the present to make goods and services valued in real terms up to a factor of 100 can certainly be called an "improvement" and "frenetic" without violating the norms of language. In any case, "market-tested improvement and supply" slants the case less than does the word "capitalism" as it is commonly understood. "Capitalism" insists on the erroneous conviction of the early economists (including my present hero Smith and my former hero Marx) that piling brick on brick is what made us rich. (If you still believe that capital *accumulation* is the master spring of the modern world, I invite you to study my *Bourgeois Dignity* [2010], especially chapters 14–19; and William Easterly's *The Elusive Quest for Growth* [2001], which shows that "capital fundamentalism" was the chief error of postwar aid to poor countries.) The great Marxist sociologist Immanuel Wallerstein, for example, was perhaps being a trifle careless when he wrote in 1983 that "the word capitalism is derived from capital. It would be legitimate therefore to presume that capital is a key element in capitalism."[11] No, it would not. What we now in retrospect *say* about the modern world does not *by virtue of the very saying* make it true. That we insist on ruminating on something called "capital" does not imply that its accumulation was in fact unique to modernity. It does not make true the Master's words: "Accumulate, accumulate! That [in the opinion of the classical economists whom Marx was attacking, but agreeing with them on the centrality of capital and its 'endless' accumulation] is Moses and the prophets."[12]

Accumulated capital, after all, depreciates. Therefore a long-term accumulation, the piling up of capital over centuries, does not happen. With rare outliers of durability such as Roman roads or the Great Wall or the treeless environment caused by the firestick of the Aborigines, most physical investments in houses and machines and drained fields require frequent renewal, or else they fall victim to entropy: they fall apart, quickly. This is what is erroneous about the late Charles Tilly's thinking, which accorded great importance to accumulations happening in this or that town centuries ago. After all, a Milanese or Amsterdamer building made in 1600 or 1800 is gone by now—unless it has been repaired and restored over and over since then. Anyone who has replaced the roof of a house knows that a house is a continuing accumulation, not to be acquired unmodified from centuries ago. "Lay not up for yourself treasures upon earth, where moth and rust do corrupt," said Jesus. St. Augustine was eloquent on the point: "All things pass away, fly away, and vanish like smoke; and woe to those who love such things!"[13]

What does *not* vanish like smoke is knowledge, or the tacit knowledge transmitted in practice, or the bookable knowledge of the formula for aspirin, or the procedure for appeal to habeas corpus transmitted in libraries. Well, not always. Jared Diamond notes the forgetting of the bow-and-arrow among the aboriginal settlers of Australia.[14] And, amazingly, the formerly Roman Britons lost their knowledge of the potter's wheel after the legions withdrew.[15] The baths at Bath during Roman times were stoked with coal, the use of which the formerly Roman Britons then promptly forgot.

But *only* knowledge has even a chance of accumulating permanently, as a few economists, such as my student Paul Romer, have realized at last, after economists tried and tried to make the routine accumulation of capital instead of the mysterious ways of human creativity into the hero of modernity. (But then Romer turns it back into routine capital accumulation that would arise in any large city, from Ur to Constantinople—but didn't. Oh, Paul.)

*   *   *

Not so long ago, both India and China, in which nearly four out of every ten humans live, were considered hopeless. That's what we were taught in the 1960s as eager young students of economics. Massive capital investment by the West and North in the East and South, we were taught, might alleviate a little the (pretty hopeless) condition of the Hindus and Confucians, but almost everyone in intellectual authority thought that real change would be a matter of centuries, not a few generations.

At the Milan meetings of the International Economic History Association in September 1994, I asked the brilliant Uruguayan economic historian, Luis Bértola—later a beloved colleague at Gothenburg University—how long he thought it would take his country to catch up to the North. "Two centuries," he gloomily replied, infected by the "new growth theory" of the economists. A theory, it seems, can drive even a superb scientist to distraction. Such theoretical distraction is contradicted by most of the historical evidence, from Germany in the nineteenth century to Taiwan in the twentieth, namely, that a country honoring and liberating its bourgeoisie can achieve a modern standard of living for even its very poor in a couple of generations. Three at most.

True, as the economic historians Stanley Engerman and the late Kenneth Sokoloff argued in 2012, the Caribbean and Latin America—and the places in the United States where slavery or peonage was profitable—got societies in which liberty and dignity for common people was systematically denied, leaving such societies lagging behind the North even now. Imagine, for example, a United States without the North. It would have been a nation of slave power, in which slave owners worked to keep the poor in their place. The Southerners tried, then and later; they and other hardy Republicans are still trying to deny poor people the vote.

But despite Bértola's understandable vexation with its long-run consequences, such deeply embedded inegalitarianism also can change, and rapidly. The cases of change confirm by contraries the emphasis on northwest European liberty and dignity for ordinary people after 1600. Hierarchy at least between market and government changed in China after 1978, and it changed sufficiently in (of all caste-obsessed places) India. By 2018 the once-hopeless China will no longer be eligible for World Bank loans, because it will have entered, on average across its unequal breadth, the "high income group," at about a third of the present level of U.S. income. India leads the world in computer services, and will lead in medical tourism and perhaps even in chains of the Best Exotic Marigold Hotels.

The uplifting of the Great Enrichment to more than ten or thirty or even one hundred times the world's pre-1800 level gives every sign of spreading in the next fifty years to the rest of humanity. Our cousins the poor will inherit the earth. For almost all of us recently, the situation has been getting better and better, and doing so in more and more places. Within a couple of generations, almost all the world's poor will have lifted themselves up, building a house for Mr. Biswas. What can stop it is wrapping progress tightly in environmental green tape, or in the older red-colored tape of regulation, or more directly, by commencing to shoot ourselves in the feet and in the heads—the way the wise and genetically special and instrumentally rational and so very modern-minded and disenchanted Europeans did in August 1914, dragging the rest of us into the mad quarrel.

Indignantly opposing such optimism about the economic and cultural possibilities for our grandchildren have been Seven Old Pessimisms, and now an Eighth New One. The old pessimism of 1848 said that the poor were fated by Malthusian logic to stay poor. The pessimism of 1916 said that only Europeans were genetically capable of getting out of $3-a-day poverty. That of 1933 said that anyway the getting out was finished because the Final Crisis of Capitalism was at hand. That of 1945 said that improvement was finished and stagnation was at hand, with excess savings bound to drag down income. That of 1968 said that anyway, when we got out of the (non-Final) Crisis and found that stagnation didn't happen, we would fall into a consumerism corrupting of our souls.[16] The pessimism of 1980, anticipated by J. A. Hobson and Rosa Luxemburg long before, said that anyway the consumerism in the core countries, though it had apparently *not* corrupted or immiserated the proletariat there, depended on an army of exploited people in the Southern Periphery and on their demands for *dhotis*. And the not-so-old pessimism of the 1990s—articulated about Britain as early as the 1890s in the face of the "German [Commercial] Invasion"—said that Old Europe and the (dis-)United States were doomed to fall down the league table, and "Lo, all our pomp of yesterday / Is one with Nineveh and Tyre."

The Seven Old Pessimisms, still dusted off for blog posts and newspaper editorials from both left and right, and built into most alert minds as obvious truths, immune to factual amendment, and justifying if challenged a hot indignation unaccompanied by scientific evidence, have proven mistaken. There was not much evidence in their favor, 1800 to the present. Yet the Pessimisms are wildly popular, flat-earth versions of economic history. Most people, for example, take Charles Dickens, of all people, as a scientific historian of the Industrial Revolution (about which our dear Charles knew very little). If slightly more aware, they seize on the *Communist Manifesto* of 1848, which for all its exhilaration consists largely of historical and economic error. Similarly, wise chatter among historians since the Greeks and Gibbon concerning the rise and fall of empires is taken nowadays as the Very Voice of History. Recent versions of the Voice ignore or deny the transformative character of the Great Enrichment, and declare that "like Rome" we are doomed to decline. Spooky fears about China as Numero Uno haunt the West (as a couple of decades ago fears about Japan did: hmm; any racial prejudice lurking here? Surely not). Yet such movement up and down the league tables does not detract a cent from the Enrichment. They never have: no leading country since 1800 except perhaps Argentina has actually fallen in income. Modern economic growth is not about Seventh Pessimism rankings, and was not caused by national power to do violence. It is about an irreversible arrival of the poor at $33 and then $80 and then $120 per capita, out of their own efforts made productive by accepting the Bourgeois Deal, letting the middle class innovate for the long-run good of us all.

The New and Eighth Pessimism of our own times—that environmental decay is irreversible (the Eighth is accompanied usually by a revival of the First, that limited resources make population growth impoverishing)—will probably prove mistaken, too. In the 1960s and 1970s, the environmentalists told us that Lake Erie was dead, passed on, bereft of life, metabolic processes finished, an ex-lake. They said that its decline from pollution had become irreversible. Now people swim in it.

The revival of the First Pessimism in this connection is well illustrated by the strange career of the biologist Paul Ehrlich (b. 1932). In 1968, on the first page of *The Population Bomb*, he declared that "The battle to feed all of humanity is over." "In the 1970s and 1980s hundreds of millions of people will starve to death. . . . At this late date nothing can prevent a substantial increase in the world death rate. . . . Nothing could be more misleading to our children than our present affluent society. They will inherit a totally different world. . . . We are today involved in the events leading to famine and ecocatastrophe."[17] None of Ehrlich's predictions has proven correct even approximately. India is now a net exporter of grain. The world death rate from the 1960s to the 2000s declined by a third. Birth rates worldwide are falling. Great amounts are being spent now on ecological protection, with encouraging success. Sharply more people than in 1968 live in affluent societies. Population growth has yielded sharply *rising* per capita income.

Yet nearly half a century after making some of the worst scientific predictions of his generation—outdoing in this respect even the proud physicists missing dark matter and the proud economists missing the Great Recession—people still heed what Ehrlich says. It is a remarkable performance, worth bottling and selling. Ehrlich has been saying since the 1960s the same thing, over and over: the sky is falling, the sky is falling. Such is our delight in pessimistic tales that we are still listening, thrilled to be In The Know.

*   *   *

True, in the nineteenth century and most of the twentieth, places like China and India experienced relative to the West a "Great Divergence."[18] Until 1492, and in many ways until 1800, as Joseph Needham showed, China was the most technologically advanced country in the world, contrary to the Eurocentric notion that the West was ever ingenious. Most of the best technologies, such as blast furnaces, were Chinese inventions (or in this particular case of large-scale production of iron, also West African). Anesthesia is among the few dozen or so most important European inventions of the nineteenth century—but the Chinese were doing operations with anesthesia by drug and acupuncture more than two thousand years earlier.[19] Hundreds of years before the West, the Chinese invented and used locks on canals, the canals themselves being gigantically longer until the nineteenth century than any in Europe. It is probably merely a lack of scholarly effort in Needham's style that leaves the impression that South Asia was *not* ahead of the West circa 1700. After all, South Asians (as before them Meso-Americans) invented place value in counting, and crucible steel. And the Arabs further west added their own inventions, such as the university, dazzling the primitive Franks. But after 1700 the West caught up smartly to best practice elsewhere, and streaked ahead.[20]

The Divergence is puzzling, probably explained by the comparative slowness with which improvements in northwestern Europe piled up at first, and certainly afterward by the traditionalist, elitist, socialist obstruction of market tests in many places. But now the Divergence is over, or can be over in a couple of generations—if, that is, people will adopt the liberty and dignity that produces market-tested improvements, such as the liberty to open a new convenience store or the dignity accorded engineers inventing a new digital camera. Allowing people under law to decide for themselves, and honoring in society their decisions and outcomes, also underlies routine supply, such as running a clothing store with diligence or drilling for oil with intelligence. Look at, say, Singapore (which, alas, does *not* have a political democracy), once Asian-poor, whose income per capita is now higher than that of the United States. Or look at Taiwan and South Korea (by now thankfully fully democratic; the efficacy of the earlier state intervention in the economy in the two has been exaggerated in many leftish accounts).

Yet the economists the learned Robert Gordon and the even more learned Tyler Cowen have argued recently that countries like the United States on the frontier of improvement are in for a slowdown.[21] Maybe. They would both acknowledge, of course, that so have many other learned economists predicted in the past couple of centuries, to find their predictions falsified once again by the Great Enrichment. The classical economists of the early nineteenth century, of whom Marx was an example, expected landlords to engorge the national product. (Marx illogically supposed that wages would fall and yet profits would fall, too, yet Capital would engorge the national product, and improvement of technique would occur.) But as the historian and essayist Thomas Babington Macaulay wrote in 1830, "On what principle is it that, when we see nothing but improvement behind us, we are to expect nothing but deterioration before us?"[22] He wrote further: "If we were to prophesy that in the year 1930 a population of fifty million, better fed, clad, and lodged than the English of our time, will cover these islands, that Sussex and Huntingdonshire will be wealthier than the wealthiest parts of the West Riding of Yorkshire now are, that machines constructed on principles yet undiscovered will be in every house, many people would think us insane."[23] Later in the nineteenth century and especially in the socialist-tending days of the mid-twentieth, it was usual to deprecate such optimism, and to characterize Macaulay in particular as hopelessly "Whiggish" and bourgeois and progress-minded and pro-improvement. He certainly was all that, a bourgeois to the core.

Yet, Whiggish and bourgeois and progress-minded and vulgarly pro-improvement though he was, he was in his prediction exactly right, even as to British population in 1930. (If one includes the recently separated Republic of Ireland, he was off by less than 2 percent.)

And Gordon and Cowen would not deny that we have before us fifty or a hundred years in which the now *poor* countries such as South Africa and Brazil and Haiti and Bangladesh will catch up to what is in the rich countries after all a stunningly successful level of average income. Nowadays, with China and India taking up 37 percent of world population, and income per capita in these two pretty-good-free-market and therefore quickly-catching-up places growing at 5 to 12 percent per capita per year, the average income per capita in the world (all the economists agree) is rising faster than ever before in history.[24] Use your recent mastery of the Rule of 72. At 7 percent per year, real income will double in 72 divided by 7 years, or a little over 10 years; at 12 percent it will double in 6 years (because, class, 72 divided by 12 is 6 exactly). Even at the modest 4 percent per year that the World Bank (implausibly) reckons China may experience out to 2030, the result will be a populace twice as rich.[25] China and India during their decades-long socialist experiments in the 1950s and 1960s and 1970s were so badly managed that there was a great deal of ground to make up merely by letting people open shops and factories where and when they wanted to. Certainly no genetics implies that Chinese or Indians should do worse than Europeans permanently. No imaginable limit to world growth is therefore close at hand, and by "close" I mean "in your lifetime, or even that of your grandchildren."

*   *   *

Why northwestern Europe? It was not racial or eugenic, a hardy tradition of scientific racism after 1870 to the contrary (scientific racism revived nowadays by some economists and evolutionary psychologists exhibiting a dismaying insensitivity to the history of eugenics). Nor was it English common law, or European individualism, or the traditions of the Germanic tribes in the Black Forest, as Romantic Europeans have been claiming now for two centuries. That much is obvious, if the obviousness were not plain from the recent explosive economic successes of highly non-European and non-Germanic places such as India and China, and before them of Korea and Japan, and for a long time the economic successes of *overseas* versions of all kinds of ethnic groups, from Jews in North Africa to Parsees in England to Old Believers in Sydney.

Yet it is still an open question, a mystery, why China, for example, did not originate modern economic growth on the scale of the Great Enrichment—which, by now, you know I claim is one of the chief outcomes of a bourgeois civilization. China had enormous cities and millions of merchants and security of property and a gigantic free trade area when bourgeois northern Europeans were still hiding in clusters of a very few thousand behind their tiny city walls, raising barriers to trade in all directions. Internal barriers to trade in China there were, but centrally and uniformly imposed, and nothing like the chaos of local tariffs in Europe.[26] China had village schools, and by early modern standards had high rates of literacy and numeracy. Until the fall of the Ming (1644), it had "undoubtedly had the highest level of literacy in the world."[27] Chinese junks gigantically larger than anything the Europeans could build until the coming of iron hulls in the nineteenth century were making occasional trips to the east coast of Africa before the Portuguese managed by a much shorter route to get there in their own pathetic caravels. Yet, as the Chinese did not, the Portuguese persisted in sailing, at least for a long while, naming, for example, the southeast African province of KwaZulu-Natal, far around the Cape of Good Hope, for the festival of Christ's Nativity of 1497, on which they first got there, and inspiring other Europeans to scramble for empire and trade. "We must sail," sang Luis Camões, the Portuguese Virgil, in 1572. Gnaeus Pompey's ancient declaration, *Navigare necesse est; vivere non est necesse* (sailing is necessary; living is not) was adopted all over Europe, from Bremen to Rotterdam. And so they did sail. No one else did, at least not with the loony passion of the Europeans—especially not the technologically brilliant Chinese, except for their vigorous commerce across the Indian Ocean and with Japan. If China had sailed at a European level, North and South America would now be speaking a version of Cantonese.

Perhaps the problem was precisely China's unity, as against the scramble of Europe at the time, Genoa against Venice, Portugal against Spain, England against Holland. The Ming and the Mughal empires were rhetorically unified, the way any large, one-boss organization, such as a modern university, thinks it is. A "memorandum culture," such as Confucian China (or rather more paradoxically the modern university), has no space for rational discussion, because the monarch does not *have* to pay attention.[28] Consider your local dean or provost, immune to reason in an institution allegedly devoted to reason. "Rational discussion is likely to flourish most," Barrington Moore has noted, "where it is least needed: where political [and religious] passions are minimal" (which would not describe the modern university).[29]

The historical sociologist Jack Goldstone has noted that

> China and India had great concentrations of capital in the hands of merchants; both had substantial accomplishments in science and technology; both had extensive markets. Eighteenth-century China and Japan had agricultural productivity and standards of living equal or greater than that of contemporary European nations. . . . Government regulation and interference in the economy was modest in Asia, for the simple reason that most economic activity took place in free markets run by merchants and local communities, and was beyond the reach of the limited government bureaucracies of advanced organic societies to regulate in detail. Cultural conservatism did keep economic activities in these societies on familiar paths, but those paths allowed of considerable incremental innovation and long-term economic growth.[30]

Well, they allowed *Smithian* "long-term economic growth"—but nothing like the explosion of the Great Enrichment. And that is the puzzle.

Yet "institutions" do not solve it.

The ingenious Swedish historian Erik Ringmar's answer to the question "Why Europe?" starts from the simple and true triad of points that all change involves an initial reflection (namely, a reflection that change is possible, no easy step), an entrepreneurial moment (putting the imagined change into practice), and "pluralism" or "toleration" (I would call it a part of the ideology of the Bourgeois Era: some way of counteracting the push-back that the naturally conservative majority of humans will give to moving their cheese).[31]

"The argument," though, "requires one more component before it is complete," writes Ringmar, and unhappily he then imparts a Northian twist to the history: the additional component, he claims, is "institutions." "Contemporary Britain, the United States or Japan are *not* modern because they contain individuals who are uniquely reflective, entrepreneurial or tolerant."[32] True: the psychological hypothesis one finds in Weber or the psychologist David McClelland or the late historian David Landes does not stand up to the evidence, as for example the success of the overseas Chinese, or indeed the astonishingly quick turn from Maoist starvation in mainland China to 9 or 10 percent rates of growth per capita, or from the Hindu rate of growth and the license Raj in India after Independence to growth rates per capita since 1991 over 6 percent. Why would *psychology* change so quickly?

Unhappily, Ringmar contends in Northian style, "A modern society is a society in which change happens automatically and effortlessly because it is institutionalized."[33] One is reminded of Mae West's old witticism: "I approve of the institution of marriage. But I'm not ready for an institution." The trouble with the claim of "institutions" is, as Ringmar had noted earlier in another connection, that "it begs the question of the origin."[34] It also begs the question of enforcement. "The joker in the pack," writes Eric Jones in speaking of the decline of guild restrictions in England, "was the national shift in elite opinion, which the courts partly share." "The judges often declined to support the restrictiveness that the guilds sought to impose. . . . As early as the start of seventeenth century, towns had been losing cases they took to court with the aim of compelling new arrivals to join their craft guilds. . . . A key case concerned Newbury and Ipswich in 1616. The ruling in this instance became a common law precedent, to the effect that 'foreigners,' men from outside a borough, could not be compelled to enrol as freemen."[35] It was an ideological change, first in Holland and then in British North America and Scotland, not an ideologically unsupported change in institutions, that made the modern world.

Some might say that the dismissal of all causes except rhetoric, especially of the scientific revolution, a better enforcement of property rights, and the Protestant ethic, is overblown, and unnecessary to a minimal version of my point. Yet I have said at length in *Bourgeois Dignity* why I think the scientific revolution is itself overblown—though indeed it was an instance of a new liberal rhetoric, challenging authority the way the Reformation did. High science becomes *economically* significant only after about 1900. And, again in *Bourgeois Dignity* and also in *Bourgeois Equality*, I give ample reasons to doubt that there was indeed a "better enforcement of property rights" after, say, 1689. And, further, it has been shown over and over since 1905, by scholars more qualified to speak on the matter than I, that Weber's notion of the Protestant ethic is wholly mistaken theologically and economically. But the basic point stands: none of this would have mattered if a new liberal ideology had not triumphed.

*   *   *

There grew up in Britain during the early eighteenth century a group of interests that had by then a stake in free markets, and all the more so eighty years later in the expanding free trade area of the United States. Article I, section 10 of the U.S. Constitution declares that "no state shall, without the consent of the Congress, lay any imposts or duties on imports or exports." When the new rhetoric gave license for new businesses, the businesses could enrich enough people to create their own vested interests for opposing a mercantilist plan for local greatness through monopoly. If the blue laws now enforced in the state of Indiana were relaxed, the grocery stores would in a while form an interest group preventing the reimposition of the law about *cold* beer sales that has so far artificially favored liquor stores. In the past few centuries, such new interests have bred toleration for creative destruction, for unpredictable lives, and for most people having much more than their grandparents. It is unlikely therefore that India will return to over-regulation and protectionism even after Manmohan Singh has left the scene, or that any future government of China will reverse the market-tested reforms. As North, Wallis, and Weingast put it, "Creative economic destruction produces a constantly shifting distribution of economic interests, making it difficult for political officials to solidify their advantage through rent-creation."[36]

The running of markets and exchange in *towns*, and therefore what I am calling the strictly bourgeois life—not merely its hunter-gatherer anticipations—is of course not ancient, because towns date from settled agriculture. What is now Oman at the eastern tip of Arabia was by 2500 B.C.E. a middleman between the Indus Valley civilization hundreds of miles to the east in what is now Pakistan and the Sumerian civilization hundreds of miles northwest up the Persian Gulf in what is now Iraq. Monica Smith notes of India in the Early Historic Period (the first few centuries B.C.E. and C.E.), that, despite feeble states, "archaeological and historical documentation indicates a thriving trade in a variety of goods," supported by such nonstate activities as merchant guilds forming "guild armies" to protect trade and pilgrims (compare the hanse towns of late medieval Europe with their fleets for suppressing piracy).[37] Her town of Kaudinyapura in central India, for example, with about 700 souls, consumed sandstone (for grinding pestles), mica (to make pottery shine), and rice, none of which were available locally: merchants brought them from at least fifty miles away. As Adam Smith said, "When the division of labor has been once thoroughly established . . . every man thus lives by exchanging, or becomes in some measure a merchant, and the society itself grows to be what is properly a commercial society."[38] The point is that "commercial society" with its bourgeois specialists in commerce is by no means a late "stage" in human history. It comes with towns, and is anticipated by trade even without towns.

*   *   *

What changed in Europe, and then the world, was not the material conditions of society, or "commercialization," or a new security of property, but the *rhetoric* of trade and production and improvement—that is, the way influential people talked about earning a living, such as Defoe, Voltaire, Montesquieu, Hume, Turgot, Franklin, Smith, Paine, Wilkes, Condorcet, Pitt, Sieyes, Napoleon, Godwin, Humboldt, Wollstonecraft, Bastiat, Martineau, Mill, Manzoni, Macaulay, Peel, and Emerson. And then almost everyone commenced talking this way, with the exception of an initially tiny group of anti-bourgeois clerisy gathering strength after 1848, such as Carlyle, List, Carey, Flaubert, Ruskin, and Marx. The bourgeois talk was challenged mainly by appeal to traditional values, aristocratic or religious, developing into theorized nationalism, racism, socialism, eugenics, and environmentalism.

The change, the Bourgeois Revaluation, was the coming of a business-respecting civilization, accepting of the Bourgeois Deal: "You let me, a bourgeoise, make market-tested improvements, and in the third act of the drama I will make all of *you* richer." Much of the elite, and then also much of the nonelite of northwestern Europe and its offshoots, came to accept or even admire the bourgeois values of exchange and improvement. Or at least they did not attempt to block them, and even sometimes honored them on a scale never before seen. Especially they did so in the new United States. Likewise, the elites and then the common people in more of the world, and now, startlingly, in China and India and Brazil, undertook to respect or at least not to utterly despise and overtax the bourgeoisie. Not everyone did, even in the United States, and there's the rub, and the promise.

The Industrial Revolution and the modern world, in other words, did not arise in the first instance from a quickening of the capitalist spirit or the Scientific Revolution or an original accumulation of capital or an exploitation of the periphery or imperialistic exploitation or a rise in the savings rate or a better enforcement of property rights or a higher birthrate of the profit-making class or manufacturing activity taking over from commercial activity, or from any other of the mainly materialist machinery beloved of economists and calculators left and right. The machines were not necessary. There were substitutes for each of them, as Alexander Gerschenkron argued long ago.[39]

Surprisingly, what seem at first the most malleable things—words, metaphors, narratives, ethics, and ideology—were the most necessary. In the First Industrial Revolution there were no substitutes for bourgeois talk. Followership after the first revolution has been another matter, and can omit the talk, at least for a while. With techniques borrowed from bourgeois societies, a Stalin could suppress bourgeois talk and yet make a great deal of steel. In 1700, however, the absence of the new dignity for merchants and inventors in Britain would have led to the crushing of enterprise, as it had always been crushed before. Governments would have stopped improvement to protect the vested interests, as they always had done. Gifted people would have opted for careers as soldiers or priests or courtiers, as always. The hobby of systematic (it was called "scientific") inquiry that swept Britain in the early eighteenth century would have remained in the parlor, and never transitioned to the mill. In France and Italy that is what happened, and it would have gone on happening without the stimulus of the British example, and behind the British the Dutch.

The talk mattered, whether or not it had exactly its intended effect. In the late eighteenth century, a male and female public that eagerly read Hannah More and William Cowper created middle-class values in hymns and novels and books of instruction, "an expanding literate public seeking not only diversion but instruction."[40] Similarly, the Abbé Sieyes's essay of 1789, *What Is the Third Estate?*, had a lasting impact on French politics. In *A Rhetoric of Bourgeois Revolution*, the historian William Sewell argues that "the literary devices that characterized Sieyes's rhetoric of social revolution quickly became standard elements in a revolutionary rhetorical lexicon. His language, it seems fair to say, had . . . enduring and powerful effects on French political culture."[41] As Tocqueville famously put it in 1856, "Our men of letters did not merely impart their revolutionary ideas to the French nation; they also shaped the national temperament and outlook on life. In the long process of molding men's minds to their ideal pattern their task was all the easier since the French had had no training in the field of politics, and thus they had a clear field."[42] Even in the North American British colonies from Vermont to Georgia and in the new nation made out of them—places with a good deal of local experience in the field of politics—the *rhetoric* of the American Declaration of Independence, or the Gettysburg Address, or the Four Freedoms speech, or the I Have a Dream speech, had lasting enduring and powerful effects in molding people's minds.[43] The word's the thing.

Modernity did not arise from the deep psycho-social changes that Max Weber posited in 1904–1905. Weber's evidence was of course the talk of people: after all, talk is the natural sort of evidence for such an issue. But he believed he was getting deeper, into the core of their psychosocial being. Yet it was not a Protestant ethic or a change in acquisitive desires or a rise of national feeling or an "industrious revolution" or a new experimental attitude or any other change in people's deep behavior as individuals that initiated the new life of market-tested improvement. These were not trivial, and were surely the flourishing branches of a new bourgeois civilization. They were branches, however, not the root. People have always been proud and hard-working and acquisitive and curious, when circumstances warranted it. From the beginning, for example, greed has been a sin, and prudent self-interest a virtue. There's nothing Early Modern about them. As for the pride of nationalism, Italian cities in the thirteenth century, or for that matter Italian parishes anywhere until yesterday, evinced a local "nationalism"—the Italians still call the local version *campanilismo*, from *campanile*, the church bell tower from which the neighborhood takes its daily rhythms—that would do proud a patriotic Frenchman of 1914. And as for the Scientific Revolution, it paid off late, very late. Without a new dignity for the bourgeois engineers and entrepreneurs, its tiny payoffs in the eighteenth and nineteenth centuries would have been disdained, and the much later and then larger payoffs postponed forever.

Yet Weber was correct that cultures and societies and economies require an animating spirit, a *Geist*, an earnest rhetoric of the transcendent, and that such rhetoric matters to economic performance.[44] (Weber's word *Geist*, by the way, is less incense-smelling in German than its English translation of "spirit." *Geisteswissenschaften*, for example, literally in English a very spooky sounding "spirit sciences," is the normal German word for what American academics call the "humanities," the British "arts.") The *Geist* of improvement, though, is not deep. It is superficial, located in the way people talk.

Such a rhetoric can be changed. For example, the conservatives in the United States during the 1980s and 1990s attacked the maternal metaphor of the New Deal and the Great Society, replacing it with a paternal metaphor of discipline.[45] In China the talk (and admittedly also the police action) of the Communist Party down to 1978 stopped all good economic improvement in favor of backyard blast furnaces and gigantic collective farms. Afterward the regime gradually allowed improvement, and now China buzzes with talk of this or that opportunity to turn a *yuan*. So does India now, with the appropriate change in currency and ultimate goals. Sometimes, as around the North Sea in 1517 to 1789, the rhetoric can change even after it has been frozen for millennia in aristocratic and then also in Christian frames of anti-bourgeois talk. Rhetoric-as-cause lacks Romantic profundity. But for all that it is more encouraging, less racist, less nationalistic, less deterministic.

Consider twentieth-century history in the anglosphere. Look at how quickly under McKinley, then Teddy Roosevelt, and then Woodrow Wilson, a previously isolationist United States came to carry a big stick in the world, to the disgust of libertarian critics like H. L. Mencken and latterly Robert Higgs.[46] Look at how quickly the rhetoric of working-class politics changed in Britain between the elections of 1918 and 1922, crushing the great Liberal Party. Look at how quickly the rhetoric of free speech changed in the United States after 1919, through the dissenting opinions of Holmes and Brandeis.[47] Look at how legal prohibitions in Britain directed at advertisements for jobs or housing saying "Europeans only," which had been commonplace in the 1960s, changed the conversation. (As late as 1991, such rhetoric was still allowed in Germany. A pub in Frankfurt had a notice on the door, *Kein Zutritt für Hunde und Türken*: "No entry for dogs and Turks.")[48] Look at how quickly American apartheid changed under the pressure of the Freedom Riders and the Voting Rights Act. Racist talk and racist behavior, of course, didn't vanish overnight in any of these countries. But the racist talk could no longer claim the dignity of law and custom, and the behavior itself was on the run. Witness Barack Obama. Look, again, at how quickly employment for married women became routine. Simone de Beauvoir, Betty Friedan, and other carriers of feminism mattered.[49] Look at how quickly in Australia, under Bob Hawke and Paul Keating in the 1980s, the protectionist "Federation Settlement" dating from the early 1900s was dropped. Look at how quickly under New Labour the nationalizing Clause IV of the British Labour Party fell out of favor. Tony Blair and his rhetoric of realism mattered. One can reasonably assert some material causes for parts of all these, surely. But rhetoric mattered, too, and was subject to startlingly rapid change.

David Landes asserted in 1999 that "if we learn anything from the history of economic development, it is that culture makes all the difference. (Here Max Weber was right on.)"[50] That seems to be mistaken, if "culture" here means, as Landes does intend it to mean, historically deep national characteristics. We learn instead that superficial *rhetoric* makes all the difference, refigured in each generation. That's a much more cheerful conclusion than that the fault that we are underlings is in our ancient race or class or nationality, not in our present speech. As the economists William Baumol, Robert Litan, and Carl Schramm put it in 2007, "There are too many examples of countries turning their economies around in a relatively short period of time, a generation or less [Korea, Singapore, Thailand, Ireland, Spain]. . . . These successes cannot be squared with the culture-is-everything view."[51] The same could be said of countries turning their politics around in a short period of time, with little change in deep culture: after World War II, a defeated Germany, an enriched Taiwan, at length a Franco-less Spain, then a Russia-freed Ukraine. Culture is not much to the point, it would seem—unless, indeed, "culture" is understood as "the rhetoric people presently find persuasive." In which case, yes, right on.

The argument here is that, contrary to a notion of essences derived from a Romantic theory of personality—and contrary to the other side of the Romantic coin, a notion of pre-known preferences derived from a utilitarian theory of decision-without-rhetorical-reflection—what we do is to some large degree determined by how we talk to others and to ourselves. That is to say, it is a matter of public ethics, such as the new acceptance of the Bourgeois Deal, or the honoring of a free press, or an egalitarian ethos of letting ordinary people have a go. As Bernard Manin put it, "The free individual is not one who already knows absolutely what he wants, but one who has incomplete preferences and is trying by means of interior deliberation and dialogue with others to determine precisely what he does want."[52] Manin points out that *avant les lettres,* in 1755, Rousseau mixed the Romantic and the utilitarian hostilities to such a democratic rhetoric into a nasty and influential concoction, which precisely denied deliberation and rhetoric.[53] Just vote, or discern without voting, the General Will.

The ethical and rhetorical change that around 1700 began to break the ancient restraints on improvement, whether restraints from the old knights or the new monopolists, was liberating and it was Enlightened and it was liberal in the sense of putting equal liberty first. And it was successful. As one of its more charming conservative enemies put it:

> Locke sank into a swoon;
> The Garden died;
> God took the spinning-jenny
> Out of his side.[54]

The German Reformation, the Dutch Revolt, the English and American and French Revolutions bred a new cheekiness among the commoners, unique for a while to northwestern Europe. (The Renaissance, seen usually as a birth of individuality, is not one of the founding Rs [Reformation, Revolt, and Revolution]; it was anti-bourgeois, anti-commoner, a celebration of the glittering lives of Federigo da Montefeltro of Urbino or Cosimo de' Medici of Florence. No wonder the formerly bourgeois northern Italians fell deeply in love with aristocracy and military uniforms and the staging of deadly and then comical duels.) To the three Rs was then added a fourth, a Revaluation of a bourgeoisie newly prevented from exercising ancient monopolies and therefore forced by the market test of profit to improve. The liberty and dignity accorded to improvers stimulated also the age of exploration and the scientific revolution and the Scottish Enlightenment, and what we are here concerned with, the greatest of these, the Industrial Revolution and its outcome, the Great Enrichment.

It is merely a materialist-economistic prejudice to insist that such a rhetorical change from aristocratic-religious values to bourgeois values *must* have had economic or biological roots. The political scientist and historian John Mueller argues that war, like slavery or the subordination of women, has become slowly less respectable in the past few centuries.[55] Habits of the heart and of the lip change. In the seventeenth century a master could routinely beat his apprentice. Now he will go to jail for doing it. Such changes are not *always* caused by interest or by the logic of class conflict. The Bourgeois Revaluation also had legal, political, personal, social, class, gender, religious, philosophical, historical, linguistic, journalistic, literary, artistic, and accidental roots. The philosopher Charles Taylor attributes the rhetorical change to the Reformation, which is true in its Radical forms, Anabaptist and Jansenist and Quaker. The economist Deepak Lal, relying on the legal historian Harold Berman, and paralleling an old opinion of Henry Adams, sees the change in the eleventh century, in Gregory VII's assertion of Church supremacy.[56] Perhaps. The trouble with such earlier and broader origins is that modernity came from Holland and England, not, for example, from thoroughly Protestant (if not Radical) Sweden or East Prussia (except Kant), or from thoroughly Church-supremacist Spain or Naples (except Vico). As scene, yes, certainly; as action, no.

It is better to locate the widespread taking up of the politically relevant attitudes later in European history, around 1700. Such a dating fits better with the new historical finding that until the eighteenth century, places like China, say, did not look all that less rich or even in many respects less free than Europe.[57] In Europe the scene was set by the affirmations of ordinary life, and ordinary death, in the upheavals of the Reformation of the sixteenth century, the Dutch Revolt and the French Huguenots/Jansenists, and the two English Revolutions of the seventeenth century. The *economically* relevant change in attitude occurred in the seventeenth and early eighteenth centuries with the novel ruminations around the North Sea—embodied literally in the novel as against the romance—affirming as the transcendent *telos* of an economy an ordinary instead of a heroic or holy life. It was, Taylor remarks, "the sanctification of ordinary life."[58]

The old bourgeoisie and the aristocracy claimed to flee from the dishonor of improvement and trade. Even the late scholastic intellectuals, for all their admirable rhetorical seriousness, did not get their hands dirty. It was sixteenth-century Dutch and English merchants, with their ink-stained hands, who developed the notion of an experimental and observing life. The honor of kings and dukes and bishops was to be devalued. The devaluation of courts and politics followed, slowly.

What followed at length in India and elsewhere was acceptance of the Bourgeois Deal, and the market-tested improvement and supply characteristic of an enriching modern world. Long may it triumph, for the good of the wretched of the earth.

Notes

1. Nirad C. Chaudhuri, *A Passage to England* (London: Macmillan, 1959), 178; see also his chapter 5, "Money and the Englishman." Chaudhuri was a professor of English literature who made his first trip to England after the War.

2. Quoted in Deepak Lal, *Reviving the Invisible Hand: The Case for Classical Liberalism in the Twentieth Century* (Princeton. N.J.: Princeton University Press, 2006), 166.

3. Angus Maddison, *Contours of the World Economy, 1–2030 AD* (Oxford: Oxford University Press, 2007), 174.

4. For Mexico and India in 2003, see ibid., 382.

5. Matthew Connelly, *Fatal Misconception: The Struggle to Control World Population* (Cambridge, Mass.: Harvard University Press, 2008), chap. 4.

6. Deirdre N. McCloskey, "Happyism: The Creepy New Economics of Pleasure," *New Republic*, June 28, 2012.

7. Isaiah Berlin, *The First and the Last* (New York: New York Review Press, 1999), 59.

8. "China Experiments with Free Trade Zone," *Chicago Tribune*, sec. 2, p. 6, October 1, 2013. That the news was buried on the last page of the business section shows how routine the liberalization of China and India has become.

9. I am indebted to Marlies Mueller for reminding me of Popper's usage.

10. See the lucid treatment in Richard E. Wagner, "*ORDO* Liberalism and the Social Market Economy," in *Economics and Religion: Are They Distinct?*, ed. H. Geoffrey Brennan and A. M. C. Waterman (Dordrecht: Kluwer, 1994), 121–38. The capitalization and italicization of *ORDO* refers to the title of a yearbook published from 1948 by the Freiburg [Germany] School of economists recommending *Ordnungpolitik*, "order policy."

11. Immanuel Wallerstein, *Historical Capitalism* with *Capitalist Civilization* (London: Verso, 1995), 13. So, since the word astrology is derived from the Latin for star, it would be legitimate to presume that stars are a key element in human fate.

12. Karl Marx, *Capital: A Critique of Political Economy*, vol. 1., 3rd ed., trans. and ed. Samuel Moore and Edward Aveling (1887; repr., New York: Modern Library, 1906), chap. 24, §3.

13. Augustine, *Tractate 7* (John 1:34–51).

14. Jared Diamond, *Guns, Germs, and Steel: The Fates of Human Societies* (New York: Random House, 1997), 258.

15. David Gilmour, *The Pursuit of Italy: A History of a Land, Its Regions and Their Peoples* (London: Allen Lane Penguin, 2011), citing Bryan Ward-Perkins, *The Fall of Rome and the End of Civilization* (New York: Oxford University Press, 2005).

16. Edward Shils, "Dream and Nightmares: Reflections on the Criticism of Mass Culture," *Sewanee Review* 65, no. 4 (Oct.–Dec. 1957): 490. He writes that the ex-Marxists "criticize the aesthetic qualities of a society which has realized so much of what socialists once claimed was of central importance, which has, in other words, overcome poverty and long arduous labor."

17. Paul R. Ehrlich, *The Population Bomb*, rev. ed. (Jackson Heights, N.Y.: Rivercity Press, 1975), xi.

18. Kenneth Pomeranz, *The Great Divergence: China, Europe, and the Making of the Modern World Economy* (Princeton, N.J.: Princeton University Press, 2000).

19. Gwei-djen Lu and Joseph Needham, "Acupuncture and Major Surgery," in *Celestial Lancets: A History and Rationale of Acupuncture and Moxa* (London: RoutledgeCurzon, 2002), 218–30.

20. Joseph Needham, *Science and Civilization in China*, 27 vols. (Cambridge: Cambridge University Press, 1954–2008).

21. Robert Gordon, "Is U.S. Economic Growth Over? Faltering Innovation Confronts the Six Headwinds," closed access paper, National Bureau of Economics Research, Working Paper no. 18315, 2012; Tyler Cowen, *The Great Stagnation: How America Ate All the Low-Hanging Fruit of Modern History, Got Sick, and Will (Eventually) Feel Better* (New York: Dutton, 2011).

22. Thomas Babington Macaulay, "Southey's Colloquies on Society," in *Critical, Historical, and Miscellaneous Essays by Lord Macaulay* (Boston, 1860), 1:186–87.

23. Ibid., vol. 1, ii, 185.

24. Population shares from Maddison, *Contours of the World Economy*, 378.

25. *Wall Street Journal*, October 7, 2013, A14.

26. Frederick W. Mote, *Imperial China, 900–1800* (Cambridge, Mass.: Harvard University Press, 1999), 362, on the Southern Sung—but, he notes, only beginning then.

27. Ibid., 373, 775.

28. Barrington Moore Jr., "Rational Discussion: Comparative Historical Notes on Its Origins, Enemies, and Prospects," in Barrington Moore Jr., *Moral Aspects of Economic Growth and Other Essays* (Ithaca, N.Y.: Cornell University Press, 1998), 148, 151. For an instance in China, see Mote, *Imperial China*, 335, on the career of the philosopher Chen Liang (1143–1194) in the Southern Sung.

29. Moore, "Rational Discussion, " 156.

30. Jack A. Goldstone, "The Problem of the 'Early Modern' World," *Journal of the Economic and Social History of the Orient* 41, no. 3 (1998): 276.

31. Erik Ringmar, *Why Europe Was First: Social Change and Economic Growth in Europe and East Asia, 1500–2050* (London: Anthem, 2007).

32. Ibid., 31.

33. Ibid., 32.

34. Ibid., 24.

35. Eric L. Jones, *Locating the Industrial Revolution: Inducement and Response* (London: World Scientific, 2010), 102–3.

36. Douglass C. North, John Joseph Wallis, and Barry R. Weingast, *Violence and Social Orders: A Conceptual Framework for Interpreting Recorded Human History* (Cambridge: Cambridge University Press, 2009), 25.

37. Monica L. Smith, "The Role of Ordinary Goods in Premodern Exchange," *Journal of Archaeological Method and Theory* 6, no. 2 (1999): 121.

38. Adam Smith, *An Inquiry into the Nature and Causes of the Wealth of Nations*, ed. R. H. Campbell, A. S. Skinner, and W. B. Todd (1776; repr., Indianapolis: Liberty Classics, 1982), bk. 1, chap. 4, para. 1.

39. Alexandr Gerschenkron, *Economic Backwardness in Historical Perspective* (Cambridge, Mass.: Harvard University Press, 1962).

40. Leonore Davidoff and Catherine Hall, *Family Fortunes: Men and Women of the English Middle Class, 1780–1850* (Chicago: University of Chicago Press, 1987), 162.

41. William H. Sewell, *A Rhetoric of Bourgeois Revolution: The Abbé Sieyes and What Is the Third Estate?* (Durham, N.C.: Duke University Press, 1994), 198.

42. Alexis de Tocqueville, *The Old Régime and the French Revolution*, trans. Stuart Gilbert (Garden City, N.Y.: Anchor Doubleday 1956), 146–47. I owe the citation to Clifford Deaton.

43. See Gary Wills. *Lincoln at Gettysburg: The Words that Remade America* (New York: Simon & Schuster, 1992).

44. Virgil Storr makes this point in the context of the economy of Barbados. Virgil Storr, "Weber's Spirit of Capitalism and the Bahamas' Junkanoo Ethic," *Review of Austrian Economics* 19, no. 4 (2006): 289–309.

45. George Lakoff, *Moral Politics: How Liberals and Conservatives Think*, 2nd ed. (Chicago: University of Chicago Press, 2002).

46. Robert H. Higgs, "The Complex Course of Ideological Change," *American Journal of Economics and Sociology* 67, no. 4 (2008): 547–66; Higgs, *Delusions of Power: New Explorations of the State, War, and Economy* (Oakland, Calif.: Independent Institute, 2012).

47. *Whitney v. California*, 274 U.S. 357 (1927).

48. John Ardagh, *Germany and the Germans*, rev. ed. (London: Penguin, 1991), 297.

49. Deirdre N. McCloskey, "Paid Work," in *Women in Twentieth-Century Britain: Social, Cultural and Political Change*, ed. Ina Zweiniger-Bargielowska (London: Longman/Pearson Education, 2001), 165–82.

50. David S. Landes, *The Wealth and Poverty of Nations: Why Some Are So Rich and Some So Poor* (New York: Norton, 1998).

51. William Baumol, Robert E. Litan, and Carl J. Schramm, *Good Capitalism, Bad Capitalism, and the Economics of Growth and Prosperity* (New Haven, Conn.: Yale University Press, 2007), 122.

52. Bernard Manin, "On Legitimacy and Political Deliberation," trans. Elly Stein and Jane Mansbridge, *Political Theory* 15 (1987): 338–68.

53. Ibid., 364.

54. William Butler Yeats, "Fragments," in *The Poems*, ed. Daniel Albright (1928; repr., London: Everyman, 1992), 211.

55. John E. Mueller, "Why Isn't There More Violence?," *Security Studies* 13 (Spring 2004): 191–203.

56. Deepak Lal, *Unintended Consequences: The Impact of Factor Endowments, Culture, and Politics on Long-Run Economic Performance* (Cambridge, Mass.: MIT Press, 1998). For a summary, see Lal, *Reviving the Invisible Hand*, 5, 155.

57. Pomeranz, *The Great Divergence*, and others.

58. Charles Taylor, *Sources of the Self: The Making of the Modern Identity* (Cambridge, Mass.: Harvard University Press, 1989), 23; Charles Taylor, *A Secular Age* (Cambridge, Mass.: Harvard University Press, 2007), 179.

Bibliography

Adhia, Nimish. "The Role of Ideological Change in India's Economic Liberalization." *Journal of Socioeconomics* 44 (2013): 103–11.

Ardagh, John. *Germany and the Germans*. Rev. ed. London: Penguin, 1991.

Augustine, St., *Tractate 7* (John 1: 34–51).

Baumol, William, Robert E. Litan, and Carl J. Schramm. *Good Capitalism, Bad Capitalism, and the Economics of Growth and Prosperity*. New Haven, Conn.: Yale University Press, 2007.

Berlin, Isaiah. *The First and the Last*. New York: New York Review Press, 1999.

Chaudhuri, Nirad C. *A Passage to England*. London: Macmillan, 1959.

Connelly, Matthew. *Fatal Misconception: The Struggle to Control World Population*. Cambridge, Mass.: Harvard University Press, 2008.

Cowen, Tyler. *The Great Stagnation: How America Ate All the Low-Hanging Fruit of Modern History, Got Sick, and Will (Eventually) Feel Better*. New York: Dutton, 2011.

Davidoff, Leonore, and Catherine Hall. *Family Fortunes: Men and Women of the English Middle Class, 1780–1850*. Chicago: University of Chicago Press, 1987.

Diamond, Jared. *Guns, Germs, and Steel: The Fates of Human Societies*. New York: Random House, 1997.

Easterly, William. *The Elusive Quest for Growth: Economists' Adventures and Misadventures in the Tropics*. Cambridge, MA: MIT Press, 2001.

Ehrlich, Paul R. *The Population Bomb*. New York: Ballantine Books, 1968.

Engerman, Stanley L., and Kenneth L. Sokoloff. *Economic Development in the Americas Since 1500: Endowments and Institutions*. Rev. ed. Jackson Heights, N.Y.: Rivercity Press, 1975.

Gerschenkron, Alexander. *Economic Backwardness in Historical Perspective*. Cambridge, Mass.: Harvard University Press, 1962.

Gilmour, David. *The Pursuit of Italy: A History of a Land, Its Regions and Their Peoples*. London: Allen Lane Penguin, 2011.

Goldstone, Jack A. "The Problem of the 'Early Modern' World." *Journal of the Economic and Social History of the Orient* 41, no. 3 (1998): 249–84.

Gordon, Robert J. "Is U.S. Economic Growth Over? Faltering Innovation Confronts the Six Headwinds." Closed access paper, National Bureau of Economics Research Working Paper no. 18315, 2012.

Higgs, Robert H. "The Complex Course of Ideological Change." *American Journal of Economics and Sociology* 67, no. 4 (2008): 547–66.

———. *Delusions of Power: New Explorations of the State, War, and Economy.* Oakland, Calif.: Independent Institute, 2012.

Jones, Eric L. *Locating the Industrial Revolution: Inducement and Response.* London: World Scientific, 2010.

Lakoff, George. *Moral Politics: How Liberals and Conservatives Think.* 2nd ed. Chicago: University of Chicago Press, 2002.

Lal, Depak. *Reviving the Invisible Hand: The Case for Classical Liberalism in the Twentieth Century.* Princeton, N.J.: Princeton University Press, 2006.

———. *Unintended Consequences: The Impact of Factor Endowments, Culture, and Politics on Long-Run Economic Performance.* Cambridge, Mass.: MIT Press, 1998.

Landes, David S. "Technological Change and Industrial Development in Western Europe, 1750–1914." Cambridge Economic History of Europe 6. Cambridge: Cambridge University Press, 1965.

———. *The Unbound Prometheus: Technological Change and Industrial Development in Western Europe from 1750 to the Present.* Cambridge: Cambridge University Press, 1969.

———. *The Wealth and Poverty of Nations: Why Some Are So Rich and Some So Poor.* New York: Norton, 1998.

Lu, Gwei-djen, and Joseph Needham. "Acupuncture and Major Surgery." In Lu and Needham, *Celestial Lancets: A History and Rationale of Acupuncture and Moxa,* 218–30. London: RoutledgeCurzon, 2002.

Macaulay, Thomas Babington. *Critical, Historical, and Miscellaneous Essays by Lord Macaulay.* 3 vols. 1830. Repr., Boston, 1860.

Maddison, Angus. *Contours of the World Economy, 1–2030 AD.* Oxford: Oxford University Press, 2007.

Manin, Bernard. "On Legitimacy and Political Deliberation." *Political Theory* 15, no. 3 (1987): 338–68. Trans. Elly Stein and Jane Mansbridge, from "Volonté générale ou délibération? Esquisse d'une théorie de la délibération politique." *Le Débat,* January 1985.

Marx, Karl. *Capital: A Critique of Political Economy.* Vol. 1. 3rd ed. Translated and edited by Samuel Moore and Edward Bibbins Aveling. 1887. Repr., New York: Modern Library, 1906.

McCloskey, Deirdre Nansen. *Bourgeois Dignity: Why Economics Can't Explain the Modern World.* Chicago: University of Chicago Press, 2010.

———. *The Bourgeois Virtues: Ethics for an Age of Commerce.* Chicago: University of Chicago Press, 2006.

———. "Happyism: The Creepy New Economics of Pleasure." *New Republic,* June 28, 2012.

———. "Paid Work." In *Women in Twentieth Century Britain: Social, Cultural and Political Change*, edited by Ina Zweiniger-Bargielowska, 165–82. London: Longman/ Pearson Education, 2001.

———. *The Treasured Bourgeoisie: How Markets and Improvement Became Ethical, 1600–1848, and Then Suspect.* Chicago: University of Chicago Press, 2015.

Moore, Barrington, Jr. *Moral Aspects of Economic Growth and Other Essays.* Ithaca, N.Y.: Cornell University Press, 1998.

Mote, Frederick W. *Imperial China, 900–1800.* Cambridge, Mass.: Harvard University Press, 1999.

Mueller, John. *War and Ideas: Selected Essays.* New York: Routledge, 2011.

Mueller, John E. "Why Isn't There More Violence?" *Security Studies* 13 (Spring 2004): 191–203.

Needham, Joseph. *Science and Civilization in China.* 27 vols. Cambridge: Cambridge University Press, 1954–2008.

North, Douglass C., John Joseph Wallis, and Barry R. Weingast. *Violence and Social Orders: A Conceptual Framework for Interpreting Recorded Human History.* Cambridge: Cambridge University Press, 2009.

Pomeranz, Kenneth. *The Great Divergence: China, Europe, and the Making of the Modern World Economy.* Princeton, N.J.: Princeton University Press, 2000.

Popper, Karl. *The Open Society and Its Enemies.* London: Routledge, 1945.

Ringmar, Erik. *Why Europe Was First: Social Change and Economic Growth in Europe and East Asia, 1500–2050.* London: Anthem, 2007.

Sewell, William H. *A Rhetoric of Bourgeois Revolution: The Abbé Sieyes and What Is the Third Estate?* Durham, N.C.: Duke University Press, 1994.

Shils, Edward. "Dream and Nightmares: Reflections on the Criticism of Mass Culture." *Sewanee Review* 65, no. 4 (Oct.–Dec. 1957): 587–608.

Smith, Adam. *An Inquiry into the Nature and Causes of the Wealth of Nations.* Edited by R. H. Campbell, A. S. Skinner, and W. B. Todd. 2 vols. 1776. Repr., Indianapolis: Liberty Classics, 1982.

Smith, Monica L. "The Role of Ordinary Goods in Premodern Exchange." *Journal of Archaeological Method and Theory* 6, no. 2 (1999): 109–35.

Storr, Virgil Henry. "Weber's Spirit of Capitalism and the Bahamas' Junkanoo Ethic." *Review of Austrian Economics* 19, no. 4 (2006): 289–309.

Taylor, Charles. *A Secular Age.* Cambridge, Mass.: Harvard University Press, 2007.

———. *Sources of the Self: The Making of the Modern Identity.* Cambridge, Mass.: Harvard University Press, 1989.

Tocqueville, Alexis de. *The Old Régime and the French Revolution.* Translated by Stuart Gilbert. 1856. Repr., Garden City, N.Y.: Anchor Doubleday, 1955.

Wagner, Richard E. "ORDO Liberalism and the Social Market Economy." In *Economics and Religion: Are They Distinct?*, edited by H. Geoffrey Brennan and A. M. C. Waterman, 121–38. Dordrecht: Kluwer, 1994.

Wallerstein, Immanuel. *Historical Capitalism with Capitalist Civilization.* London: Verso, 1995.

Ward-Perkins, Bryan. *The Fall of Rome and the End of Civilization.* New York: Oxford University Press, 2005.

Wills, Gary. *Lincoln at Gettysburg: The Words that Remade America.* New York: Simon & Schuster, 1992.

Yeats, William Butler. *The Poems.* Edited by Daniel Albright. 1928. Repr., London: Everyman, 1992.

CHAPTER 9

Adam Smith and a New Public Imagination

Fonna Forman

My great-grandfather Abe Kaiman arrived in the United States from Kolno, Poland, in the early 1920s, alone at age fourteen, and made his way to Milwaukee, Wisconsin, where I was born and raised. He was determined to land in Milwaukee because in 1910 the city had elected America's first socialist mayor, Emil Seidler. The rust belt labor activists and immigrant intellectuals who got him elected were committed to an agenda of "public enterprise"— improved public works, public health, public schools, public parks, public libraries, public transportation, public vocational training, and even public natatoria.[1] Over the next five decades, Milwaukee became a model of honest, frugal government, committed to the well-being of the laboring class and to a higher conception of the common good, led by a series of activist mayors with a robust public mandate. Mayor Frank Zeidler (1948–1960) characterized Milwaukee as a "Cooperative Commonwealth" rooted in education and progressive reform.

Soon after his arrival, my great-grandfather joined and eventually became a leading voice in the local chapter of Der Arbiter Ring, the Jewish Workmen's Circle, a labor movement established in 1900 by Eastern European Jewish immigrants, which provided social services and unemployment relief to new arrivals adapting to life in America. Over time, and for the remainder of his life, Abe was a leader in the Milwaukee Transit Union, and opened a small shop that sold tires and motor oil. Family lore has it that he was very bad at business, and that the shop was little more than a front for the meetings that convened over many decades in its back rooms.

When Grandpa Abe died, I was beneficiary of his two prized possessions: a photograph of him taken in 1926 at the funeral of Eugene Debs (wearing Debs's overcoat!) and a small diamond ring that he bought for my great-grandmother years later, after saving his pennies in this new American reality. Debs and the diamond, together, have always struck me as emblematic of the Jewish experience in America, and of their unique place in the history of American capitalism. By the end of Abe's life, Jews in America were rapidly entering the middle class; the European Socialist agenda gave way to an American Democratic one. My great-grandfather found a better life in America than the pogroms of Europe that drove him here, no doubt. And he was determined that his children would study, and prosper, and have an easier path. And they have. But what I remember most about him, beneficiary in this as well, I suppose, was his worry that other immigrant groups in America were not finding the successes that his children did. To this day, this noble preoccupation endures in the Jewish Workmen's Circle. As descendants of immigrants, they remain committed to the ideals of a "progressive, diverse and inclusive society" and to "remain a bulwark in the fight for the dignity and economic rights of immigrants, fairness in labor practices, decent health care for all Americans, in short, for the very promises that brought our organization's founders to this nation in the first place."[2]

Progressive Lineages

Much of my research as an intellectual historian has focused on Adam Smith, to recuperate the ethical, social, and spatial dimensions of his thought in support of a more public agenda.[3] It would have been an easier task to engage Rousseau or Kant to support my interests in public culture and in designing public policy oriented toward more equitable and just outcomes in society. But I decided to tackle the father of classical economics, because a good deal of his thought has gone missing in ideological appropriations of his legacy over the last two centuries—by both the Left and the Right. In my work I have emphasized a variety of themes: Smith's reflections on the degradations of poverty and human deprivation, public goods and the need for robust public investment in human well-being, and Smith's localism and the importance of local social norms and civic culture in his thought.

The present chapter, on the subject of markets and morals, is an occasion to revisit Adam Smith and to further my argument that a good deal of his thinking has been lost and much of it abused. I would like to focus specifically on a dimension of Smith's ethics concerned with human well-being and public investment in increasingly complex societies. I will draw on passages from Smith's ethical treatise, *Theory of Moral Sentiments* (1759), and also his economic treatise, the *Wealth of Nations* (1776), to demonstrate that Smith had more to say about public ethics and public investment than both his advocates and detractors over the centuries would have us believe. In this context, I will explain why I, as a scholar of Smith, have become increasingly interested in cities in recent years and been inspired by salient examples of equitable urbanization in Latin America. Here I will explore a tradition of public thinking about urban life that has been steadily retreating in Europe and the United States, in favor of more overtly private agendas in the city. Medellín and Bogotá, Colombia, and indeed, Milwaukee, Wisconsin, and many other American municipalities in the first half of the twentieth century, reorganized themselves to produce more equitable ends in the city. They became more inclusive, more agile, more transparent and accountable, and committed themselves to investing public resources to catalyze bottom-up capacities.[4] It is a tradition worth exploring for the impact it had on the quality of urban life for all.

Adam Smith as a Public Thinker

Adam Smith might be the most widely misunderstood and abused figures in all of modern thought. As Amartya Sen put it, "some men are born small and some achieve smallness . . . but Adam Smith has had much smallness thrust upon him."[5] Surely this was truest when the economists held sway over Smith's legacy. But there has been a massive revisionist project in recent decades to rescue Smith's legacy from ideological debates over capitalism and to recover him as an eighteenth-century moral and political philosopher— instigated by Donald Winch in the 1970s and carried forward by a surge of scholarship across the humanities and social sciences by Knud Haakonssen, Istvan Hont, Nick Phillipson, Emma Rothschild, Charles Griswold, Sam Fleischacker, the "New Voices,"[6] and many others. I see my own work as very much in this vein.

It has been striking to me how late modern views on private property have fundamentally broken from the classical liberal idea that wealth is embedded in a social system of ethical responsibility. The conventional view of Smith is obviously not without basis. His book the *Wealth of Nations*, published in 1776, is a manifesto of open markets and small states; where justice is "negative," confined to the protection of property; where humans are calculating creatures motivated primarily by self-interest; and where social bonds are a product of "enlightened selfishness"—in other words not intrinsic but instrumental, the result of cost-benefit calculation.

But the conventional interpretation of Smith neglects what he actually said about human motivation, as well as the historical circumstances that provide context for what he wrote about the state and markets. Smith in fact was a moral philosopher by training, not an economist. While he wrote a major treatise on economy in 1776, he also wrote another book, an ethical treatise called the *Theory of Moral Sentiments*—which was revised five times over thirty-one years, between its first appearance in 1759 and its final, dramatically revised sixth edition in 1790, the year of Smith's death.

In *Moral Sentiments*, Smith presented an empirical portrait of human motivation that seems at odds with the utilitarian portrait conventionally attributed to him today. He opened the treatise as follows: "However selfish soever man may be supposed, there are evidently some principles in his nature, which interest him in the fortune of others, and render their happiness necessary to him, though he derives nothing from it except the pleasure of seeing it."[7] *Moral Sentiments* is an extended reflection on what this means. It is a settled fact among Smith scholars today that the ethical themes of *Moral Sentiments* are the motivating center of Smith's intellectual life, though this more contextual reading of Smith has not yet worked its way into public knowledge, which has been dominated by paradigms of privatization and supply-side economics and a denigration of the welfare state.

Writing in the eighteenth century, Adam Smith argued that modern society cohered after the dissolution of traditional forms of authority (kings, churches, static feudal hierarchy) because our relations with one another are regulated naturally by what Smith called our "moral sentiments"—what we might think of as our social or collective sentiments. The *Theory of Moral Sentiments* contains a brilliant account of social coordination as an emergent social phenomenon, a view that cognitive scientists and neuro-researchers are confirming today with increasingly sophisticated diagnostic technologies in the lab. But Smith, as an eighteenth-century Scottish empiricist, did not know what mirror neurons were; he had no fMRI to observe the function of our brains. He studied human behavior the only way he could—by observing and describing in rich detail the texture of social life among the people around him, how social cooperation in small spaces actually seemed to work. And he did so in notoriously colorful illustrations that delighted his eighteenth-century audience. Indeed, Smith was really, at root, a social theorist, a theorist of collective sentiment and action, and a public theorist—an economist who thought deeply about the sorts of public investments states needed to make in order to sustain those collectivities in increasingly complex futures.

It turns out that even the *Wealth of Nations* itself contains a far more complex set of ideas than is often acknowledged. Without actually reading the book, one might not know that Smith was a vicious critic of greedy accumulation, of the commodification of human relationships, and of the degradation of the working poor in early industrial capitalism. Smith was also among the century's most vocal critics of European slavery and empire. A compelling case can be made that his distaste of state power in the eighteenth century was rooted largely in this, since state policy was too easily hijacked by the vile agendas of international trading companies like the East India Company. It is a delicious irony of history, and an uncomfortable biographical fact for many, that Smith ended the last twelve years of his career, as his father had, working as a customs commissioner, a proud tax collector in the Scottish customs house, the very agent of British mercantilism.

Most astonishing of all, perhaps, Smith devoted an entire section of his seminal *Wealth of Nations*, indeed, the longest section of this biblical economic treatise, Part V, to elaborating the state's provision of public goods, the necessity of progressive taxation and taxation on luxury goods for redistribution to the poor, and the necessity of producing citizens who are civically engaged with one another, and aware enough to collectively constrain the vices and corruptions of their leaders. In Smith's eighteenth-century context, he was laying a foundation for what today we might call "civic culture." Moreover, Smith spoke explicitly about public goods, public space, and public health and public education—the basket of provisions that private entities do not have proper incentives to carry out well.[8] He spent dozens of pages, in fact, discussing the virtues of public education, essential to countering the dehumanizing effects of industrialization and the enervation and alienation of the working poor. He also noted that the needs for public revenue would become more acute as countries over time became larger and more opulent.

While Smith obviously could not foresee our challenges today, and while it would be implausible to argue that his thought is either a cause or a cure for them, his reflections on the compatibility of free markets with robust investment in public goods are provocative for our own thinking. He is Adam Smith, after all, and his public thinking has been neglected over the last two centuries, as his thought has been spun by neoliberals and their critics, both equally bent on severing capitalism from its ethical roots. Re-engaging Smith's public moments enables us to resuscitate elements of early capitalism that have been lost—elements within its own history that might temper its impact today on the least well off among us.

The key today, I will argue, is to actively resist the steady decline of civic life, the encroachment into public space and the usurpation of public goods that have accompanied the triumph of privatization and free market thinking. Nowhere is the decline of public thinking more evident than in our cities, where this effect has been particularly devastating. The decline of public thinking has prompted municipal planning departments to "unplug" from communities and neighborhoods at the margins of predictable zones of investment, resulting in dramatically uneven urban growth in cities across the world, from Nairobi to New York City. From the perspective of social justice, how can cities organized around private interest possibly absorb the dramatic urbanization of the world's poorest people, pouring into cities at a rate of 77 million each year?[9] The explosion of slums at the periphery of cities across the planet is a humanitarian crisis of gargantuan proportion that global cities today are entirely unprepared to confront. The problem is rapidly accelerating as political conflict and climate change make life increasingly unstable for vulnerable people across the globe.

Where might we look to recover a new public imagination, to resuscitate Adam Smith's commitment in the *Wealth of Nations* to public goods, and to maintaining an ethical social order in which the lives of the most vulnerable among us are improved?

Interlude: An Engaged Public Practice

My research as a political theorist has become increasingly practical and engaged in recent years. In 2011 I founded the UC San Diego Center on Global Justice, which facilitates research on global poverty and development, with an emphasis on collective action at the community scale.[10] While the Center is home to many initiatives related to global ethics and cooperation (the conventional terrain of global justice), the majority of our projects "localize the global" by focusing on real-world interventions at local scale. One primary research track in recent years has focused on equitable urban development, with a particular emphasis on the San Diego-Tijuana metropolitan region. As a scholar of Adam Smith, I became interested in cities, since I believe that the clash between competing interpretations of his thought, and the peril of embracing the most sterile version of his economic model without understanding the constraints of his ethics, manifest most vividly in places where extreme wealth and extreme poverty and deprivation coexist in close proximity. For Smith, in *Theory of Moral Sentiments*, what we *see* has a more poignant effect on our moral sensibilities and thus a more compelling claim on our ethical responsibilities, than what we merely hear about or read about, or simply know about. As I've argued in much of my work, proximity matters for Smith in the realm of the ethical. He was a localist, in this sense. And there is no space more dense with the drama of human contrasts than the twenty-first-century city.[11]

The border cities of San Diego and Tijuana together comprise the largest binational metropolitan region in the world, with more border crossings per year than any other checkpoint on the planet. While the region has become a zone of great economic prosperity for some, it is also a microcosm of all of the deprivations globalization has inflicted on the world's poorest people, intensified by two geopolitical institutions: first, the North American Free Trade Agreement (NAFTA), that seduces multinationals to set up factories (or *maquiladoras*) on the periphery of Tijuana, where they generate massive profits freed from any constraints on labor or environmental practices; and second, an increasingly militarized political border that disrupts the social, economic, and environmental ecologies that define this region. The San Diego-Tijuana metropolitan region exemplifies the global phenomenon of uneven urban growth of the last decades, as some of the poorest informal settlements of Latin America sit just minutes away from the mega-wealthy suburban paradise of what is sometimes called "America's finest city."

The border wall is as much a mental as a physical barrier. For the majority of San Diegans without affective ties to Tijuana, the wall has become as invisible as the lives behind it. My students at the University of California, San Diego are astonished to discover that an informal settlement of 85,000 people, the Los Laureles canyon on the periphery of Tijuana—indeed, the "last slum of Latin America"—sits just twenty miles from our campus on the eucalyptus-scented bluffs of La Jolla. For San Diegans with affective ties to Mexico, the wall reinforces separation from home. The sense of dislocation and loss typically experienced by immigrants is reinforced in our region by the disruption of family and communal life that the intensification of surveillance since 9/11 has inflicted on those who travel north in search of dollars. For Tijuana residents with wealth and privilege, the wall is a porous inconvenience that can be traversed. While the tightening of border security after 9/11 became an onerous obstacle to the free flow of goods and services, the cross-border business community lobbied Congress and stewarded "smart border" policies and practices to speed things up, and have advanced plans for cross-border rail, cross-border meeting spaces.[12] In 2015, a long-anticipated bridge was built across the border, connecting the Tijuana airport with a parking lot on the U.S. side. The $120 million enclosed, windowless 390-foot structure allows ticketed passengers to leave their cars in the United States, and after paying $18, walk directly to their gate on the Tijuana side. The bridge also reduced northbound border wait-times for arriving passengers, making Tijuana Airport a continental hub for Latin American business and tourists arriving in Southern California. Obviously the real estate developers who stewarded this project were motivated by little more than profit, but the gesture itself was radical, resonant with the proposal made in the 1970s by renowned progressive urbanists Kevin Lynch and Donald Appleyard, in their commissioned report on the future of the San Diego-Tijuana region, *Temporary Paradise*.[13] There they argued that the future of the two cities depended on shared understanding of regional assets, and that the boundaries of collaborative action should be determined not by artificial jurisdictional lines but by the natural topology and hydrology of the territory. Today, the business-supported airport bridge is the only piece of formal infrastructure, beyond Homeland Security, that traverses the line.

For the great majority of Tijuanenses and other Central American refugees and U.S. deportees who will never visit that airport, or carry the documentation needed to walk across that radical bridge, the wall remains impermeable. It reinforces inferiority and marginality and sets up an impenetrable barrier to hope.

The research I discuss in this chapter has evolved through my partnership with urbanist and architect Teddy Cruz, who is best known for his studies of informal urbanization in the neighborhoods flanking the U.S.-Mexico border.[14] Our collaboration fuses my work in social and political theory—and my interests in poverty, inequality, human rights, and global justice—with Cruz's work on public architecture and equitable urbanization, and his intensely local focus on the border region. Our projects investigate the convergence of formal and informal strategies in designing more equitable cities—what we call the "top-down" and "bottom-up."[15] By formal, or "top-down," we mean the policies and investments of formal institutions. Top-down refers to bodies of governance, like municipalities, planning departments, and redevelopment agencies, but also cultural and educational institutions that exert influence in planning decisions. By informal, or bottom-up, we mean the social, moral, economic, environmental, spatial, and democratic activities, practices, and knowledges that circulate every day in the life of cities, beyond the planning logics of formal institutions. We have been particularly interested in researching bottom-up creativity, entrepreneurialism and resilience in communities navigating conditions of scarcity. Like Smith, who was continually amazed by the ingenuity of the entrepreneur, our assumption is that there is huge creativity and knowledge embedded in the informal strategies through which vulnerable communities adapt and survive. Our work documents and translates those activities and knowledges to formal bodies charged with designing more inclusive and equitable urban policy.

Too many cities today have unplugged from the marginalized informal sectors—through sheer neglect, through sham advocacy planning processes, through policy that constrains informal practices, and through surrendering to the agendas of private developers, who whitewash urban informality beneath a picturesque veneer, gentrifying urban neighborhoods to make them attractive to the "creative class" and to hipsters and young cosmopolitans seeking a more urban way of life.[16]

We have been investigating municipalities that have resisted this conventional path, and have integrated top-down and bottom-up approaches to producing more equitable cities, pursuing strategies that range from transforming municipal bureaucracy into a more efficient, transparent, accountable, and inclusive system; to developing innovative civic engagement and public space projects; to investing in infrastructural improvements in the most marginalized zones of a city to stimulate inclusive economic flows; to experimenting with economic models that enable communities to steward their own development, for their own future.

In 2012 Cruz and I were summoned by the mayor of San Diego to design and direct an urban think tank housed inside his office.[17] Our goal in the Civic Innovation Lab was to create an agile unit, beholden to no city department and no corporate interest, that would experiment with public space and civic engagement as strategies of equitable economic development in diverse neighborhoods long neglected by municipal investment. We identified projects that enabled us to push against the policies and processes of a reactive, regulatory planning culture in the city, and the developer interests that have historically dominated it. We were also tasked with advancing a new cross-border municipal agenda with our counterparts in Tijuana, to frame a new era of cooperation between the cities, and to stimulate new thinking about equitable economic development across the border region.

Latin America and the Search for a
New Public Imagination

Our work in the Tijuana-San Diego border region sits at the threshold between Latin America and the United States, both physically and intellectually. We have discovered that some of the most compelling examples of equitable urbanization have emerged from Latin America in the last half century, as cities across the continent mobilized alternative strategies of development to counter the impact of structural adjustment on public goods, most frequently associated with Cold War dictators and oligarchy. There is no other continental region in the world with so many examples of municipalities resisting national economic commitments by investing in local participatory processes, primarily in the informal sectors of society, to rethink public infrastructure and social service at the scale of the city.

In recent years, my research collaboration with Cruz has focused on translating these cases into new paradigms of public housing, public infrastructure, property, and citizenship, inspiring "other" modes of intervention into the contemporary city. Urban development across the world today tends to be controlled by a few actors—typically an alliance among private developers, housing authorities, and municipalities, frequently supported enthusiastically by corporate sponsors, and a public culture saturated with consumerist imaginaries. Opening alternative, more public avenues of urbanization might seem unattainable in this climate, but there are examples of success—where more democratic forms of urbanization, enabled by diverse social networks, informal economies, and imaginative forms of public participation, have produced more wealth, and more equitable outcomes in the city.

There is a long line of Latin American examples, dating back to São Paulo's SESCs (Serviço Social do Comércio)—privately run institutions that work tightly with the municipality to promote culture, education, and healthy living in urban communities. Founded in 1946, these public-private entities have since spread throughout Brazil. Today the city of São Paulo alone has fifteen SESCs in operation. In the 1970s, Mayor Jaime Lerner intervened in the urban fabric of Curitiba, Brazil, with a series of low-tech acupunctural gestures designed to ignite civic participation.[18] These interventions paved the way for the renowned Curitiba Bus Rapid Transit (BRT) system, which became emblematic across the world of intelligent mass transportation in the next decades. Curitiba became one of greenest cities in the world, with more green space per person than any other Latin American city. Much of this investment was produced through creative incentive programs, such as exempting private landowners from various state and federal land taxes by developing public parks on their land. In 1988, Curitiba had five parks and five forests; today, it has twenty-one parks and fifteen forests, all protected by the Municipal Secretariat of Environment (Secretaria Municipal do Meio Ambiente). Thanks to its heavy investment in public spaces as well, Curitiba has more than 450 public squares and more than 400 small public gardens where residents can walk, exercise, and interact.[19]

Another well-known example of equitable urbanization was the participatory budgeting experiments of Porto Alegre, Brazil, in the 1980s that enabled citizens to decide through deliberative community processes how a percentage of the city budget would be allocated. Participatory budgeting has since been adapted to cities across the world, from the Dominican Republic to rural India to Chicago, producing more equitable public spending patterns and a more robust culture of civic awareness and neighborhood agency.

This Latin American tradition of urban experimentation inspired the celebrated urban transformations of Bogotá and Medellín, Colombia, as well as well-documented strategies of participatory urbanization in Cali, La Paz, Mexico City, and Quito. Among these I will present the cases of Bogotá and Medellín. They are the most far-ranging and comprehensive in their strategies, and most striking in the transformations that occurred. They are also the two cases with which I am most familiar, having researched and collaborated in recent years with the key political and civic actors in each.

Case Study I. Bogotá: Changing Cities, Norms First

Bogotá, Colombia, in the 1990s is probably the best-known example of equitable urbanization to emerge from Latin America. Antanas Mockus became mayor in 1995 at a moment of intense violence and urban chaos in Bogotá. Mockus, a professor of philosophy at the National University of Bogotá, was inspired by the tradition of participatory urbanization across the continent, but he infused these lessons with a richer understanding of individual and social behavior, and the power of performative artistic interventions to transform urban life. As he put it when we last talked, "We seek that the diverse social actors can meet and find each other, and achieve, among all, a reasonable discussion about the consequences of a particular proposed measure to be achieved. That is what it is usually done according to the legacy of participatory budgeting from Porto Alegre . . . or the French social contract. But personally I added to this the topic of mutual regulation and reciprocal expectations. I proposed that all citizens could participate in the transformation of their own behavior."[20] Mockus has become legendary for the distinctive ways he intervened in the behavioral patterns of the city to reduce violence and lawlessness, improve quality of life for the poor, and reconnect citizens with their government and with each other.

There is a saying that Latin America is the only place in the world where mayors win elections on platforms of raising taxes. From the start, Mockus had committed his administration to an "ideal of justice" grounded in "social equity" and the "redistribution of wealth." As he described his mandate: "Those who have come to the world at a disadvantage, those who live in extreme poverty and lack the means to have access to health services, or to adequate nutrition and education, have an inalienable right to a minimum standard of living. These minimum conditions must be sufficient for each to be able to begin building their own life as they imagine and desire it."[21]

But his social priorities were not only about providing social service and public infrastructure from the top down. While public provision was essential to reducing poverty in the city and restoring human dignity in marginalized neighborhoods, Mockus was equally committed to behavioral intervention at the level of urban social norms.[22] For Mockus governance is as much about changing patterns of public trust and social cooperation from the bottom up as it is about changing urban policy from the top down. He wrote: "As mayor I assumed a fascinating pedagogical task: learning and teaching in a community of seven million people. I decided to confront the culture of the city, its languages, perceptions, customs, clichés and especially people's excuses."[23] Meeting urban violence with stricter penalties, for example, will not work. Law and order solutions do not "interiorize" new values among the public. As mayor of Bogotá, Mockus declared emphatically the moral norms that should regulate our relations: that human life is sacred, that radical inequality is unjust, that adequate education and health are human rights, that gender violence is intolerable, and so on. And he developed a corresponding urban pedagogy of performative interventions to demonstrate precisely what he meant, inspiring generations of civic actors, urbanists, and artists across Latin America and the world to think more creatively about engaging social behavior.

One of Mockus's first acts of office was the distribution of "citizenship placards" across the city with a giant thumb that could be used to communicate approval and disapproval to one another. Elsewhere I have written about the Smithian implications of this performative gesture of social regulation, using others as mirrors for our own conduct.[24] Critics raised their eyebrows, but the changes were palpable: people began to look at each other and recognize each other. People began to understand that their behavior was interconnected, and through this simple performative gesture of holding up a thumb, up or down, participants slowly and without realizing it, decided together the kind of city they wanted to inhabit. In a very short period of time, a new sense of civic connectedness began to emerge in a city that had fallen into complete dysfunction and violence.

Throughout his political career, Mockus staged ingenious stunts to access the hearts and minds of the citizens of Bogotá. For example, he campaigned for office shamelessly darting through the city in a red cape and tights, with a large C plastered on his chest—for "Super Citizen." He believed in modeling desired behavior by, for example, riding his bicycle everywhere he went; or showering on public television to demonstrate how to turn off the water when soaping up; or pouring a barrel of drinking water down a toilet to demonstrate how much water is lost with each flush. Very early in his administration, Mockus replaced the corrupt downtown traffic police force with a troupe of 500 street mimes, in whiteface, who stood on street corners and shamed traffic violators by blowing whistles, pointing, and holding up signs of disapproval: "incorrecto!" To many it looked like a circus, and Mockus drew criticism, but through this act of public shaming, the mimes were instituting a new social norm of compliance with traffic signs. And it worked. Their antics became a citywide sensation; everyone was watching on television, and traffic fatalities declined by 50 percent in Mockus's first administration. Mockus won the hearts of citizens as he accompanied his bottom-up normative interventions with massive top-down municipal investment in social service and public works, improving people's lives in very tangible ways. Naysayers could not deny the proof: during Mockus's first administration, murders were reduced by 70 percent and traffic fatalities by 50 percent, tax collection nearly doubled, water usage decreased by 40 percent, while water and sewer services were extended to nearly all households.

While Bogotá's transformation has been spotty in the decades since, it is nevertheless difficult to imagine that Mayor Enrique Peñalosa's celebrated multi-nodal transportation system—the Transmileno bus rapid transit system, bicycle hub network, and Ciclovia—could have succeeded without the normative shifts that Mockus's behavioral interventions initiated, and the public trust in institutions and culture of taxation that they enabled.[25]

Case Study II. Medellín's New Deal

Medellín was regarded the most violent city in the world in the late 1980s and early 1990s. The home of Pablo Escobar, the city was a battleground of drug lords, paramilitary groups, and left-wing guerrillas. After the assassination of Escobar, a series of progressive mayors in Medellín committed themselves to tackling violence and poverty not through conventional tactics of "law and order" but through municipal experiments in "social urbanism," an approach to collaborative and transparent urban planning coined by the city's director of urban projects, Alejandro Echeverri (2005–2008). As a method, social urbanism is committed to the simultaneous development of infrastructure and social capital. It coordinates cross-sector investments in massive public infrastructure and public education and social services typically in the poorest and most violent sectors of a city, and simultaneously cultivates a vibrant, bottom-up citizenship culture, working closely with embedded neighborhood-based agencies to rebuild public trust and a sense of collective hope.[26] Medellín is perhaps the most comprehensive case of equitable urbanization in the Latin American tradition I have been describing, since it wove together various experimental strands of equitable urbanization drawn from continental lineages, from the participatory energies of Porto Alegre, to the green acupunctural interventions and massive public transportation infrastructure of Curitiba, to the mobilization of citizenship culture inspired by Mockus's ingenuity in Bogotá. It is not insignificant that a lineage of civic philanthropists were also inspired by the cross-sector investments in public infrastructure during the American New Deal.[27]

Medellín has received significant global attention in recent years for the successful transformations that took place there, with frequent stories in major newspapers, as well as global prizes like the Urban Land Institute's "Most Innovative City" award in 2013. Medellín was also the site of the UN-Habitat World Urban Forum in April 2014. It is gratifying that global institutions have acknowledged the excellence of Medellín's architectural and infrastructural interventions in the most vulnerable sites across the city. These beautiful egalitarian architectural gestures have had a dramatic positive impact on reducing on poverty and crime and improving public health.[28]

But there are problems with the conventional narrative about Medellín, which tends to tell a story about economic development stewarded by public-private partnerships that expanded public transport, opened markets, and attracted foreign investment. The economic development narrative also misses the role of the bottom-up, making the marginalized informal *comunas* of the city seem like needy recipients of top-down planning and charitable intervention. What makes Medellín's transformation distinctive is the explicitly egalitarian commitments that motivated it—and the political and civic processes through which the municipality enabled historically marginalized sectors of the city to become active agents in a participatory process of rebuilding the future.

We wanted to translate these processes, so that Medellín might become intelligible, not only as a set of buildings, structures, and spaces but primarily as an imaginative set of political and civic processes organized around the urgency of poverty and violence. It is essential to understand, then, just *how* the city managed to reorient resources on such a massive scale toward sites of greatest need. What must a city do? How does government need to transform? What kinds of institutional intersections are necessary? What is the role of the bottom-up in enabling these interventions to succeed and sustain themselves over time?

We began to work closely with former mayor Sergio Fajardo (2004–2007) and his director of urban projects, architect and Professor Alejandro Echeverri, to produce a relational map of the political and civic processes that enabled the transformation of Medellín, and the dramatic reduction of violence and poverty that followed. Echeverri was the lead city planner, or "urban curator," during Fajardo's administration, responsible for advancing "social urbanism" as a strategy, and for leading many of Medellín's most emblematic spatial and public projects. Together, we conducted dozens of interviews with individuals involved in Medellín's history of transformation, from mayors to social workers, from artists and academics to civic philanthropists, since what happened there was a complex process of negotiation and collaboration across institutions and publics. We translated these stories and anecdotes, stitched them together, and mapped them out in the Medellín Diagram.[29] It is not by emulating buildings and transport systems that cities across the globe can begin to approximate the inclusive urbanization that transformed this city. The key is to understand the political and civic processes through which institutions reimagined themselves and facilitated public redistribution of knowledges and resources.

Conclusion: Civic Lessons

What all these Latin American examples share is their commitment to public investment and improving the quality of urban life for all, an orientation that has gone missing from American public discourse in the last decades. When Cruz and I were summoned by the mayor of San Diego in 2012 to develop an agile unit in his office to experiment with public space and civic engagement in marginalized neighborhoods, we wanted to model our lab after the municipal think tanks of Bogotá and Medellín during the administrations of Antanas Mockus and Sergio Fajardo—Bogotá for its strategies of infiltrating the behavioral patterns of civic dysfunction with performative gestures designed to change social norms, and Medellín for its collaborative model of governance and intervention.[30] In the last years we have been partnering with the main actors in these now legendary stories, to better understand how we might "translate" and adapt their lessons to our own distinctive context.

I began this chapter describing my work to rescue Adam Smith's legacy for a more public agenda. The stakes of misinterpreting his thought have become very concrete for me, as a political theorist working in sites of poverty, in an era of declining public investment. I have become particularly interested in investigating sites where competing interpretations of Smith's thought are fraught with implications for human well-being.

Latin America may be the most interesting case, where the tension manifests as eruptions of democratic energy across the continent (the sort exemplified by the administrations of Mockus and Fajardo) to challenge privatization that, particularly in its Chilean "Chicago Boys" variety, takes Smith's *Wealth of Nations* as its holy grail. Indeed, *neoliberalismo* is a rich terrain for engaging the tortured legacy of Adam Smith, and the subject of markets and morals more generally, for in the Latin American context, privatization has historically involved collusion between international banks, national governments, and multinational corporations, with the consequence of divesting local citizens of their public rights over natural resources like metals and water. It was a strategy fueled in the 1970s by Cold War anxieties, which produced sinister alliances between American presidents and genocidal dictators like Pinochet in Chile and Rios Mont in Guatemala, who reduced all social resistance to communism, whether located in aboriginal communities or university classrooms, and carried out genocide in the name of freedom. As the Cold War ended, the strategy continued, driven now by little more than the naked greed of global capitalism.

Adam Smith, who stood firm against the abuses of international trading companies in the eighteenth century, the multinationals of his own day, and who condemned imperial exploits, would never have supported the structural adjustment schemes of the 1990s across Latin America, would never have tolerated the collusion of state and corporate interests, and the pockets that were lined, and would never—ever—have tolerated the crimes inflicted against local people and the decimation of their small scale economies and ways of life. My Adam Smith is standing with the people of Cochabamba, fighting against Bechtel and the Bolivian government for public water rights.

Notes

My great thanks to Arthur Melzer and Steve Kautz for inviting me to be a part of this collection. My thanks also to those at Michigan State who helped workshop an earlier version of this chapter; to Jim Tully and his colleagues at the University of Victoria who engaged this work and improved my thinking and for demonstrating in theory and practice what "public philosophy" can do; to Antanas Mockus, Sergio Fajardo, Alejandro Echeverri, and many friends and colleagues in Bogotá and Medellín for their inspiration and support; and to Teddy Cruz for his public imagination, for demonstrating what political theory can *do*, and for his partnership in the many projects I discuss in this essay.

1. John Gurda, "Here, Socialism Meant Honest, Frugal Government," *Milwaukee Journal Sentinel*, April 4, 2009; John Gurda, "Socialism Before It Was a Four Letter Word," *Milwaukee Journal Sentinel*, April 3, 2010.

2. https://circle.org/who-we-are/our-history/.

3. Fonna Forman, *Adam Smith and the Circles of Sympathy: Cosmopolitanism and Moral Theory* (Cambridge: Cambridge University Press, 2010).

4. For more on connecting the top-down with the bottom-up, see Fonna Forman and Teddy Cruz, "Changing Practice: Engaging Informal Public Demands," in *Other Markets: A Reader*, ed. Helge Mooshammer, Peter Mörtenböck, Teddy Cruz, and Fonna Forman (Rotterdam: nai010 Publishers, 2015). See also Teddy Cruz and Fonna Forman, *Top-Down / Bottom-up: The Political and Architectural Practice of Estudio Teddy Cruz + Fonna Forman* (Berlin: Hatje Cantz, forthcoming).

5. Amartya Sen, *The Idea of Justice* (Cambridge, Mass.: Belknap Press of Harvard University Press, 2009), 186.

6. Leonidas Montes and Eric Schliesser, eds., *New Voices on Adam Smith* (London: Routledge, 2006).

7. Adam Smith, *The Theory of Moral Sentiments*, ed. D. D. Raphael and A. L. Macfie, vol. 1 of *The Glasgow Edition of the Works and Correspondence of Adam Smith* (1759; repr., Indianapolis: Liberty Press, 1982), 9.

8. Regarding health, Smith was referring to public intervention during a health crisis, like a plague, where the good of all was jeopardized. But his reasons here are consistent with his general reasons for all the public provisions he discusses: notably, that the public must step in when there is insufficient private incentive or capacity to carry out activities essential to public well-being, and necessary to presrving freedom in society.

9. http://www.un.org/ga/Istanbul + 5/booklet4.pdf.

10. We organize interdisciplinary research teams that respond to challenges posed to us by community-based NGOs and governments. Our focus is poverty and other obstacles to human flourishing. The Center is committed to *collaborative* problem solving with communities. We engage communities as research partners, rejecting the conventional university models of "community service" that typically take the shape of humanitarian aid, or applied research, in which universities provide charity or services, or else engage communities as laboratories for testing academic or scientific knowledge. We also reject the "bucket theory" of development that sees communities as empty receptacles waiting to be filled with our knowledge.

11. A central theme in Forman, *Adam Smith and the Circles of Sympathy*.

12. http://www.smartbordercoalition.com/.

13. David Appleyard and Kevin Lynch, *Temporary Paradise? A Look at the Special Landscape of the San Diego Region* (Report to the City of San Diego, September 1974).

14. Teddy Cruz, "Spatializing Citizenship: Marginal Neighborhoods as Sites of Production," in *Territories of Poverty*, ed. Ananya Roy and Emma Shaw Crane (Athens: University of Georgia Press, 2015).

15. See Cruz and Forman, *Top-Down / Bottom-Up*.

16. Richard Florida, *The Rise of the Creative Class and How It's Transforming Work, Leisure, Community, and Everyday Life* (New York: Basic Books, 2002). Florida's optimism has been recently tempered in *The New Urban Crisis: How Cities Are Increasing Inequality, Deepening Segregation, and Failing the Middle Class—and What We Can Do About it* (New York: Basic Books, 2017).

17. See "One Mayor's Downfall Killed the Design Project That Could've Changed Everything: Public Interest Design's Wild Ride into City Hall," *Next City*, February 23, 2015, http://nextcity.org/features/view/teddy-cruz-fonna-forman-civic-innovation-san-diego-public-interest-design.

18. See Jaime Lerner, *Urban Acupuncture: Celebrating Pinpricks of Change That Enrich City Life* (Washington, D.C.: Island Press, 2014).

19. Josephine d'Allant, "Can Biking and Walking Save Lives in Cities in the Global South?" *Huffington Post*, August 13, 2014.

20. Antanas Mockus, Interview with Teddy Cruz and Fonna Forman, Bogotá, July 24, 2015.

21. Antanas Mockus, "Bogotá's Capacity for Self-Transformation and Citizenship Building," unpublished paper, 1–29, at 6–7.

22. This discussion of Mockus and social norms is drawn from Fonna Forman, "Social Norms and the Cross-Border Citizen: From Adam Smith to Antanas Mockus," in *Rethinking Cultural Agency: The Significance of Antanas Mockus*, ed. Sebastian Cuellar and Carlo Tognato (Cambridge, Mass.: Harvard University Press, forthcoming).

23. Antanas Mockus, "Building 'Citizenship Culture' in Bogotá," *Journal of International Affairs* 65, no. 2 (Spring/Summer 2012): 143–46.

24. Forman, "Social Norms and the Cross-Border Citizen."

25. In 2013, we brought Antanas Mockus and his Bogotá-based nonprofit Corpovisionarios to the U.S.-Mexico border to help us cultivate a new citizenship culture grounded in a moral claim that human beings, regardless of formal legal citizenship, regardless of race, have dignity, and deserve equal respect and basic quality of life. In collaboration with Mockus and his NGO, Corpovisionarios, and with generous funding from the Ford Foundation, we produced a Binational Citizenship Culture Survey, an instrument that measures what Mockus calls "citizenship culture" in the San Diego-Tijuana border region. Working with the municipalities of San Diego and Tijuana, as well as diverse stakeholders from both sides of the border, we spent nearly a year

designing a survey that was responsive to the needs and challenges, as well as the resources and aspirations, of this distinctive binational region. Our claim has always been that the wall cannot disrupt the informal normative, social, economic, and environmental flows that define our region. The purpose of the survey was to identify these informal flows to compel a new era of public self-knowledge and cross-border municipal collaboration. The most exciting finding of the survey was that publics on both sides of the border trust each other and want more cooperation on a variety of public issues than anyone on either side realized. The survey is a powerful tool for those of us eager to reduce poverty, and pursue strategies of equitable economic development in the U.S.-Mexico border region. For further discussion of the Bi-National Citizenship Culture survey, see Forman, "Social Norms and the Cross-Border Citizen." See also the video produced for *Visualizing Citizenship*, Yerba Buena Center for the Arts, San Francisco, curated by Lucía Sanromán (March 2017), https://www.youtube.com/watch?v = XZNKjPQ-6dc&t = 198s (accessed June 1, 2017). See also "New San Diego-Tijuana Survey Holds Mirror Up to Border Cities," *Next City*, February 25, 2015, http://nextcity.org/daily/entry/binational-survey-san-diego-tijuana-border-antanas-mockus; and "Survey Says San Diegans, Tijuanans Want More Cross-Border Collaboration," *San Diego Union Tribune*, June 19, 2015 (radio and print), http://www.kpbs.org/news/2015/jun/19/survey-says-san-diegans-and-tijuanans-want-more-cr/.

26. For more, see Fonna Forman and Teddy Cruz, "Global Justice at the Municipal Scale: The Case of Medellín, Colombia," in *Institutional Cosmopolitanism*, ed. Luis Cabrera (New York: Oxford University Press, forthcoming).

27. For discussion, see Forman and Cruz, "Global Justice."

28. Magdalena Cerda et al., "Reducing Violence by Transforming Neighborhoods: A Natural Experiment in Medellín, Colombia," *American Journal of Epidemiology* 175, no. 10 (2012): 1045–53.

29. The Medellín Diagram was first presented in April 2014 in the Medellín Museum of Modern Art on the occasion of the Seventh UN-Habitat World Urban Forum, which was hosted in Medellín. It was co-produced by Fonna Forman and Teddy Cruz, in collaboration with Alejandro Echeverri and graphic designer Matthias Goerlich of Studio Matthias Goerlich / Frankfurt. See "La experiencia de Medellín es ahora una guía," *El Colombiano*, April 10, 2014. The first articulation of the Medellín Diagram can be found online, in both Spanish and English, at www.Medellín-diagram.com. The Medellín Diagram was further elaborated and exhibited in Fall 2014 in *Citizen Culture*, curated by Lucía Sanromán in the Santa Monica Museum of Art; in the Shenzhen Architectural Biennial exhibition, *Radical Urbanisms*, curated by Alfredo Brillembourg and Herbert Klumpner (December 2015); and most recently at *Visualizing Citizenship*, Yerba Buena Center for the Arts, San Francisco, curated by Lucía Sanromán (March 2017), https://www.youtube.com/watch?v = z89ixMyyElo.

30. Fonna Forman and Teddy Cruz, "Latin America and a New Political Leadership: Experimental Acts of Co-Existence," in *Public Servants: Art and the Crisis of the*

Common Good, ed. Johanna Burton, Shannon Jackson, and Dominic Wilsdon (Cambridge, Mass.: MIT Press, 2017).

Bibliography

Appleyard, David, and Kevin Lynch. *Temporary Paradise? A Look at the Special Landscape of the San Diego Region*. Report to the City of San Diego, September 1974.

Cerda, Magdalena, Jeffrey D. Morenoff, Ben B. Hansen, Kimberly J. Tessari Hicks, Luis F. Duque, Alexandra Restrepo, and Ana V. Diez-Roux. "Reducing Violence by Transforming Neighborhoods: A Natural Experiment in Medellín, Colombia." *American Journal of Epidemiology* 175, no. 10 (2012): 1045–53.

Cruz, Teddy. "Spatializing Citizenship: Marginal Neighborhoods as Sites of Production." In *Territories of Poverty*, edited by Ananya Roy and Emma Shaw Crane. Athens: University of Georgia Press, 2015.

Cruz, Teddy, and Fonna Forman. *Top-Down / Bottom-Up: The Political and Architectural Practice of Estudio Teddy Cruz + Fonna Forman*. Berlin: Hatje Cantz, forthcoming.

d'Allant, Josephine. "Can Biking and Walking Save Lives in Cities in the Global South?" *Huffington Post*, August 13, 2014.

Florida, Richard. *The New Urban Crisis: How Our Cities Are Increasing Inequality, Deepening Segregation, and Failing the Middle Class—and What We Can Do About It*. New York: Basic Books, 2017.

——. *The Rise of the Creative Class and How It's Transforming Work, Leisure, Community, and Everyday Life*. New York: Basic Books, 2002.

Forman, Fonna. *Adam Smith and the Circles of Sympathy: Cosmopolitanism and Moral Theory*. Cambridge: Cambridge University Press, 2010.

——. "Social Norms and the Cross-Border Citizen: From Adam Smith to Antanas Mockus." In *Rethinking Cultural Agency: The Significance of Antanas Mockus*, edited by Sebastian Cuellar and Carlo Tognato. Cambridge, Mass.: Harvard University Press, forthcoming.

Forman, Fonna, and Teddy Cruz. "Changing Practice: Engaging Informal Public Demands." In *Other Markets: A Reader*, edited by Helge Mooshammer, Peter Mörtenböck, Teddy Cruz, and Fonna Forman. Rotterdam: nai010 Publishers, 2015.

——. "Global Justice at the Municipal Scale: The Case of Medellín, Colombia." In *Institutional Cosmopolitanism*, edited by Luis Cabrera. New York: Oxford University Press, forthcoming.

——. "Latin America and a New Political Leadership: Experimental Acts of Co-Existence." In *Public Servants: Art and the Crisis of the Common Good*, edited by

Johanna Burton, Shannon Jackson and Dominic Wilsdon. Cambridge, Mass.: MIT Press, 2017.

Gurda, John. "Here, Socialism Meant Honest, Frugal Government." *Milwaukee Journal Sentinel*, April 4, 2009.

——. "Socialism Before It Was a Four Letter Word." *Milwaukee Journal Sentinel*, April 3, 2010.

Lerner, Jaime. *Urban Acupuncture: Celebrating Pinpricks of Change That Enrich City Life*. Washington, D.C.: Island Press, 2014.

Mockus, Antanas. "Bogotá's Capacity for Self-Transformation and Citizenship Building." Unpublished paper.

——. "Building 'Citizenship Culture' in Bogotá." *Journal of International Affairs* 65, no. 2 (Spring/Summer 2012): 143–46.

Montes, Leonidas, and Eric Schliesser, eds. *New Voices on Adam Smith*. London: Routledge, 2006.

Sen, Amartya. *The Idea of Justice*. Cambridge: Mass.: Belknap Press of Harvard University Press, 2009.

Smith, Adam. *The Theory of Moral Sentiments*. Edited by D. D. Raphael and A. L. Macfie. Vol. 1 of *The Glasgow Edition of the Works and Correspondence of Adam Smith*. 1759. Reprint, Indianapolis: Liberty Press, 1982.

PART III

Revisiting Locke, Montesquieu,
and Smith

CHAPTER 10

Capitalism and the Moral Sentiments

Peter McNamara

The Global Financial Crisis of 2008 and the accompanying deep recession have shaken faith in the capitalist system across the globe and especially in the American variety of capitalism. What seemed like inevitable processes a little over a decade ago—globalization and the spread of free trade under American leadership to name the most important—seem now to be much more contingent phenomena. These developments call into question not just the economic prospects for global capitalism but also many of the moral and political hopes associated with the capitalist project. A period of great optimism, especially in the years after the collapse of the Soviet Union, has given way to caution and even outright pessimism. Ought we any more to confidently think of the West—its distinct combination of liberalism, democracy, and capitalism—as the future?

As a contribution to thinking through this situation, I propose to outline and contrast the moral psychologies of two of the most important intellectual architects of capitalism: John Locke and Adam Smith. The discussion that follows does not settle the matter of whose moral psychology is better. Its goal is the preliminary and more limited one of raising a serious question about Adam Smith. The last thirty years has seen a remarkable resurgence of interest in Smith. This resurgence has coincided with the dominance of so-called "neoliberalism" in the arena of economic policy. But Smith's resurgence is not solely or even chiefly a matter of economic policy. Much of the interest in Smith is in his moral and political philosophy. In contrast to both the abstract *homo economicus* of mainstream economics and the "blank slate" theory of Locke, many believe Smith's account of human nature is thicker and more robust and, moreover, that Smith's account of human nature and especially human sociability is confirmed by recent developments in the fields of anthropology, biology, and evolutionary psychology. Smith's account of human nature points not only to the naturalness of commercial society but also to the compatibility of commercial society, what we would call capitalism, with an enlightened and humane moral code. The question I wish to ask was captured in a famous quip by Walter Bagehot, one of the early and most influential editors of *Economist* magazine. Summing up Smith's intellectual project, he described it as having "the immense design of showing the origin and development of cultivation and law; or, as we may perhaps put it, not inappropriately, of saying how, from being a savage, man rose to be a Scotchman."[1] Now Bagehot had a penchant for seeing thinkers in racial and ethnic terms, but I do not think this habit is relevant here. His point is a simple but potentially telling one. Smith over-generalized about humankind—about human nature—on the basis of insufficient information and drew in the end what were essentially parochial conclusions. Is this true?

The argument is organized as follows. First, I discuss Smith's moral theory and some of the reasons for its current appeal. Second, I outline Locke's alternative moral psychology as it is expressed in his major philosophical work, *An Essay Concerning Human Understanding*.[2] The final section further develops Locke's moral psychology by way of a comparison between Smith and Locke on the respective roles of the family and society in the emergence of the moral sentiments.[3] What will become clear is that Locke comes very close to elaborating a theory of moral sentiments but he stops short in certain critical respects that are highly relevant to our overall theme.

Smith Resurgent

Smith's *Theory of the Moral Sentiments* grows out what Knud Haakonssen has appropriately called a "social theory of the self."[4] Yet it is, at the same time, a theory grounded in a claim that certain fixed principles of human nature that are the foundations of our moral opinions. The *Theory of Moral Sentiments* begins with such a declaration. "How selfish soever man may be supposed, there are evidently some principles in his nature, which interest him in the fortunes of others, and render their happiness necessary to him, though he derives nothing from it except the pleasure of seeing it" (TMS I.I.i.1). Indeed, one might say that Smith comes close to erasing the distinction between the social or conventional and the natural or universal. Our capacity for moral judgment and the norms that constitute morality grow out of a process of continued interaction with and learning from others. Without such interaction we would be, more or less, without moral concepts. Smith explains that we first experience moral judgment through our judgments of others. Such judgments are made possible by our ability to enter into the passions of the actor. Approval takes place when we are able to enter into, in the sense of feeling the same or, more precisely, an analogous passion in ourselves. Disapproval is signified by our inability to experience such a commonality of feeling. It is our imagination, specifically, our capacity for what Smith calls "sympathy" (I.I.i.5), that makes possible such experiences. Though the product of the imagination, Smith understands such experiences to be powerful and natural and, therefore, a fixed principle of our nature. Sympathy allows us to enter into the "situation" of others (I.I.i.7). We find joy in their joy and pain in their pain. Smith argues that we can fully sympathize only with moral behavior—not with the joy of a successful criminal or with the pain of that criminal later undergoing deserved punishment. Hence, for Smith, it is sympathy that makes possible the *moral* sentiments. As noted, we arrive at our understanding of what is moral by modulating our behavior in accord with what others can sympathize with. We are moved to do this by our desire for approval, what Smith calls mutual sympathy, by which he means a genuine harmony or concord of feeling among human beings. From mutual sympathy we derive a genuine pleasure, one that is unrelated to our desire for any external reward. Contrary to the view of Hobbes, human beings really do take pleasure in each other's company. We are social animals. When someone laughs at your joke, you feel pleasure not simply because your vanity has been gratified or because you have attained a certain amount of power and status but because you really enjoy the company of—the mutual sympathy with—your friends.[5]

Now Smith is aware that sympathy does not always lead to moral sentiments, but in these cases he contends that the "wisdom of nature"[6] is such that these anomalies are beneficial to society and sometimes even to morality itself. We sympathize with the rich and the great even though they do not always display good character. Smith argues that this helps social stability (I.iii.2.3). Furthermore, Smith claims that when weighing behavior we tend to focus on results. A well intentioned action that fails through absolutely no fault of the doer is not praised as much as one that succeeds, if it is praised at all. This anomaly has the good tendency of steering us away from futile attempts at benevolence (II.iii.3). One last example: we feel more for those we know and who are near us than those we don't know and who are far away, even though all are human beings and all entitled to respect and concern. This moral anomaly has the good effect of focusing our attention on those whom we can truly and efficiently help rather than those we can't.[7] Human beings in their glories and in their apparent failings are truly "fitted by nature" for society (II.iii.1).

Smith's account of sympathy is one of two key contributions to moral theory; the other is his account of the impartial spectator. As noted, our awareness that we judge others is soon followed by an awareness that our own actions are the subject of frank judgments by others. We seek their approval, Smith says, because it is pleasurable to us and because their disapproval is both unpleasant and threatening to us. Smith does not, however, reduce morality to the mere search for the approval of others. Rather, as he famously explains, we are not satisfied with approval that is undeserved, nor are we simply satisfied with the approval of the actual observers, the spectators, of our conduct. Beyond what Smith sees as the uncertain and variable and, therefore, unsatisfying praise of actual spectators, Smith argues that we seek the surer and, therefore, more satisfying praise of the impartial spectator. We hypothesize an impartial and informed observer of our conduct and seek through our actions the approval of this construct of our intellect and imagination. It is the impartial spectator that helps us make the tough calls and hard decisions. The impartial spectator is in effect Smith's interpretation of the phenomenon of conscience. He develops this interpretation without the aid of revealed religion and with only the most limited, one might even say perfunctory, theological basis in rational deistic religion.[8]

Three features of Smith's theory make it especially appealing. First, Smith elaborates his moral theory without recourse to the ideas that had made problematic earlier moral theories, such as innate ideas, a specific faculty of the moral sense, a rationally knowable natural law, or a divine law. Second, Smith's theory has a flexibility to it that is both morally and politically appealing. Moral judgment is explained in such a way that it takes into account the particular circumstances of each case and, furthermore, Smith allows room for moral judgment to evolve as society evolves. In both cases the problems associated with invariable and universalistic moral norms are avoided. Indeed, moral judgment results from an interactive, negotiated process among equal individuals. Last, Smith argues that the socialization process that gives rise to morality is not merely conventional. It is, he argues, grounded in nature, especially in our desire for mutual approbation, our desire to praiseworthy and not just praised, and, perhaps most fundamentally, in our natural resentment at injustice.

Locke's Blank Slate and the Evolution of Moral Opinions

With this summary of Smith's moral theory in hand, let us now turn in somewhat greater detail to Locke. This more extensive treatment is necessary for two reasons. First, Locke's moral psychology is premised on his idea of the *tabula rasa* or blank slate, an idea that few today give any credit.[9] It is important then to begin with this now controversial idea so as to make clear what Locke meant by it and its connection to his attack on innate ideas. Second, one striking but seldom acknowledged feature of Locke's moral psychology is that starting from the *tabula rasa* foundation Locke comes very close to elaborating something that is startlingly close to a theory of moral sentiments. This kind of argument appears in both *Essay Concerning Human Understanding* and *Some Thoughts Concerning Education*.

Accounts of Locke's argument in the *Essay* are often put in too broad a terms. Locke does not use the term blank slate in the *Essay* but he does use the equivalent terms "empty cabinet" and "white paper" (I.ii.15, I.iii.22, II, II.i.2).[10] In all cases he is referring to the human *understanding*, not to human *nature* as a whole. Furthermore, with regard to the human understanding, Locke's argument is really against the concept of innate *knowledge*.[11] The human understanding is an "empty cabinet" that is over time furnished with ideas that come from experience and reflections on that experience. According to Locke, we have no innate speculative or moral knowledge. Conscience, which Locke defines as "nothing else, but our own Opinion or Judgement of the Moral Rectitude or Pravity of our own Actions" (I.iii.8), provides no certainty in moral matters. When Locke speaks of true moral knowledge he has in mind something that is universal, obligatory, and clear-cut. An inkling, a disposition, or an inclination does not rise to the level of knowledge. Even if there were a principle that met these stringent criteria, this would not *prove* it innate because there exists an alternative explanation for how we came by such a principle, namely, the "new way of ideas"[12] put forth by Locke in the *Essay*. There is, however, no such principle, according to Locke. Children, idiots, savage peoples, that is, those closest to a natural state, know nothing of the principles said to be innate. Innate principles, according to

Locke, should possess a vividness and clarity that acquired principles lack. Locke deploys his rhetorically most powerful argument when he chronicles the great diversity of human moral opinion. There is, he argues, simply no moral principle that is *universally* agreed upon by *all* men. Locke recounts a seemingly endless list of atrocious human behavior: rapine and plunder, infanticide, geronticide, euthanasia, cannibalism, bestiality, just to mention the most shocking. Locke's point is not that human beings sometimes commit great crimes, but rather that there are entire societies where such actions are not even looked upon as crimes.

Toward the end of Book I, Chapter iii, Locke turns to providing a psychological explanation of the innatist position. The innatist position is no mere philosophical or theological doctrine. It is rather a reflection or product of what Locke portrays as a basic feature of the human mind. Human beings can neither go about their daily business nor achieve *"quiet in their minds"* without *"some Foundation or Principles to rest their thoughts on.* There is scarce anyone so floating and superficial in his Understanding, who hath not some reverenced propositions, which are to him the Principles on which he bottoms his Reasonings; and by which he judgeth of Truth and Falsehood, Right and Wrong" (I.iii.24). These principles, however wrong or strange, are often considered "sacred" and men "will sooner part with their lives" than doubt them (I.iii.21). Where do these "bottoms" come from? Locke gives a memorable explanation. It is one that is quite damning for the advocates of innate ideas. But it is also one that paves the way for something very close to a theory of moral sentiments. That men would die for a "sacred opinion," however wrong or strange, is, for Locke, not hard to explain. Consider, he says, "the *ways*, and steps *by which*" these *"Doctrines"* enter the understanding. Even though derived "from no better original, than the Superstition of a Nurse, or the Authority of an old Woman," they, by "length of time, and consent of Neighbours, *grow up to the dignity of Principles* in Religion or Morality." Through a process of witting and unwitting social reinforcement, these doctrines of "Religion or Manners, come, by these means, to have the reputation of unquestionable, self-evident, and innate Truths" (I.iii.22). When grown to adulthood, the individual's memory of this early education fades and, not recalling the origins of these doctrines, he comes to believe that these doctrines *"were certainly the impress of God and Nature* upon [his mind]; and not taught [him] by anyone else" (I.iii.23). Once one has imbibed doctrines in this way, it is very difficult to think beyond them. Most men lack the leisure to do so, but those who do have it also confront very great obstacles. To begin with, a man would have to be willing to "shake the foundations of all his past thoughts and Actions." In addition, there would be the "shame" of breaking with his past views and, more importantly, there would be the "reproach" earned by departing from the "received opinions of [his] Country or Party," especially when these opinions are thought to be the "Standards set up by God in our minds" (I.iii.26).

Locke promises to give in Books II–IV a new foundation for knowledge including moral knowledge. Although he makes good on this promise of a new foundation, he leaves a reader dissatisfied in one fundamental respect: he famously does not even outline the general contours of the genuine morality. The reader is left to his own devices, confident in the awareness, made possible by Locke, that nature has provided him with the reasoning capacity to figure out the law of nature—the true guide for morality. Locke's failure to even sketch the genuine morality of the law of nature takes on a somewhat different light when we consider more closely what he has to say about the actual codes of morality that have prevailed in different parts of the earth and at different times. Rather than the apparent moral chaos that Locke emphasizes in Book I, there is in fact a considerable amount of order and regularity.[13] The volume and intensity of his portrayal of human diversity tends at first to drown out this other line of argument.

While there are no innate moral principles, there are "innate practical Principles" (I.iii.3), what Locke calls "Principles of Actions lodged in Men's Appetites" (II.iii.13). These are "Inclinations of the Appetite to good," the primary of which are "a desire for happiness, and an aversion to Misery." These innate practical principles "do continue constantly to operate and influence our Actions." Furthermore, these principles "may be observ'd in all Persons and all Ages, steady and universal." They are the "constant Springs and Motives of all our Actions, to which, we perpetually feel them strongly impressing us" (I.iii.3). These are, however, not "impressions of Truth." The difficulty with such principles of action is that if "left to their full swing, they would carry men to the over-turning of all Morality" (I.iii.13). The question is whether there is a power, absent knowledge of the law of nature, that can step in to regulate these principles of action. Locke shows that a combination of self-interest and concern for reputation is sufficient in many cases.

Locke begins by noting that even associations of thieves require certain rules of order to preserve their societies. These are "Rules of convenience within their own communities" (I.iii.2) and not true moral laws, but they arise of necessity and are effective. It is not just gangs of thieves who develop such rules. Locke says soon after that "a great part of Mankind give Testimony to the Law of Nature" by holding to "several Moral Rules," which receive from "Mankind, a very general Approbation." The reason:

> For God, having, by an inseparable connexion, joined *Virtue* and public happiness together; and made the Practice thereof, necessary to the preservation of Society, and visibly *beneficial* to all, with whom the Virtuous Man has to do; it is no wonder that everyone should, not only allow, but recommend, and magnifie those Rules to others, from whose observance of them, he is sure to Reap advantage to himself. He may, out of Interest as well out of Conviction; cry up that for Sacred; which if once trampled on, and prophaned, he himself cannot be safe and secure. (I.iii.6)

When Locke returns to this evolutionary line of argument later in the *Essay*, it is in the context of his discussion of law and moral relations. As noted, he believes human beings are moved by love of good and fear of evil or, what is the same, pleasure and pain. Whether something is morally good or evil depends only on "the Conformity or Disagreement of our voluntary Actions to some Law, whereby Good or Evil is drawn on us, from the Will and Power of the Law-maker" (II.xxviii.5). Locke distinguishes three types of moral law: the divine law, which is only truly made known by either reason or revelation; the civil law; and the law of opinion or reputation. When discussing these three kinds of law, Locke makes the somewhat surprising observation that the seemingly impressive sanctions attached to the first two kinds of laws are seldom well weighed: "The Penalties that attend to the breach of God's Laws, some, nay, perhaps, most Men seldom seriously reflect on: and amongst those that do, many, whilst they break the Law, entertain Thoughts of future reconciliation, and making their Peace for such Breaches. And as to the Punishments due from the Laws of the Commonwealth, they frequently flatter themselves with hopes of impunity" (II.xviii.12). With the third kind of law, the law of reputation, however, "no Man scapes" punishment (II.xviii.12).

Locke's explanation of the sanctions mechanism of the law of reputation is particularly important for our comparison with Smith. When individuals enter political society, they give up to the government the right to use force against their fellow citizens, "yet they retain still their power of Thinking well or ill; approving or disapproving of the actions of those whom they live amongst, and converse with: And by this approbation and dislike they establish amongst themselves, what they will call *Vertue* and *Vice*" (II.xviii.11). This "power" that is retained by individuals in society is both remarkably strong and uniform in its results. As noted, no one escapes the "Censure and Dislike" of those he offends. More important, there is not "one of ten thousand, who is stiff and insensible enough, to bear up under the constant Dislike, and Condemnation of his own Club. . . . [N]o Body, that has the least Thought or Sense of a Man about him, can live in Society, under the constant Dislike, and ill Opinion of his Familiars, and those he converses with" (II.xxviii.12).

In this later discussion, Locke amplifies his remarks in Book I. He grants that there are occasional differences from person to person and society to society, but he maintains that there has been considerable uniformity as regards notions of virtue and vice. To drive home his point he cites Virgil, Cicero, and St. Paul. How is this possible? Locke explains:

> [N]othing can be more natural, than to encourage with Esteem and Reputation that, wherein every one finds his advantage; and to blame and discountenance the contrary: 'tis no Wonder, that Esteem and discredit, Vertue and Vice, should in a great measure every-where correspond with the unchangeable Rule of Right and Wrong, which the law of God hath established; there being nothing that so visibly, and directly secures, and advances the general Good of Mankind in this World, as Obedience to the Laws, he has set them, and nothing breeds such mischief and confusion as to neglect them. (II.xxviii.12)

Thus, what is striking about the outcome of the law of reputation is not just the uniformity that it produces but also that this uniformity is such that it falls pretty much within "the true Boundaries of the Law of Nature" (II.xxviii.11). This state of affairs comes about—one might say it is brought about by nature—despite the absence of genuine knowledge of the law of nature on the part of individuals, the church, or the government.

Thus, Locke provides an evolutionary account of morality that explains the emergence of moral rules in terms of human needs and social pressures. At times, he sounds decidedly Smithian, especially when he is discussing the work done by the desire for esteem. What Locke does not say is that this evolutionary process culminates in a *liberal* society. We will return to this difference with Smith in our conclusion.

Locke and Smith on Moral Education of the Young

Much of the psychological analysis outlined above is deployed in *Some Thoughts Concerning Education* for the purpose of governing the moral education of the young. The contrast between Smith's short but revealing account in *Theory of Moral Sentiments* of the beginnings of moral education and Locke's longer account of the same stage brings to the fore certain fundamental differences in their outlooks on the place of morality in nature. These differences make clear the reason that Locke does not develop a theory of moral sentiments in the Smithian sense. Locke's account emphasizes the extraordinary care that must be taken in the management of a child's passions if they are to learn to love liberty and virtue. By so doing Locke also makes clear how easy it is to depart, either slightly or grossly, from the ways of liberty and virtue.

Smith identifies "self-command" as the moral capacity that allows us to put aside our present, perhaps very strong inclinations and instead pursue the course of virtue. We acquire self-command not through study but through "that great discipline which Nature has established for the acquisition of this and of every other virtue; a regard to the sentiments of the real or supposed spectator of our conduct" (III.iii.21). Smith remarks at one point that "domestic education"—education in or close to the home—is the "institution of nature," whereas public education is the "contrivance of man" (VI.ii.1.10). Though this sounds similar to Locke's very strong defense of private education in *Some Thoughts* (see, e.g., STCE 70), closer inspection shows significant differences. Smith explains that the relationship between parents and children is likely to lead to only very limited degrees of self-command: "While it remains under the care of such partial protectors, its anger is the first and, perhaps, the only passion which it is taught to moderate" (III.iii.22). Smith believes that it is when the child is away from the care of parents and nurses that he enters the "great school of self-command." "When it is old enough to go to school, or to mix with its equals, it soon finds that they have no such indulgent partiality. It naturally wishes to gain their favour, and to avoid their hatred or contempt. Regard even to its own safety teaches it to do so; and it soon finds that it can do so in no other way than by moderating, not only its anger, but all its other passions, to the degree which its play-fellows and companions are likely to be pleased with" (III.iii.22). The pleasure of knowing that we are the objects of approval of real spectators or of the impartial spectator compensates us for the hardships we must undergo in order to act virtuously.

For Locke, matters are neither quite so simple nor quite so natural. Natural endowments and the natural course of things do not so directly lead to virtue. He addresses the same fundamental problem in moral education as Smith: how to put aside our immediate passions and desires in the interest of something higher? Early moral education involves, in the ideal case described in *Some Thoughts*, a careful "design" (STCE 59), "ordered" (STCE 60) by the child's parents. Crucial parts of this design necessitate deceiving the child, at least for a time, about the true relationship between morality and nature. Locke's education begins with careful and at times rigorous attempts to assist the child to master bodily pleasures and pains. Gentlemen should treat their children "as the honest farmers and substantial yeoman do theirs" (STCE 4). This training is essential but preliminary to the real substance of moral education, which is centered on the mind rather than the body.

The critical first step in Locke's educational program is for parents to establish their authority over the child. "Fear and awe" begin this authority, and although it is later mixed with "love and friendship," the child does not lose his sense of dependency on and "reverence" for his parents (STCE 42, 99). Parents should begin this process as early as possible so that the child becomes unaware through forgetting the origins of parental authority. Awe before parents will then seem "natural" (STCE 44). As in the *Essay*, Locke asserts that reward and punishment are the only motives for a "rational creature" (STCE 54). He rejects as dehumanizing and counterproductive corporal rewards and punishments. The "great secret of education," he says, is to make use of esteem and disgrace, the "most powerful incentives." The difficulty is to bring the child's mind to "relish" them (STCE 56).[14]

Locke believes that children are "very sensible of *praise* and commendation" at an early age. Parents should utilize every opportunity to "*caress and commend them when they do well*" and "*show a cold and neglectful countenance to them upon doing ill.*" These methods will be more effective than "threats or blows" (STCE 57). Locke does not, however, believe that this is enough to make children *relish* praise. He suggests further that steps be taken to make sure that the rewards of esteem be accompanied by other kinds of incentives, "not as particular rewards and punishments of this or that particular action, but as necessarily belonging to and constantly attending one who by his carriage has brought himself into a state of disgrace or commendation." This he believes will bring him to "conceive that those that are commended and esteemed for doing well will necessarily be beloved and cherished by everybody *and have all other good things in consequence of it*" (STCE 58, emphasis added). Shame and the deprivation of other good things ought to follow bad conduct. There is not, however, a perfect symmetry between esteem and disgrace. Locke warns that great care must be taken in inflicting shame on the child. "Shame in children has the same place that modesty has in women, which cannot be kept and often transgressed against" (STCE 60). Care must be taken to husband the child's sense of his own reputation. Locke counsels at times a certain amount of appropriately concealed indulgence toward transgressions such as lying and excuses.[15]

Once a child's mind has been brought to relish esteem and to dread disgrace, Locke says "you may turn them as you please, and they will be in love with all the ways of virtue" (STCE 58). This does not mean, however, that esteem and disgrace are sufficient incentives required to promote virtue. Consider Locke's account of what turns out to be the critical and foundational virtue of liberality.[16] The transformation required by the exercise of this virtue should not be underestimated. From the position of a dependent and grateful recipient of his parents' benefactions, the child must now become a happy giver. Locke suggests the following strategy. The child ought to be encouraged to give, but that things be so arranged that he experience very little or no pain in giving. Indeed, liberality "should be encouraged by great commendation and credit and constantly taking care that he loses nothing by his liberality. Let all the instances he gives of such freeness be always repaid, and with interest" (STCE 110). In a practical, though not in a theoretical, sense the virtue of liberality grounds the virtues of justice and humanity. The child's willingness to allow others their due and treat them with respect critically depends on his conviction that not only will this cost him nothing but that he will somehow gain from it.

The highly contrived character of the parents' design indicates that family life is not a microcosm of nature as a whole. One delicate task for the child's tutor is to introduce him to knowledge of "the world." Among the qualifications Locke requires of a tutor is that he know "the ways, the humors, the follies, the cheats, the faults of the age and particularly of the country he lives in." He must reveal this "knowledge of the world as it really is" to the young man as he becomes fit to receive it. Locke prefers this approach to that favored by many parents, particularly fathers, of putting the child in the "company" of large numbers of children so that he might learn to be "bolder and better able to bustle and shift amongst boys his own age." Fathers are tempted in this direction by seeing that "fortune is often most successfully courted by bold and bustling men" (STCE 70). Locke believes that on balance it is better to protect a child from the "infection" and "contagion" of company (STCE 68, 69). We are all a "sort of chameleons" (STCE 67), he says, and children even more so. Whatever skills are gained from consorting with his fellows, these are more than offset by the bad behaviors learned from them. The attainment of such knowledge of the world need not of course lead to the over-turning of virtue. Indeed, one purpose of teaching the young man the cheats and traps of the world is to equip him with knowledge of what is necessary to protect his reputation for virtue in the face of such threats. Concern for his good reputation along with the moral capacities he has learned allow him to maintain his bearings, not unlike the way in which Smith believes that the sentiments of the impartial spectator operate as a check on conduct.

Conclusion

Who has the better moral psychology? Does the answer to this question have implications for the future prospects for capitalism? Obviously, the first of these questions cannot be answered here. Indeed, it is not a question that can be answered simply at a theoretical level. A full investigation would have to take into account the findings of modern science and social science.[17] Our discussion of the differences between Locke and Smith does shed considerable light on the second question. By way of a conclusion, a summary of the key differences between Locke and Smith allows us to raise in a fuller way the criticism implied in Bagehot's quip about Smith. Bagehot implied that Smith had drawn essentially parochial and largely optimistic conclusions about the progress of civilization.

There are two critical differences between Smith and Locke relevant to our present inquiry. They revolve around, first, their respective confidence in socialization, and, second, their views on the naturalness of a liberal society. Locke's educational treatise makes great use of the emotions of esteem and disgrace and at times in a very Smithian way. He explains the complex psychological machinery that leads human beings to take the opinions of others into account when governing their own behavior. This machinery, if well developed and managed, facilitates the creation of a complex second nature capable of a life of virtue, even in the face of conflicts between virtue, on the one hand, and interest and passion, on the other. Yet there is a decisive difference between Smith and Locke that is captured in the gulf between Smith's confidence in socialization as the route to morality and Locke's insistence on carefully protecting the child from the influence of society. The cause of this disagreement would seem to be located in Locke's anxiety that the child's character be secured before he enters the world. Locke's education requires a careful nurturing of the child's sense of self by making it the possessor of a reputation. The self must first be firmly established before there can truly be *self*-esteem, *self*-command, and so on. Without this, the young person might be concerned about his reputation but without a true sense of self, and, chameleon like, simply take on the color of the surrounding society. Smith, on the other hand, assumes that there is a more natural path to good character through the process of socialization itself. Locke sees the process of forming a truly liberal personality as much more difficult.[18]

A similar divergence from Smith is visible in Locke's evolutionary account of morality. Our basic human needs lead all societies to establish certain rules of conduct roughly in line with the genuine laws of nature. A concern for reputation and a fear of social disapproval play a role in creating these rules and enforcing them. While it is "natural" (ECHU II.xxviii.12) for societies to evolve sets of rules similar to the law of nature, Locke does not say that it is natural for these to correspond to those of a liberal society. One must assume that some societies will remain closer to gangs of robbers, and that even complex societies need not be fully liberal. Smith, in contrast, contends that the commercial progress of society allows the moral sentiments fully to unfold by creating the kind of equality that goes along with economic independence and by allowing the humane virtues to flourish. With regard to the latter, Smith observes that in civilized societies "the mind is at liberty to unbend itself, and to indulge its natural inclinations in all those respects" (TMS V.2.9).[19]

A related issue is that of the problem of accounting for seeming extreme departures from ordinary moral norms. "Can there be," Smith asked, "a greater barbarity . . . than to hurt an infant?" Yet Smith acknowledges that the practice of infanticide has been widespread even in the western world. He explains such departures in terms of the effect of what he called "custom."

For example, in the case of the "polite and civilized Athenians," infanticide was once thought necessary because of the conditions of extreme poverty. He explains its continuance, though it was clearly no longer necessary, in the civilized nations of the ancient world, as the effect of "uninterrupted custom" (TMS V.2.15). The power of custom is such that even the enlightened of the time did not register an objection. Smith laments that "Aristotle talks of it as what the majistrate on many occasions ought to encourage. The humane Plato is of the same opinion, and, with all that love of mankind that seems to animate his writings, nowhere marks this practice with disapprobation" (TMS V.2.15). The question is whether Smith's explanation is adequate. Smith characterizes departures, such as infanticide, as "particular usages," by which he meant isolated exceptions that do not affect his general argument. Locke, in contrast, needed to posit no such explanation for dramatic departures from what might seem to be self-evident moral norms. The "busie mind of Man" (as he puts it in his *First Treatise*, §58) is eternally capable of such enormities and society of sanctioning them.

As noted, answering the question of who has the better moral psychology is beyond the scope of our present venture. Nevertheless, we can say with confidence that the answer to that question does have significant implications for the prospects for capitalism and especially the moral and political hopes that many of its proponents associate with it. The answer bears on whether we see liberal moral sensibilities as natural (in the sense of intrinsic) to capitalism, on how difficult it is to make those sensibilities flourish, and on how durable those sensibilities are once they have been established. Reading Smith would have us be optimistic. Reading Locke would have us be more cautious.

Notes

1. "Adam Smith as a Person," in *The Works and Life of Walter Bagehot*, vol. 7, ed. Mrs. Russell Barrington (London: Longmans, Green, 1915), 8. Bagehot admired the *Wealth of Nations* but had a low opinion of the *Theory of Moral Sentiments* and Smith's penchant for grand historical theorizing.

2. Many fine studies of Smith's moral theory have appeared in recent years. See, for example, Charles Griswold, *Adam Smith and the Virtues of Enlightenment* (Cambridge: Cambridge University Press, 1999); Samuel Fleischacker, *A Third Concept of Liberty: Judgment and Freedom in Kant and Adam Smith* (Princeton, N.J.: Princeton

University Press, 2000); Emma Rothschild, *Economic Sentiments: Adam Smith, Condorcet, and the Enlightenment* (Cambridge, Mass.: Harvard University Press, 2001); James Otteson, *Adam Smith's Marketplace of Life* (New York: Cambridge, 2002); Craig Smith, *Adam Smith's Political Philosophy* (London: Routledge, 2006); Jerry Evensky, *Adam Smith's Moral Philosophy* (Cambridge: Cambridge University Press, 2007); Ryan Patrick Hanley, *Adam Smith and the Character of Virtue* (New York: Cambridge University Press, 2009); Fonna Forman-Barzilai, *Adam Smith and the Circles of Sympathy* (New York: Cambridge University Press, 2010).

3. References to the *Essay* are to the edition by Peter H. Nidditch (Oxford: Oxford University Press, 1975) and to the *Thoughts* to that by Ruth Grant and Nathan Tarcov in *Some Thoughts Concerning Education and of the Conduct of the Understanding* (Indianapolis: Hackett, 1996). References to Smith are to *The Theory of Moral Sentiments* (Indianapolis: Liberty Fund, 1982).

4. Knud Haakonssen, *Natural Law and Moral Philosophy* (Cambridge: Cambridge University Press, 1996), 131.

5. Cf. Hobbes, *On the Citizen*, ed. and trans. Richard Tuck and Micahel Silverthrone (Cambridge: Cambridge University Press, 1998): "So clear is it from experience to anyone who gives any serious attention to human behavior, that every voluntary encounter is a product either of mutual need or of the pursuit of glory."

6. See II.iii.3.4; VI.ii.1.4; VI.ii.20.

7. For these arguments, see TMS I.iii.2.3, II.iii3, and VI.ii.intro.3.

8. For these arguments, see TMS III.ii–iii.

9. See, e.g., Paul H. Rubin, *Darwinian Politics: The Evolutionary Origin of Freedom* (New Brunswick, N.J.: Rutgers University Press, 2002), ix: "The notion that human beings are born as blank slates (*tabula rasa*, to use Locke's Latin phrase) is no longer intellectually respectable among serious people."

10. He uses blank slate in his early *Essays on the Law of Nature* and in a draft of the *Essay*.

11. Nathan Tarcov, *Locke's Education for Liberty* (Chicago: University of Chicago Press, 1984), 109.

12. This was Locke's critic, Bishop Stillingfleet, characterization of the *Essay*.

13. This point is well recognized by Peter Myers, *Our Only Star and Compass: Locke and the Struggle for Political Rationality* (Lanham, Md.: Rowman and Littlefield, 1999), 150–52. My account, however, makes a "[r]easonable moral consensus" more "immanent" in the ordinary course of nature than does Myers (cf. 151). See also Daniel Carey, "Locke's Anthropology: Travel, Innateness and the Exercise of Reason," *Seventeenth Century* 19, no. 2 (2004): 263, who notes Locke's "sociological" approach. I use the term "evolutionary" because Locke's argument covers difference between societies and differences between stages of society.

14. Tarcov infers from this that the desire for esteem is neither natural nor innate. *Locke's Education for Liberty*, 101.

15. See STCE 131–32. For perceptive commentary, see ibid., 181–83.

16. For comment on this point, see ibid., 141–49.

17. With respect to modern science, it is worth noting that many of the objections made to Locke in his own time are not dissimilar to objections made to the blank slate today. Modern science tells us that there are many features of our biological nature that prompt (e.g., oxytocin) or facilitate (e.g., mirror neurons) sociability. Locke's contemporary critics also pointed to various inclinations and disposition that are the basis of moral opinions. As John Yolton thoroughly documents, Locke showed an extraordinary disinterest in these types of criticism. The critics simply missed his point, he thought. *John Locke and the Way of Ideas* (Oxford: Oxford University Press, 1956), 14–15, 58–59. Locke might be just as dismissive of today's critics of the blank slate.

18. At bottom there would seem to a fundamental difference as to the nature of the self and personal identity. Locke treats these problems at length in the *Essay*. Locke's distrust of the imagination is a further complicating factor. For suggestions along these lines see Jonathan Lamb, *The Evolution of Sympathy in the Long Eighteenth Century* (London: Pickering and Chatto, 2009), 5–7, 56, 84. Samuel Fleischacker describes Smith's unconcern for the anxieties about personal identity one finds in Locke and Hume. "Adam Smith and Cultural Relativism," *Erasmus Journal of Philosophy and Economics* 4, no. 2 (2011): 29.

19. Lisa Herzog discusses this point at length in "Adam Smith's Account of Justice Between Naturalness and Historicity," *Journal of the History of Philosophy* 52, no. 4 (2014): 703–26. Herzog questions the coherence of Smith's overall argument.

Bibliography

Bagehot, Walter. "Adam Smith as a Person." In *The Works and Life of Walter Bagehot*, edited by Mrs. Russell Barrington, vol. 7. London: Longmans, Green, 1915.

Carey, Daniel. "Locke's Anthropology: Travel, Innateness and the Exercise of Reason." *Seventeenth Century* 19, no. 2 (2004): 260–85.

Evensky, Jerry. *Adam Smith's Moral Philosophy*. Cambridge: Cambridge University Press, 2007.

Fleischacker, Samuel. "Adam Smith and Cultural Relativism." *Erasmus Journal of Philosophy and Economics* 4, no. 2 (2011): 20–41.

———. *A Third Concept of Liberty*. Princeton, N.J.: Princeton University Press, 2000.

Forman-Barzilai, Fonna. *Adam Smith and the Circles of Sympathy*. Cambridge: Cambridge University Press, 2010.

Griswold, Charles. *Adam Smith and the Virtues of Enlightenment*. Cambridge: Cambridge University Press, 1999.

Haakonssen, Knud. *Natural Law and Moral Philosophy.* Cambridge: Cambridge University Press, 1996.

Hanley, Ryan Patrick. *Adam Smith and the Character of Virtue.* Cambridge: Cambridge University Press, 2009.

Herzog, Lisa. "Adam Smith's Account of Justice Between Naturalness and Historicity." *Journal of the History of Philosophy* 52, no. 4 (2014): 703–26.

Hobbes, Thomas. *On the Citizen.* Edited and translated by Richard Tuck and Micahel Silverthrone. Cambridge: Cambridge University Press, 1998.

Lamb, Jonathan. *The Evolution of Sympathy in the Long Eighteenth Century.* London: Pickering and Chatto, 2009.

Locke, John. *Essay Concerning Human Understanding.* Edited by Peter H. Nidditch. Oxford: Oxford University Press, 1975.

———. *Essays on the Law of Nature.* Edited by W. von Leyden. Oxford: Clarendon Press, 2002.

———. *Some Thoughts Concerning Education and Of the Conduct of the Understanding.* Edited by Ruth Grant and Nathan Tarcov. Indianapolis: Hackett, 1996.

Myers, Peter. *Our Only Star and Compass: Locke and the Struggle for Political Rationality.* Lanham, Md.: Rowman and Littlefield, 1999.

Otteson, James. *Adam Smith's Marketplace of Life.* New York: Cambridge, 2002.

Rothschild, Emma. *Economic Sentiments: Adam Smith, Condorcet, and the Enlightenment.* Cambridge, Mass.: Harvard University Press, 2001.

Rubin, Paul H. *Darwinian Politics: The Evolutionary Origin of Freedom.* New Brunswick, N.J.: Rutgers University Press, 2002.

Smith, Adam. *The Theory of Moral Sentiments.* Glasgow, 1759.

Smith, Craig. *Adam Smith's Political Philosophy.* London: Routledge, 2006.

Tarcov, Nathan. *Locke's Education for Liberty.* Chicago: University of Chicago Press, 1984.

Yolton, John. *John Locke and the Way of Ideas.* Oxford: Oxford University Press, 1956.

CHAPTER 11

Markets and Morality
in the Enlightenment: Neglected Aspects
of Montesquieu's Case for Commerce

Andrew S. Bibby

Recent advances in the empirical study of the economics of religion have yielded a few notable generalizations. The most interesting empirical finding is the apparent discovery of a positive relationship between religious values and free markets, with economic growth as the most obvious social benefit.[1] Researchers recognize that the field of the economic study of religion is plagued by empirical uncertainties and theoretical clarity.[2] Yet the findings re-raise a set of old but important questions. What values are required for commercial society to emerge? What moral attitudes are necessary for commercial society to thrive?

This essay looks to Enlightenment political thought for clarification and insight. Answering these kinds of questions requires not only more and better empirical models, but also a renewed emphasis on theoretical and analytical clarity, especially in three areas: (a) the moral and religious conditions of commercial society; (b) the processes and channels through which culture acts on the economy; (c) the resources available to a liberal society for the cultivation of healthy or sensible attitudes in regard to the promises and pitfalls of commercial modernity.

The analysis of the relationship between morality and markets does not begin in the Enlightenment. But it is during the Enlightenment era that this relationship is first explored in a rigorous or systematic way. The two most commonly cited authors are Adam Smith (1723–1790) and David Hume (1711–1776). Less commonly referenced is the French liberal political philosopher Montesquieu (1689–1755), whose work, I will argue, constitutes the first major attempt to articulate the "two-way" relationship between commerce and society in the modern era.

The first section of this chapter shows why the standard account of Enlightenment thinking on the subject of secularization is incomplete. The second section analyzes Montesquieu's *The Spirit of the Laws* to help explain the persistence of religion in commercial modernity, despite or in contrast to the powerful claims of the proponents of secularization, that is, that commerce undermines traditional religious morality. The concluding section argues that Montesquieu's "two-way" analysis of the relationship between commerce and religion is useful in explaining both the growth of capitalism in the West and the religiously inspired reactions to it.

Economy and Religion

The study of the connection between free markets and religious morality is an old subject.[3] The study of the *effects* of religious morality on society and economics, however, is both new and controversial. Writing in 1989, Michael McConnell and Richard Posner identified three objections to the "economic approach" to religion and religious issues. First, one should expect resistance to the very idea of applying economic approaches to "nonmarket" behavior. The proper domain of economic analysis is not morality or religion, but explicitly "economic" markets, where one can assume that human beings engage naturally in profit-maximizing behavior. Religious morality is not (or should not be) reducible to standard market explanations, like the rewards or perceived benefits of religious participation and belief. Second, the economics of religion as an empirical field lacks reliable data. The paucity of the economic studies of religion "lends credence to the supposition that religion must lie outside the domain of economics."[4] Finally, economics is suspect from a religious point of view. It is a "form of applied utilitarianism," which embodies its own system of values: scientific, rationalistic, and even "antireligious." Economics, viewed normatively, is a kind of secular faith that can have little to say about religiously motivated activities. At best it may have little explanatory value; at worst it may distort or corrupt the subject it seeks to explain.

The field of economics and religion has its own internal problems, in addition. As Iannacone has explained, the field is divided into at least three separate strands, each with its own methods (and in some cases radically different purposes).[5] The subfield known as "Economic Analyses of Religion," for example, applies methods from economics to explain patterns of religious behavior. "Religious Economics," by contrast, draws on sacred writings and theological principles to "promote or criticize economic polices." A third area, "The Economic Consequences of Religion," places particular emphasis on the social and economic consequences of religious practice and belief.

My interest in the following is strictly limited to this third area of study, that is, to the economic and social consequences of religion. Readers may be familiar with this tradition by way of Max Weber or by virtue of the sizable literature on the highly contested Protestant Ethic thesis. According to proponents of Weber's thesis in *The Protestant Ethic and the Spirit of Capitalism* (first published in 1904–1905), the Protestant Reformation triggered a "mental revolution," which in turn made possible the advent of modern commercial capitalism. Christianity, for Weber, was a "social bond of world-encompassing brotherhood." It was not greed or unbridled avarice that brought about the age of capitalism. Rather, worldly commercial success required restraint, a "rational tempering" of humanity's "irrational impulse." These traits could be supplied by Protestant theology, which emphasized personal diligence, frugality, thrift, individual responsibility, and "the moral approval it granted to risk- taking and to financial self-improvement."[6]

It would not be possible to summarize the criticism of Weber's thesis here. A few points may be noted in passing. Critics pointed out, for example, that many of the capitalist institutions Weber identified as crucial to his thesis *preceded* the Protestant Reformation. Capitalism had flourished, some claimed, in the Middle Ages and in the Italian city-states, which were Catholic.[7] Others noted that Weber may have exaggerated the extent to which Protestant theologians understood, let alone promoted modern economic institutions and behaviors, such as public credit and lending at interest. Economic historians pointed out that many of the regions cited by Weber did not conform to Weber's model, or in many cases, directly contradicted his thesis.[8]

But if Weber was wrong in his specific claims, the spirit of his search was not altogether misplaced. The stress on spiritual rather than material factors was at the very least a useful rebuttal to Marxian historical materialism. Weber's work also served as a corrective to negative attitudes toward commercial republicanism, a form of government (and a way of life) often viewed by intellectuals as antithetical to religious morality and poisonous to republican virtue.[9] Weber's essential claim is still worth pursuing: do religious beliefs matter for economic outcomes?[10]

We can now turn to a closer look at the example of Montesquieu, whose economic writings are not well known, but which have had a surprisingly prominent effect on the development of modern liberal political economy.[11] Political theorists will be familiar with Montesquieu's analysis of the distinction between old republics devoted to virtue and modern England, a popular commercial monarchy devoted to liberty. Political scientists and historians will likewise be familiar with Montesquieu's defense of England's separation of powers in Book 11 of *The Spirit of the Laws*. Others may be acquainted with Montesquieu's famous defense of commerce in Book 20: "Commerce cures destructive prejudices, and it is an almost general rule that everywhere there are gentle mores, there is commerce and that everywhere there is commerce, there are gentle mores."

For some of Montesquieu's admirers, the above statement was not only the most interesting of Montesquieu's claims in the fourth part of *The Spirit of the Laws*, but also among the most influential arguments of the French Enlightenment. Albert Hirschman, for example, has argued that Montesquieu was the most powerful advocate of the idea that commerce "softens" or "polishes" mores. Montesquieu, more than any writer of the era, Hirschman argued, gave life to the expression *doux commerce*.[12]

Long before the *doux commerce* hypothesis became synonymous with Montesquieu's case for commerce, however, Montesquieu himself had shown that markets are "embedded" (as economists might say) in culture. In fact, Montesquieu was thoroughly convinced that the strength of the *doux commerce* thesis rested on a prior expectation that free market "mores" would be esteemed, valued, and articulated in the "spirit" of the society in which they were embedded. In other words, the *doux commerce* thesis does not even begin to capture the complexity of the Enlightenment case for commerce, explored further below. One consequence of this oversimplification was that by the nineteenth century, this claim had become low-hanging fruit for a range of anti-market critics. The most influential critique came from Karl Marx, who suggested that capitalist society would ultimately self-destruct by undermining or neglecting its own moral foundations.[13]

Secularization in the Enlightenment:
The Case of Montesquieu

Montesquieu's formulation successfully captured the spirit of the Enlightenment case for commerce: free markets *do* have a tendency to violate pure mores, but they also soften barbarous ways of life, while providing powerful incentives for other positive social traits. Do free markets promote virtue? The moderate Enlightenment answer to this question is fairly well understood: No, they do not, if virtue is defined as public self-sacrifice, monarchical honor, or communal piety. But for theorists like Montesquieu, the justification for virtue understood in these terms is weak. The "spirit of commerce" provides a substitute for a different set of less noble but more reliable virtues. It brings *en train* "the spirit of frugality, economy, moderation, work, wisdom, tranquility, order, and rule." Yes, then, commerce corrodes traditional political virtue. But this is precisely why, on practical *and* moral grounds, the critics of traditional political virtue endorsed it.

Montesquieu is a peculiar case. As Kingston notes, there is no scholarly consensus on the precise meaning of Montesquieu's modernity, nor is there even a provisional consensus on Montesquieu's own view of religion.[14] While I do not read Montesquieu as ambivalent on the advantages of commercial modernity, it is fair to be cautious or wary of using Montesquieu as a representative of an extreme secular "Enlightenment." Montesquieu has been viewed as a deist, for example, by Faguet and Shklar; as a follower of Erastianism by Fletcher; as a Machiavellian by Bianchi; as a traditional defender of Christian principles by Shackleton.[15] Others have read Montesquieu as a radical and subversive proponent of modern secularization, an interpretation that would put him much closer to Voltaire and Hobbes as a "commercial secularist." Andrea Radasanu, for example, claims that Montesquieu views man's natural condition as one of religious indifference.[16] Montesquieu's project would be to recover humanity's natural secularism "through the artifice of economic institutions."[17]

While I personally find the latter view persuasive, the "commercial secularist" reading of Montesquieu has at least one major defect: it fails to account for Montesquieu's lengthy examination of the causal relationship between religion and economics, especially in part five of *The Spirit of the Laws*. In these often overlooked passages, Montesquieu makes two unique claims that reveal an interesting dimension of the problem of the relation between markets and morality. First, secularization is a *tendency*, not a rule; and second, more important, secularization is *relative* to the *specific content* of religious belief.[18]

The following section illustrates Montesquieu's two-way study of the connection between markets and religious morality by identifying five major "channels." According to Montesquieu, religion affects economically relevant behavior directly and indirectly, in the following five primary channels:

1. moral and civil laws;
2. criminal laws;
3. religious beliefs, especially varying opinions about heaven, hell, and the soul;
4. religious practices, including customs and rituals;
5. religious pluralism and diversity.

Montesquieu explored each of these channels in all of his major works, including his *Persian Letters* (1721), the *Considerations on the Causes of the Greatness of the Romans and Their Decline* (1734), and the *The Spirit of the Laws* (1748). The clearest and most systematic overview is to be found in Books 24 and 25 of *The Spirit of the Laws*. Here Montesquieu appraises major world religions in terms of their social and economic effects, providing what might be the most sophisticated analysis of religion from a sociological point of view in the Enlightenment era.

Goodness and Gain

Religion operates on society through different channels, but perhaps none more profoundly than through the moral laws. For Montesquieu, moral laws are provided by philosophy, and are intertwined with religious duties. They are categorically distinct from physical laws, which are "invariable" (I.1). Moral laws are related to economy, therefore, because they govern the fundamental principles and priorities of human action. They provide definition to the ambiguous terms happiness, life, property, and compassion (XXIV.8).

The most obvious way that moral laws affect economy is through the praise and blame of attitudes toward work. For a good illustration, here is Montesquieu describing the reports of the people of Pegu from an account he had read in Constantin De Renneville's *Collection of Voyages that Contributed to the Establishment of the East India Company* (1500): "The principal points of religion of the inhabitants of Pegu are, not to commit murder, not to steal, to avoid uncleanliness, not to give the least uneasiness to their neighbor, but to do him, on the contrary, all the good in their power. With these rules they think they should be saved in any religion whatsoever. Hence it proceeds that those people, though poor and proud, behave with gentleness and compassion to the unhappy" (XXIV.8). In this passage Montesquieu does not argue that religion makes the Pegu rich (as an economist of religion might say, that it "pays to pray"), only, that there are good a priori reasons to believe that there is a causal connection between religiosity and "economically important social behavior." Of course, the possibility that religion *can* constrain (from murder, theft, uncleanliness) does not mean that it always does, as Montesquieu carefully pointed out earlier (XXIV.2). But in economic matters, religious principles are often inseparable from business relations, even if—as modern studies suggest—those principles generally apply *more* to everyday interactions than they do to attitudes to capitalism, socialism, income redistribution, and so on.[19]

Fear of divine retribution, however, is not the passion to be reckoned on. The moral laws need help from and are informed also by the "maxims of philosophy." In contrast to the Platonic idea of philosophy as recollection, Montesquieu viewed philosophy as a practical reminder of humanity's basic needs (I.1). Montesquieu borrowed from Stoicism as a guide. While he found certain aspects of Stoicism "excessive," and while he criticized the Stoic goal of "knowing oneself" as an illusion, he admired the Stoics for their "practical morality," and especially for its promise as a philosophy that could ground morality in a corrupt world. It could provide a model of a kind of "natural religion," compatible with modern life, insofar—or precisely because—it encouraged healthy attitudes toward labor and work. In brief, Montesquieu found in Stoicism an example of a philosophical religion consistent with commercial mores.[20]

Montesquieu's praise of Stoicism stands in stark relief to what might be called "contemplative morality." Philosophies of contemplation, Montesquieu argued, tend to distract from the basic needs of human beings ("to preserve, to nourish, to clothe themselves, and do all the actions of society").

Religion, Montesquieu noted, "ought not to give [people] too contemplative a life" (XXIV.10). Penances, for example, should promote action and work. They should "be joined with the idea of labor, not with that of idleness; with the idea of good, not with that of supereminence; with the idea of frugality, not with that of avarice" (XXIV.12).

Punishment and Civility

Religion affects economy through the civil laws (see esp. XXIV.14–20).[21] In particular, religion affects the way citizens think about crime and punishment, especially when the civil laws are uncodified or new. Japan, for example, which was largely Shinto in Montesquieu's time but increasingly Buddhist, was characterized by "stern" civil laws. Montesquieu believed that Japan had less need for extralegal (that is, religious) "rewards and punishments." To illustrate this principle, Montesquieu uses an extreme example—a report from a thirteenth-century missionary—which describes the imbalance of religious and civil laws under the Tartars, ruled by Genghis Khan. Under the Great Khan, the civil laws carried the entire burden of legislating morality. Religious laws, by contrast, condemned the smallest and most trivial activities, which the "civil laws ought to [have] permitted." It was not a sin for the Tartars to "break their word" or to "seize upon another man's goods" or to "do an injury to a person or to commit murder." And yet it was a capital crime to "put a knife in the fire," to "lean against a whip," or to "strike a horse with the bridle" (XXIV.14).

The effect of religiosity on the civil laws is more acute when they involve deeply held opinions about heaven and hell. Common sense might suggest that a strong belief in the severity of judgment in the afterlife should be associated with better behavior, less criminality, and economic stability. Montesquieu offered the following non-intuitive hypothesis. Civil laws are *less effective in proportion to* the emphasis on rewards in heaven, as opposed to punishments in hell. To illustrate, he asks his reader to imagine a religion that places most of its emphasis on heavenly rewards. Anticipation of great heavenly rewards will encourage subjects to believe themselves to be "above the power of the legislator." One has everything to win (sensual rewards in heaven) but relatively less to lose (an ambiguous hell with no articulated stories of the nature of punishment). Consequently, those who commit egregious crimes are more likely to look upon death with contempt. As

Montesquieu phrases the rhetorical question, "How shall the man be restrained by laws who believes that the greatest pain the magistrate can inflict will end in a moment to begin his happiness in the next?" (XXIV.14).

Montesquieu did not shy away from recommending reform. Religious description of punishment, he argued, could be modified to avoid an obsessive preoccupation with judgment in the afterlife. The most harmful belief to avoid was the idea of "unexpiable crimes" (XXIV.14). A religion that make crimes impossible to atone for deprives society not only of physical work (today, restitution in the form of community service) but also of the motivation to work one's way out of a larger debt to humanity.

Interests of the Soul

The idea of immortality is also an important factor, not only for everyday economic behavior, but in the larger story of the development of modern commercial society. In short, Montesquieu tried to show that beliefs about the soul and the afterlife directly affect how one should conduct one's business in this world.[22]

Montesquieu begins with ideas about the body. One approach is to conceive of the body as a "temporary lodging." That conception, Montesquieu argues, can have a depressing effect on work, insofar it makes individuals less likely to attend to basic needs, to provide for the future, or to strive for comfort, however illusory that striving might be. On this point, religion provides a striking range of different answers on the question of the dignity of the body in relation to the soul. Montesquieu warns against the extreme case; that is, the view of the human body as merely a "house" made of "earth and dirt."

Ideas or opinions about the soul also affect attitudes toward work. Taking up the controversial idea that the soul is corporeal (or as Hobbes put it, "spirituall Bodies"), Montesquieu suggests that it is unreasonable and perhaps pernicious to expect that the soul will enjoy the same pleasures and sensations of the earthly body. Like Hobbes, Montesquieu can envision a perfected body (one that does not "marry . . . or eate and drinke . . . without the specificall eternity of generation"). Like Hobbes, Montesquieu seems to believe that the vision of a literal resurrection could lead to fanaticism: to die in the expectations of heavenly rewards. "Almost everywhere in the world, and in all times, the opinion that the soul is immortal, wrongly taken, has engaged women, slaves, subjects, and friends to kill themselves in order to go to the next world and serve the object of their respect or their love." These customs arise "less from the dogma of the immortality of the soul than from that of the resurrection of the body; a consequence has been drawn from this that after his death an individual would have the same needs, the same feelings, and the same passions as before."

While much more could be said on Montesquieu's view of the afterlife, it is clear that there is a causal link, and that the dogma of the immortality of the soul "affects men prodigiously." This is to say, opinions about the body, the soul, and heaven and hell do influence behavior in understandable—perhaps even in predictable—ways. The soul has "interests" and passions. The hope of resurrection of the body in the next life is, for Montesquieu, a powerful predictor of a society's attitude toward work in this life, and therefore a potentially significant factor in the variation in wealth and poverty among nations.

Ritual Productivity

Religious morality operates on a fourth channel, by influencing everyday business, both positively and negatively, through ceremony, ritual, practice, and tradition. Taking his cue from the eighteenth-century nobility's contempt for agricultural labor, Montesquieu looked at the example of China, where he described, suggestively, the positive effects of a religious ceremony called "opening the ground." Citing Father Du Halde's *History of China* (1738), Montesquieu related the example of emperors around the world who have used religious tradition to encourage work. In China, "the emperor is every year informed of the husbandman who has distinguished himself most in his profession; and he makes him a mandarin of the eighth order." In Persia, "the kings quitted their grandeur and pomp on the eighth day of the month, called Chorrem-ruz, to eat with the husbandmen. These institutions were admirably calculated for the encouragement of agriculture." In India, the kings used religious ceremony as a "public and solemn act" to "excite people to tillage." One emperor, Venty, "tilled the lands himself, and made the empress and his wives employ their time in the silkworks in his palace."[23]

Taking into account, no doubt, the eighteenth-century Catholic tendency to discourage literacy in the French reading public, Montesquieu also pointed to ways in which religious rituals in non-Christian traditions contributed to writing and to education. Again referring to China, he admired the "ease" that "rites" have "engraved on the hearts and minds of the Chinese." The tradition of writing took up a large part of the attention of the youth; this helped them later to "read and understand the books in which they are comprised." While the Chinese ritual precepts, have "nothing in them that is spiritual," the act of reading and the difficulty of writing itself had a positive role because, in his words, it "established emulation, banished laziness, and contributed to a love of learning" (XIV.17).

Non-Christian religious disputes also provided an important backdrop, against which Montesquieu could warn of the pernicious consequences of religious conflict for European commerce and finance. Using the example of the senseless animosity between Hindus and Muslims ("the Indians hate the Mahometans, because they eat cows; the Mahometans detest the Indians because they eat hogs"), Montesquieu subversively suggested that religious prohibitions of "indifferent things" could be explained by natural causes. The spiritual prohibition of beef and pork, for example, were economically useful in the primitive stages of each religious tradition.[24]

Avoiding Christian examples, he trivialized Muslim and Hindu belief systems to make a larger point, that religious practices can inspire aversion for things that are "in themselves indifferent." Local religious practices that seem like arbitrary prejudices to outsiders (such as the ban on pork or on beef in Islam and Hinduism) often arise *out of* economic or sociological necessity. The legislator need not legislate against the "indifferent things." But neither should the state allow religion to "inspire a horror" of things that would "[move] men away from love and pity for men."

Attachment, and Desires

Here it is appropriate to consider the relationship between devotion, attachment, and allegiance. When Montesquieu began writing the three books devoted to religious issues, in *The Spirit of the Laws*, he clearly had in mind the objection of the Protestant French philosopher Pierre Bayle, who argued that a "state formed by true Christians would not continue to exist" (see XXIV.6). Underlying Bayle's criticism of religion was the old problem of the relationship between the human and the divine laws, and underlying that, the question whether it is possible in a free society for citizens to serve two masters.

Montesquieu had explored this question decades earlier, in his *Persian Letters*. One of the characters in that novel argued that traditional Christianity tended to diminish rather than enhance civic participation. Sincere Christians thought of themselves as "travelers who should think only of another country." Pious Christians should, moreover, sacrifice temporal well-being for the sake of salvation.[25] The consequence of such reasoning was not only oppression, but economic decline. In his much discussed "population letters," Montesquieu worried openly that "otherworldliness" had depleted the economic and political strength of European monarchies while severely reducing Europe's population and labor force (*PL* 17).

When Montesquieu returned to this subject in *The Spirit of the Laws*, he did not try to solve the problem directly. Rather than opposing Christian otherworldliness, he expended his efforts instead on illustrating the varieties of reasons for attachment to religion, and correspondingly, the variety of ways in which harmful "otherworldliness" could be destroyed.

For space, it is necessary to confine this discussion to a few examples, illustrating the motives for attachment, and which themselves, I argue, point to a larger project to undermine them.[26] Montesquieu identifies the most potent ingredients in the rational and emotional concoction that contributes to powerful devotion as a combination of spiritual, psychological, and political causes. First, a religion that portrays God as a "supreme spiritual being" that is not corporeal (but that appreciates, or responds to "sensible" practices of worship) is extremely powerful.[27] Catholics fit this category more so than Protestants (XXV.2) and, according to Montesquieu, this makes them "more zealous of propagation." Second, a religion will have a more powerful hold on human beings if the god is personal, that is, if the gods take sides in human affairs.[28] Third, complexity. Religions that have "many practices" tend to increase intensity of devotion. This is primarily because they occupy more of our time, but also because they increase the frequency of our thoughts of the afterlife.[29] Fourth, hell. A religion in which the promise of everlasting torment for the wicked will help to train human efforts on activities that will save one's own soul, or deliver the enemy to justice.

Finally, we tend to be more attached to religions that provide black and white moral rules. Montesquieu calls this a "pure morality." Men may be "rascals one by one." But in groups, humans "love morality." In other words, human beings are not only moved powerfully by notions of justice; they are also moved by the praise they receive for appearing to do good. Religion helps to satisfy those yearnings. If true, it follows that human beings are drawn to religions where the righteous are rewarded, the wicked suffer, and everyone else can be forgiven. Montesquieu compares religion here to a grand morality play (see XXV.2). At theaters, we gather to cheer on the good guy, but it also feels good to see the bad guy suffer; in Montesquieu's words, we are "immensely pleased by the feeling that morality professes."

All of these causes point simultaneously to the causes of attachment *and* also to the ways in which a reformed Christianity—simpler, less sensitive to the externals of worship, more focused on grace than works—might lead to a more productive focus on success in this life.

Pluralism and Prosperity

The last third of Book 25 concerns toleration, establishment of religion, and its perpetuation (XXV.9–15). We can now turn to the connection between religious pluralism, political stability, and economic prosperity. Theorization on this connection begins with Adam Smith,[30] is extended by Tocqueville, and is expressed, most succinctly, by Thomas Jefferson, who, in 1820, on the occasion of a synagogue consecration, argued that the great "maxim of civil government" should be reversed when it comes to religion. In religion, "the maxim should read 'divided we stand, united we fall.'"[31]

Jefferson's quip is a simplification and a reduction of a similar analysis in Book V of *An Inquiry into the Nature and Causes of the Wealth of Nations*. It also does not do justice to Adam Smith's comprehensive views of the ways in which the "the pure and rational" natural religion might be encouraged. However, it serves as a fair summary of contemporary economists' views of the legacy of Smith, who, many think, first explained how "religious market structure" influenced individual belief and participation (participation as measured primarily by church attendance and religious belief).[32] At the heart of the economic reading of Adam Smith is the idea that religion is a commodity, an object of choice.[33] Unlike given identity, race, or sex, consumers of religious services choose—and change—their religion according to the availability and attractiveness of the commodity available through the marketplace. Scholars in this field often compare religion to "firms" that either flourish or fade, depending on the extent of competition in the religious marketplace—and to the extent that the services it provides will appeal to potential buyers. These religions will be "high in quality and well-aligned with individual preferences," to borrow an appropriate formulation.[34]

Montesquieu held similar views, although he, like Smith, did not view religion merely as a commodity. Still, Montesquieu can be seen working out a provisional theory of the relationship between the religious marketplace and religious belief. In the *Persian Letters*, for example, Usbek suggests that a rational and peaceful religion will only thrive under the political conditions of religious diversity and political tolerance. The key is identifying what is useful in each religion and then encouraging a political order that would bring them into maximal harmony. First, he argues, "all religions contain some precepts useful to humanity." But for these precepts to be maintained, Usbek argued, it is better for there to be *at least two religions* and preferably a multiplicity of sects. When there are two religions, the minority "as a rule" are "more valuable to their homeland" because they are able to achieve distinction "only by an affluent lifestyle, and their own prosperity, they tend to acquire wealth by hard work, and to seek out the most arduous occupations in a society."

When there are multiple religions, Usbek continues, the religions become "rivals." Jealous competition extends to everyday life, encouraging each rival sect to "be fearful of doing something that would dishonor his own side and expose it to the unpardonable scorn and criticisms of the adversary." Will this competition lead to conflict and war? "It is not the multiplicity of religions that produced [historical] wars, but the spirit of intolerance animating the religion that believed itself to be dominant" (*PL* LXXXVI).

This positive view of the multiplicity of sects is echoed by Montesquieu himself in Book 19 (XIX.27), where he famously declares that a state that provides freedom of religion will lead to either a multiplicity of sects or the acceptance of an established religion by an "indifferent" majority (XIX.27).[35] Montesquieu extended this argument further in Book 25 of *The Spirit of the Laws*: the multiplicity of sects, he claims, was key to weakening political religion while promoting tolerance in various cultures around the world (including Japan, the people of "Siam," the "Calmucks," and Calicut, who because of religious diversity, never "disputed on religion" (XXV.15).

Montesquieu is not as optimistic as some modern day economists that religious pluralism will decrease tension as a mathematical rule. As Rica complains in *Persian Letters*, multiplicity increases the number of religious factions but also the odds of religious fanaticism. This is because in any society, there is an "infinite number of unbalanced minds."[36]

Furthermore, Montesquieu does not claim that multiplicity *itself* is doing the work. Competition rarely takes place in a culture where all religions are numerically or culturally equal. More often than not, the competition takes place within a social *hierarchy*. So while the above passages clearly support an "open market" for religion, Montesquieu's theory is distinctive from the standard "market model" framework. For one, Montesquieu's model is a form of toleration that is compatible with an established (or dominant) church. Moreover, disestablishment is not the only route to privatization, tolerance, and industry. On this point, we could say that Montesquieu is somewhere between Adam Smith and David Hume. Imperfect toleration, rather than either multiplicity (Smith) or establishment (Hume), is seen as optimal, for encouraging hard work, harmony, and public prosperity.

Later in Book 25, Montesquieu will make a point of this by noting that toleration has limits: "there is a great difference between tolerating a religion and approving it" (XXV.9). Political authorities may decide what new religions can be "established" in the country (XXV.10). Finally, the state may decide on practical grounds to regulate existing religious groups. The only governing principle for Montesquieu is that regulation should be minimal; that is, limited to protecting fundamental needs of life, shelter, liberty, and the protection of property.[37]

Testing Montesquieu

How might this Montesquieuean approach contribute to the debate on the controversial relationship between competitive markets and moral behavior? In 1982, Albert Hirschman suggested three broad "rival" views of the market: as civilizing, destructive, or "feeble" in its effects on society. Building on Hirschman's framework, a close analysis of Montesquieu lends historical and theoretical weight to the "feeble" markets view, which in contrast to the "civilizing" view, treats markets as essentially good but also weak, due to the persistence of institutional, social, and cultural legacies from the feudal past (as such, it is known also as the "feeble shackles" thesis; see Fourcade and Healy). This conclusion would be significant, if only because Montesquieu—and therefore much of eighteenth-century thought—is too often interpreted (wrongly in my opinion) as the source or origin of the "civilizing" thesis, which holds that market relations make people more cordial and less likely to fight each other. Long before the *doux commerce* hypothesis became synonymous with Montesquieuean optimism, Montesquieu himself had shown that markets are "embedded" in particular cultures, and therefore highly sensitive to cultural inputs, traditions, and expectations.[38]

As argued above, the analysis of religion in part five effectively undermines this axial position. A Montesquieuean view of the two-way relationship between markets and morality could be seen, therefore, as a reminder of the richness of Enlightenment thought. It would also provide retrospective insight into the explosion of anti-market reactions in the nineteenth century to the Enlightenment case for commerce.

But was Montesquieu right? A short list of predictions could easily be generated from Montesquieu's work, many of which receive strong empirical support today. First, it is abundantly clear that social and moral orders, religion in particular, affect economics, by fostering, inhibiting, or giving "local flavor" to everyday market behaviors. Take, for example, the common-sense view of Montesquieu that religious principles encourage different kinds of moral responsibility, therefore opening up a channel for the creation and maintenance of economically productive incentives. The link between religiosity and a wide range of economically relevant behavior has been an object of study for decades now, with findings that broadly support the two-way relationship in Book 25.[39]

One area in which Montesquieu saw religion as particularly useful was as an indirect support of *law* in countries with undeveloped legal and political institutions. As a kind of legislator himself, Montesquieu recommended a gradual transformation and rationalization of religious opinion, not only because he did not think religion *would* fade away with the advent of commercial and industrial society, but because it might play a positive role as countries modernized and became increasingly bureaucratized, rationalized, urbanized, et cetera.

In other words, the upheavals of commerce—which Montesquieu rightly supported—might be less damaging to society and more effective in the long run, in the context of a political order in which religion and philosophy joined together: in encouraging good or beneficial existing civil laws; in substituting for nonexistent laws or rights; or acting as a deterrent where the civil laws are either underdeveloped or contrary to basic human rights and needs. These and similar assumptions are supported by numerous studies.

What makes Montesquieu truly unique among Enlightenment philosophers, however, is his emphasis on the *comparative* content of religious belief. As we have seen, Montesquieu was particularly worried about the promotion of religious dogma that combines sensual heavenly rewards, with no corresponding concept of civil or spiritual punishment for error. Interestingly, numerous studies have attempted to provide empirical demonstration of that insight. In the language of modern economics, different religions have different degrees of "high stakes" incentives. According to one notable report, countries with low levels of belief compared with high religious participation appear to perform worse economically than in countries with relatively higher levels of religious belief than religious participation.[40] A subsequent finding from Robert Barro confirms this connection, although reversing Montesquieu's emphasis on heaven. In Barro's words, "The stick of punishment may be more powerful compared with the carrot."

Putting aside the question of empirical accuracy, some general conclusions can be summarized now. First, Montesquieu did not share the exaggerated claim, made by the most vocal proponents of trade, that commerce was a panacea. As Montesquieu joked somewhat pessimistically, commerce will not turn "deserts into fruitful fields, villages into great cities, cottages into palaces, beggars into princes, convert cowards into heroes, blockheads into philosophers."[41]

In retrospect, Montesquieu's answer to our question, "Are Markets Moral?" was perhaps too subtle for pro-market enthusiasts of the time. He predicted that commercial society would degrade some aspects of character ("pure mores") while enhancing others ("gentle mores"). As this chapter has shown, however, Montesquieu also laid the foundations for a version of the secularization thesis that does not fit easily with modern simplified forms. The traditional secularization thesis offered only a one-way explanation of the complex interplay of markets and ethics. This optimistic, progressive, Enlightenment era prediction of the slow, but inevitable, death of religion should not be attributed to Montesquieu, even if one agrees that he is the era's most influential champion of commerce. On the contrary, he would have found it unsurprising that religion would not disappear from the world, despite profound advancements in science, political liberty, and commerce. This follows necessarily from his reversal of the causation of the commerce-religion connection. Commerce and material development might erode revealed religion's political authority *and even* its *plausibility*.[42] But Montesquieu's work on religion strikes out in a different direction, suggesting that there is a large range of "viable pathways" not only to commercial culture, but to a variety of different capitalisms.[43] This emphasis on the moral conditions of commerce does not neatly resolve the question, but it does provide an intriguing story of the surprising growth of capitalism in the West and, some would say, the equally surprising religiously inspired reactions to it.

Ultimately, it was not Montesquieu's sober assessment of the "mixed" effects of commerce that could have prevented the worst of those reactions. But his approach to the problem of religion and politics is illustrative. Today's defenders of liberal capitalism might rethink the public justification of commercial society and its benefits.[44] A successful case will depend less on the promise of the free market's material and social benefits, more on a self-critical examination of the moral causes that allow us to enjoy them.

Notes

1. See Laurence R. Iannaccone, "Introduction to the Economics of Religion," *Stanford Journal of Economic Literature* 36, no. 3 (1998): 1465–95; Robert Barro and Rachel M. McCleary, "Religion and Economic Growth," *Milken Institute Review* (June 2004): 38–45; Rachel M. McCleary, "Salvation, Damnation, and Economic Incentives," *Journal of Contemporary Religion* 22, no. 1 (January 2007): 49–74. Skeptics of these studies will point out, correctly, that correlation is not causation. Researchers are not agreed on the precise causal mechanisms. For example, one may point to the lack of engagement by researchers with questions concerning the substance of religion. As Iannaccone explains, economic research takes the "demand for religion as given" while keeping the "character of religious commodities loosely defined." "Introduction to the Economics of Religion," 1490. Although this approach streamlines research and avoids narrow formulations, it provides little insight into the difference between a prayer meeting and a book club, or church attendance and a dart league or a billiards club.

2. Laurence Iannaccone has called attention to a "poverty of theory" in the field. Are the initial results of recent findings constant over time and across countries? Is the relationship between religion and economics linear, or is there a point at which religiosity becomes a drag on growth? Are some religions superior to others in terms of their economic performance? Perhaps the most significant oversight for economists has to do with a lack of attention to the formation of beliefs. See Iannaccone, "Introduction to the Economics of Religion," 1491.

3. Montesquieu in 1748 had argued that market morality would "silence" religious and otherworldly concern for the soul. David Hume in 1757 had suggested that religion would decline in response to advances in science and education. Marx in 1859 had analyzed the decline of religion as one manifestation of a larger trend toward "modernization."

4. Richard A. Posner and Michael W. McConnell, "An Economic Approach to Issues of Religious Freedom," *University of Chicago Law Review* 56, no. 1 (1989): 1–60.

5. See Iannaccone, "Introduction to the Economics of Religion."

6. Max Weber, *The Protestant Ethic and the Spirit of Capitalism* (New York: Harper Collins, 1930).

7. See Kurt Samuelsson, *Religion and Economic Action: The Protestant Ethic, the Rise of Capitalism and the Abuses of Scholarship*, trans. E. Geoffrey French (Toronto: University of Toronto Press, 1993); also see Iannacone, "Introduction to the Economics of Religion," 1474.

8. Much of Amsterdam's wealth, for example, was centered on Catholic families. The German Rhineland was predominantly Catholic, while Catholic Belgium was one of the earliest to industrialize. See the reference to Delacroix, quoted in Iannacone, "Introduction to the Economics of Religion."

9. See William H. Swatos and Kevin J. Christiano, "Introduction—Secularization Theory: The Course of a Concept," *Sociology of Religion* 60, no. 3 (1999): 209–28.

10. See Rachel M. McCleary and Robert J. Barro, "Religion and Economy," *Journal of Economic Perspectives* 20, no. 2 (Spring 2006): 49–72. Contrast Weber's approach to a "social capital" explanation, which treats religious participation or "networking" as the key factor in promoting social and economic well-being, a view that, by and large, trivializes the role of religious belief.

11. See Andrew Scott Bibby, *Montesquieu's Political Economy* (New York: Palgrave Macmillan, 2016).

12. Albert O. Hirschman, *The Passions and the Interests: Political Arguments for Capitalism Before Its Triumph* (Princeton, N.J.: Princeton University Press, 1977), 60.

13. See Marion Fourcade and Kieran Healy, "Moral Views of Market Society," *Annual Review of Sociology* 33 (2007): 285–311. The main argument here is that the modern study of religion and economics does not begin with Adam Smith's *An Inquiry into the Nature and Causes of the Wealth of Nations* (a point that conflicts with the statements of major pioneers in the field; see, for example, Iannaccone, "Introduction to the Economics of Religion"). This chapter will show that Montesquieu is not only the first to systematically explore the effects of religion (religion as "independent variable"); he may also be the more relevant theorist for current "two-way" research on major topics like the determinants of religiosity, the emergence and evolution of religious institutions, secularization and pluralism; and the economic consequences of religion—the last being the primary focus of this chapter.

14. Rebecca Kingston, "Montesquieu on Religion and on the Question of Toleration," in *Montesquieu's Human Science: Essays on The Spirit of Laws*, ed. David W. Carrithers, Michael A. Mosher, and Paul A. Rahe (Lanham, Md.: Rowman and Littlefield, 2001), 375–408.

15. Emile Faguet, *Dix-huitième siècle* (Paris: Boivin and Compagnie, 1893); Judith Shklar, *Montesquieu* (Oxford: Oxford University Press, 1987); F. T. H. Fletcher, "Montesquieu et la politique religieuse en Angleterre au XVIIIe siècle," in *Actes du congrès Montesquieu* (Bordeaux: Delmas, 1956), 295–304; Lorenzo Bianchi, "Nécessité de

la religion et de la tolérance chez Montesquieu: la 'Dissertation sur la politique des Romains dans la religion,'" in *Lectures de Montesquieu*, ed. Edgar Mass and Alberto Postigliola (Naples: Liguori Editore, 1993), 25–39; Robert Shackleton, "La religion de Montesquieu," in *Actes du Congrès Montesquieu* (Bordeaux: Delmas, 1956), 287–336.

16. Andrea Radasanu, "Montesquieu on Ancient Greek Foreign Relations: Toward National Self-Interest and International Peace," *Political Research Quarterly* 66, no. 1 (March 2013): 3–17.

17. See Christopher Nadon, ed., *Enlightenment and Secularism: Essays on the Mobilization of Reason* (Lanham, Md.: Rowman and Littlefield, 2013), xxii. For a balanced attempt at sorting out Montesquieu's religious views, see Roger B. Oake, "Montesquieu's Religious Ideas," *Journal of the History of Ideas* 14, no. 4 (1953): 548–60. Oake does not agree that "Montesquieu's mind was as little religious as possible" (548). For a review of the French literature, see Kingston, "Montesquieu on Religion and on the Question of Toleration," 399 n. 4. Lacordaire is one of the very few who see Montesquieu as a religious thinker (he notes, in 1861, that the *Spirit of the Laws* was "la plus belle apologie du christianisme au XVIIIe siècle"). Robert Shackleton also views Montesquieu as a practicing Catholic but "with deist convictions," *Montesquieu: A Critical Biography* (London: Oxford University Press, 1961). Andrew Lynch highlights the subversive side of Montesquieu's writing on religion, which, he concludes, is good only for social utility. "Montesquieu and the Ecclesiastical Critics of l'Esprit des lois," *Journal of the History of Ideas* 38, no. 3 (1977): 495. Sanford Kessler examines Montesquieu's *Persian Letters* and concludes that Montesquieu was attempting to provide a "new theology" based on the principles of natural religion. "Religion and Liberalism in the *Persian Letters*," *Polity* 15, no. 3 (1983): 383–86. Judith Shklar follows Kessler and Lynch in regarding Montesquieu as largely an antireligious thinker. *Montesquieu*), 84. Peter Gay puts Montesquieu's views in context, and argues that he is "exceptional" among the *philosophes* for assigning Christianity to a privileged position among religions, "largely for its historical role." Still, Gay's Montesquieu is part of the majority view: religion had lost all its vitality, and remained a "harmful survival" even in the eighteenth century. *The Enlightenment: The Rise of Modern Paganism* (New York: Norton, 1995), 373n2. Kingston compares Montesquieu's views on natural law to the modern school of natural law, and though she attempts to portray Montesquieu as more friendly to religion than is generally conceded, she concludes, again in line with other scholars, that Montesquieu considered religion a "cultural artifact whose truths and doctrines are largely fashioned by humans themselves." "Montesquieu on Religion and on the Question of Toleration," 376, 380. Diana Schaub provides a sharp summary of Montesquieu's views on toleration. "Of Believers and Barbarians in Montesquieu's Enlightened Toleration," in *Early Modern Skepticism and the Origins of Toleration*, ed. Adam Levine (Lanham, Md.: Lexington Books, 1999), 225–48. Robert C. Bartlett gives an equally compelling analysis but emphasizes Montesquieu's antipathy toward religion and compares him, unrealistically, in my view, with Bayle. "On the Politics of Faith and Reason: The Project of Enlightenment in Pierre Bayle and Montesquieu,"

Journal of Politics 63, no. 1 (2001): 1–28. See Schaub, "Of Believers and Barbarians," 236–39, for a different reading of Montesquieu's attitude toward Bayle.

18. I borrow this formulation from Swatos and Christiano, "Secularization Theory."

19. See Iannacone, "Introduction to the Economics of Religion," 1477. Another example of the connection between religion and business culture can be found in Montesquieu's reading of Humphrey Prideaux's *The Old and New Testament Connected in the History of the Jews and Neighbouring Nations* (1715–1717), which he had read with great interest. There, Prideaux had described a vow of the Essenes, which served as a substitute for civil law. Lacking a complex civil code, rule of law, and property rights, the Essenes' greed was checked by religious principles. The vow helped to "observe justice to mankind, to do no ill to any person, upon whatsoever account, to keep faith with all the world, to hate injustice, to command with modesty, always to side with truth, and to fly from all unlawful gain."

20. The Stoics had "contempt" both for "pleasure and [for] pain" (XXIV.10). The Stoics did not work merely for profit (they looked upon riches and ambition as "vanity"). They labored rather for the "happiness of mankind" and for the sake of "exercising the duties of society."

21. Although Montesquieu admits that religious laws may have a "negligible" effect in cultures where the civil laws are severe (XXIV.14), few countries fall under this category.

22. Montesquieu seems to reject the possibility of a significant or consistent relationship between beliefs and economic activity, attitudes toward work, and citizenship. For example, Montesquieu points out that followers of Confucius and pre-Socratic philosophers (Zeno, in this case) did not believe in survival after death, yet these individuals had "admirable influences" on society (XIV.19). On the other hand, major world religions with sacred doctrines about the immortal soul have created "frightful consequences" (XIV.19).

23. "Further, the emperor is every year informed of the husbandman who has distinguished himself most in his profession; and he makes him a mandarin of the eighth order. Among the ancient Persians the kings quitted their grandeur and pomp on the eighth day of the month, called Chorrem-ruz, to eat with the husbandmen. These institutions were admirably calculated for the encouragement of agriculture."

24. In discussing the holy status given to cattle in Hindu "local religious law," for example, Montesquieu concludes that it is entirely appropriate to the "climate of the Indies," where it is difficult to breed cattle (XXIV.24). Quoting from François Bernier's travel memoirs, he adds the following note: "The flesh of cattle in that country is insipid, but the milk and butter which they receive from them serve for a part of their subsistence; therefore the law which prohibits the eating and killing of cows is in the Indies not unreasonable." Similarly, in discussing the religious rationale for not eating pigs, Montesquieu cites M. de Boulainvilliers, who had provided the following explanation: "[Pigs] must be very scarce in Arabia, where there are almost no woods, and hardly anything fit for the nourishment of these animals; besides, the saltiness of the

water and food renders the people most susceptible of cutaneous disorders. This local law could not be good in other countries, where the hog is almost a universal, and in some sort a necessary, nourishment."

25. See Sanford Kessler, *Tocqueville's Civil Religion: American Christianity and the Prospects for Freedom* (Albany, N.Y.: SUNY Press, 1994). Compare to *PL* 85, 119.

26. A fuller account of the battle plan for "disattachment" can be found in Bibby, *Montesquieu's Political Economy*, 106–12.

27. Part of the reason for this is that we feel pride in choosing a noncorporeal God that does not have bodily functions, Montesquieu explains. But imagine the opposite combination: an "idolatrous" god that eats, sleeps, breathes, and performs bodily functions, but that does not care, or share, that "natural penchant for things that [we feel]." This, in Montesquieu's view, is the least potent source of attachment to religion: we should lose respect for the God itself, who has our needs, and therefore is not removed from "the humiliation" of our condition.

28. This strengthens attachment because religious people naturally wish to be the object of the Creator's preferences. If he flatters our own estimation of our intelligence (in having picked the right God, for example).

29. Over time, Montesquieu argues, we become attached to those things that occupy us. It is much more difficult for Jews and Muslims to change their religion than for barbarians or savages, who "wholly occupied with hunting or warring, scarcely burden themselves with religious practices" (XXV.2).

30. Adam Smith's views on the favorable role of competition in Book V.III in regard to the religion market has inspired a whole line of research. For interest, see Rodney Stark and William Bainbridge, *A Theory of Religion* (New Brunswick N.J.: Rutgers University Press, 1996); Laurence R. Iannaccone, "The Consequences of Religious Market Regulation: Adam Smith and the Economics of Religion," *Religion and Society* 3 (1991): 156–77. For comparison and contrast from a noneconomic point of view, see Charles L. Griswold Jr., *Adam Smith and the Virtues of Enlightenment* (Cambridge: Cambridge University Press, 1999); Emma Rothschild, *Economic Sentiments: Adam Smith, Condorcet, and the Enlightenment* (Cambridge, Mass.: Harvard University Press, 2002); Samuel Fleischacker, *On Adam Smith's Wealth of Nations: A Philosophical Companion* (Princeton, N.J.: Princeton University Press, 2009).

31. See also letter from Thomas Jefferson to Dr. Jacob De La Motta, September 1, 1820, quoted in David G. Dalin, "Jews, Judaism, and the American Founding," in *Faith and the Founders of the American Republic*, ed. Daniel L. Dreisbach and Mark David Hall (Oxford: Oxford University Press, 2014), 62–83.

32. Iannaccone, "Introduction to the Economics of Religion."

33. I want to thank an anonymous reader for pushing back on the idea that Smith treated religion merely as a commodity. Rather, Smith explored the ways in which the political order encourages the "right religion," one free from "every mixture of absurdity, imposture, or fanaticism, such as wise men have in all ages of the world wished to see established." Adam Smith, *The Wealth of Nations* (New York: Modern Library,

1994), bk. 5, chap. 1. Readers more familiar with Smith's writings on religion will also recognize that Smith did not promote disestablishment simply. As with Montesquieu, Smith saw this as an ideal, but one that would require compromises with political reality.

34. McCleary and Barro, "Religion and Economy."

35. Some will make their decisions "by the light of their own mind" and others "by the caprice of fancy." The prediction here is not that the reasonable people will become secular and the fanciful people religious (which is arguably the caricature view of Enlightenment thinking on secularization).

36. See *PL* 56; Randolph Paul Runyon, *The Art of the Persian Letters: Unlocking Montesquieu's "Secret Chain"* (Newark: University of Delaware Press, 2005).

37. None of this is to suggest that Montesquieu promoted an established hierarchical church-state regime, or, as others have claimed, that he did not support the separation of church and state. Kingston, "Montesquieu on Religion and on the Question of Toleration," 397. Rather, one may read Montesquieu's limited toleration more in line with broad Lockean political principles. Where they differ, arguably, is on the idealized extent of privatization. Montesquieu, it seems, was more aggressive in promoting what one scholar has called "benign zealotry." On this last point see Bartlett, "On the Politics of Faith and Reason."

38. For an introduction to this topic, see Fourcade and Healy, "Moral Views of Market Society."

39. For a summary, see Iannaccone, "Introduction to the Economics of Religion," 1476. Of course, Montesquieu did not study drug and alcohol consumption, the correlates of education, or the effects of religion on the family. But the connection between relationship between religiosity and crime, social trust, honesty, compassion, justice, humility, and the avoidance of "unlawful gain" was virtually a commonplace among theorists of civic theology (not surprisingly, factors considered by economists as statistically significant and correlated with a healthy economic order today).

40. These and other studies are found in Robert J. Barro and Rachel M. McCleary, "Religion and Economic Growth," National Bureau of Economic Research Paper 9682 (Cambridge, Mass., 2003); also Rachel M. McCleary, "Religion and Economic Development: A Two-Way Causation," *Policy Review* 148 (2008): 45–57. Both find a "virtuous cycle" between believing and participation. With nonproductive time on their hands and grievance against society, people will engage in destructive behavior. However, a virtuous cycle occurs when people believe relative to belonging. That is, people hold religious beliefs but do not spend enormous amounts of resources (time, income, talents) on their religion. Similar reasoning is found in Book 25, as we saw, in Montesquieu's discussion of the positive impact of ceremonies, but also in his arguments for suppressing religious festivals and time devoted to worship (XXIV.23), his criticism of the magnificence and costliness of "temples" (XXV.3), the way in which "ministers of religion" are "drawn from business" and families (XXV.5), and the need to curb the "luxury of superstition," while discouraging the "burden" of "too many practices" (XXV.2).

41. See "Trade and Naval Power the Offspring of Civil Liberty only, and cannot subsist without it," Saturday, February 3, 1721, in John Trenchard, *Cato's Letters, or Essays on Liberty, Civil and Religious, and Other Important Subjects. Four Volumes in Two*, edited and annotated by Ronald Hamowy (Indianapolis: Liberty Fund, 1995), no. 64.

42. See Thomas L. Pangle, *The Theological Basis of Liberal Modernity in Montesquieu's Spirit of the Laws* (Chicago: University of Chicago Press, 2010).

43. See Fourcade and Healy, "Moral Views of Market Society."

44. Credit should be given to Fourcade and Healy for this formulation, who recommends a broader attention to "the public justification of the contemporary economic order" (286).

Bibliography

Barro, Robert J., and Rachel M. McCleary. "Religion and Economic Growth." *Milken Institute Review* (June 2004): 38–45.

———. "Religion and Economic Growth." National Bureau of Economic Research, Cambridge, Mass., 2003.

Bartlett, Robert C. "On the Politics of Faith and Reason: The Project of Enlightenment in Pierre Bayle and Montesquieu." *Journal of Politics* 63, no. 1 (2001): 1–28.

Bianchi, Lorenzo. "Nécessité de la religion et de la tolérance chez Montesquieu: la 'Dissertation sur la politique des Romains dans la religion.'" In *Lectures de Montesquieu*, edited by Edgar Mass and Alberto Postigliola, 25–39. Naples: Liguori Editore, 1993.

Bibby, Andrew Scott. *Montesquieu's Political Economy*. New York: Palgrave Macmillan, 2016.

Dalin, David G. "Jews, Judaism, and the American Founding." In *Faith and the Founders of the American Republic*, edited by Daniel L. Dreisbach and Mark David Hall, 62–83. Oxford: Oxford University Press, 2014.

Faguet, Emile. *Dix-huitième siècle*. Paris: Boivin and Compagnie, 1893.

Fleischacker, Samuel. *On Adam Smith's Wealth of Nations: A Philosophical Companion*. Princeton, N.J.: Princeton University Press, 2009.

Fletcher, F. T. H. "Montesquieu et la politique religieuse en Angleterre au XVIIIe siècle." In *Actes du congrès Montesquieu*, 295–304. Bordeaux: Delmas, 1956.

Fourcade, Marion, and Kieran Healy. "Moral Views of Market Society." *Annual Review of Sociology* 33 (2007): 285–311.

Gay, Peter. *The Enlightenment: The Rise of Modern Paganism*. New York: Norton, 1995.

Griswold, Charles L., Jr. *Adam Smith and the Virtues of Enlightenment*. Cambridge: Cambridge University Press, 1999.

Hirschman, Albert O. *The Passions and the Interests: Political Arguments for Capitalism Before Its Triumph*. Princeton, N.J.: Princeton University Press, 1977.

Iannaccone, Laurence R. "The Consequences of Religious Market Regulation: Adam Smith and the Economics of Religion." *Religion and Society* 3 (1991): 156–77.

——. "Introduction to the Economics of Religion." *Stanford Journal of Economic Literature* 36, no. 3 (1998): 1465–95.

Kessler, Sanford. "Religion and Liberalism in the *Persian Letters*." *Polity* 15, no. 3 (1983): 380–96.

——. *Tocqueville's Civil Religion: American Christianity and the Prospects for Freedom*. Albany, N.Y.: SUNY Press, 1994.

Kingston, Rebecca. "Montesquieu on Religion and on the Question of Toleration." In *Montesquieu's Human Science: Essays on The Spirit of Laws*, edited by David W. Carrithers, Michael A. Mosher, and Paul A. Rahe, 375–408. Lanham, Md.: Rowman and Littlefield, 2001.

Lynch, Andrew. "Montesquieu and the Ecclesiastical Critics of l'Esprit des lois." *Journal of the History of Ideas* 38, no. 3 (1977): 487–500.

McCleary, Rachel M. "Religion and Economic Development: A Two-Way Causation." *Policy Review* 148 (2008): 45–57.

——. "Salvation, Damnation, and Economic Incentives." *Journal of Contemporary Religion* 22, no. 1 (January 2007): 49–74.

McCleary, Rachel M., and Robert J. Barro. "Religion and Economy." *Journal of Economic Perspectives* 20, no. 2 (Spring 2006): 49–72.

Montesquieu, Baron de. *The Spirit of the Laws*. Cambridge: Cambridge University Press, 1989.

Nadon, Christopher, ed. *Enlightenment and Secularism: Essays on the Mobilization of Reason*. Lanham, Md.: Rowman and Littlefield, 2013.

Oake, Roger B. "Montesquieu's Religious Ideas." *Journal of the History of Ideas* 14, no. 4 (1953): 548–60.

Pangle, Thomas L. *The Theological Basis of Liberal Modernity in Montesquieu's* Spirit of the Laws. Chicago: University of Chicago Press, 2010.

Posner, Richard A., and Michael W. McConnell. "An Economic Approach to Issues of Religious Freedom." *University of Chicago Law Review* 56, no. 1 (1989): 1–60.

Radasanu, Andrea. "Montesquieu on Ancient Greek Foreign Relations: Toward National Self-Interest and International Peace." *Political Research Quarterly* 66, no. 1 (March 2013): 3–17.

Rothschild, Emma. *Economic Sentiments: Adam Smith, Condorcet, and the Enlightenment*. Cambridge, Mass.: Harvard University Press, 2002.

Runyon, Randolph Paul. *The Art of the Persian Letters: Unlocking Montesquieu's "Secret Chain."* Newark: University of Delaware Press, 2005.

Samuelsson, Kurt. *Religion and Economic Action: The Protestant Ethic, the Rise of Capitalism and the Abuses of Scholarship*. Translated by E. Geoffrey French. Toronto: University of Toronto Press, 1993.

Schaub, Diana. "Of Believers and Barbarians in Montesquieu's Enlightened Tolera-
    tion." In *Early Modern Skepticism and the Origins of Toleration*, edited by Adam
    Levine, 225–48. Lanham, Md.: Lexington Books, 1999.
Shackleton, Robert. "La religion de Montesquieu." In Actes du Congrès Montesquieu,
    287–94. Bordeaux: Delmas, 1956.
———. *Montesquieu: A Critical Biography.* London: Oxford University Press, 1961.
Shklar, Judith. *Montesquieu.* Oxford: Oxford University Press, 1987.
Smith, Adam. *An Inquiry into the Nature and Causes of the Wealth of Nations.* New
    York: Modern Library, 1994.
Stark, Rodney, and William Bainbridge. *A Theory of Religion.* New Brunswick N.J.:
    Rutgers University Press, 1996.
Swatos, William H., Jr., and Kevin J. Christiano. "Introduction—Secularization The-
    ory: The Course of a Concept." *Sociology of Religion* 60, no. 3 (1999): 209–28.
Trenchard, John. *Cato's Letters, or Essays on Liberty, Civil and Religious, and Other
    Important Subjects. Four volumes in Two.* Edited and annotated by Ronald Ham-
    owy. Indianapolis: Liberty Fund, 1995.
Weber, Max. *The Protestant Ethic and the Spirit of Capitalism.* New York: Harper Col-
    lins, 1930.

CONTRIBUTORS

Andrew S. Bibby is Associate Director of the Center for Constitutional Studies and Assistant Professor of History and Political Science at Utah Valley University.

Gurcharan Das is an author, commentator, public intellectual, and the former CEO of Procter & Gamble India.

Richard A. Epstein is Laurence A. Tisch Professor of Law at New York University School of Law.

Fonna Forman is Associate Professor of Political Science at UC San Diego.

Robert P. George is McCormick Professor of Jurisprudence at Princeton University.

Steven J. Kautz is Associate Professor of Political Science at Michigan State University.

Peter Augustine Lawler (deceased) was Dana Professor of Government at Berry College.

Steven Lukes is Professor of Politics and Sociology at New York University.

Deirdre Nansen McCloskey is Professor of Economics, History, English, and Communication at University of Illinois at Chicago.

Peter McNamara is Associate Professor of Political Science at Utah State University.

Arthur M. Melzer is Professor of Political Science at Michigan State University.

John Tomasi is Professor of Political Science and Philosophy at Brown University.

INDEX

Washington, George, 103
Wealth of Nations (Smith), 169, 170, 171–72, 221
Weber, Max: culture and, 157; Protestant ethic thesis of, 126, 151, 155, 211–12; psychological hypothesis of, 150; usage of "capitalism" and, 141
Weingast, Barry, 140, 152
welfare state: combining principles of use and production, 13–14; dependent on capitalism, 14; deterioration of middle-class values and, 100
What Is the Third Estate? (Sieyes), 154
What Money Can't Buy (Sandel), 74
white lies, 48
Why Some Things Should Not Be for Sale (Satz), 75–76

Wilson, Woodrow, 156
Winch, Donald, 169
Wittgenstein, Ludwig, 81
women: markets in reproductive or sexual labor of, 76; seen as oppressed by traditional family, 90; time pressure on, 99. *See also* feminists
Wood, Michael, 129
Wordsworth, William, 68, 77
work: cognitive elite and, 99, 100, 106; economic liberty of, 20, 21–22, 27, 28; Montesquieu on, 6, 215–16, 217–18, 223, 229n20
World Trade Organization, 140

Zeidler, Frank, 167
Zelizer, Viviana, 74–75

ACKNOWLEDGMENTS

This is the eighth volume of essays published by the LeFrak Forum and the Symposium on Science, Reason, and Modern Democracy. Founded in 1989 by Jerry Weinberger, Dick Zinman, and Arthur Melzer in the Department of Political Science at Michigan State University, the Symposium is a center for research and debate on the theory and practice of modern democracy. It sponsors lectures, events, publications, and teaching, as well as graduate and postdoctoral fellowships. Its specific mission is to explore the intersection of philosophy and public policy: to place theoretical issues in practical context and policy issues in philosophical perspective.

The present volume grew from an event jointly sponsored and organized with the Centre for Civil Society, one of India's leading think tanks, and held at the Habitat Centre in New Delhi. Additional essays came from a series of lectures held at Michigan State University. All of the essays appear here for the first time.

During this period, the Symposium's programming was made possible by an endowment grant from the Samuel J. & Ethel LeFrak Charitable Foundation, a "We the People" challenge grant from the National Endowment for the Humanities, and a grant from the Earhart Foundation of Ann Arbor, Michigan. We are very grateful for their generous support.

Michigan State's Department of Political Science and College of Social Science have been home to the Symposium since its founding. We thank our colleagues in these institutions. In particular, we thank former Dean Marietta Baba and her successor Rachel Croson, as well as former Department Chair Richard Hula and current Chair Chuck Ostrom. We are especially grateful to Karen Battin, the Symposium's administrative assistant, for her fine work.

In addition to the authors whose essays are included in this volume, the following individuals took part in the conference or lecture series: Punkurj Mishra, Ian Shapiro, Rajshree Chandra, Gurpreet Mahajan, Tom G. Palmer,

Neera K. Badhwar, Shikha Dalmia, Shubhashis Gangopadhyay, Christopher Lingle, Wan Saiful Wan Jan, and Jerry Weinberger. We thank them for their valuable contributions.

We owe a very fond debt of thanks to our partners at the Centre for Civil Society, especially Parth Shah, founder and president of CSS, and Baishali Bomjan, then Director of CSS Academy. They made what could have been an onerous task into a genuine pleasure.

We are grateful to Douglas Walker for help with manuscript preparation, and to Julie Shawvan for her fine index. Finally, we would like to thank Damon Linker, our editor at the University of Pennsylvania Press, for his helpful support and guidance in this project.

Lightning Source UK Ltd.
Milton Keynes UK
UKHW042116230819
348467UK00001B/475/P